Other books by David D. Burns, M.D.

Feeling Good: The New Mood Therapy (1980)

Intimate Connections (1985)

The Feeling Good Handbook (1989)

Ten Days to Self-esteem: The Leader's Manual (1993)

TEN DAYS
—TO GREAT—
SELF-ESTEEM

DAVID D. BURNS, M.D.

Vermilion
LONDON

AUTHOR'S NOTE

The ideas, procedures, and suggestions contained in this book are not intended as a substitute for consulting with a psychiatrist, psychologist, or other mental health professional. All matters regarding your mental health require professional supervision.

The names and personal details of the patients mentioned in this book have been changed to protect their identities.

You are invited to visit Dr. Burns's web site at www.feelinggood.com. This site contains much useful information including:
- how to obtain referrals for treatment by cognitive therapists around the country
- dates of upcoming lectures and workshops by Dr. Burns
- how to order a variety of audiotapes for mental health professionals and for the general public
- how to obtain *The Leader's Manual* for *Ten Days to Self-esteem*
- question and answer forum ("Ask the Guru")

9 10 8

Copyright © 1993 by David D. Burns
Introduction copyright © 1999 by David D. Burns

Published in the United States by William Morrow and Company Inc.

First published in the UK in 2000 by Vermilion, an imprint of Ebury Press, Random House, 20 Vauxhall Bridge Road, London SW1V 2SA

www.randomhouse.co.uk

Random House Australia (Pty) Limited
20 Alfred Street, Milsons Point, Sydney, New South Wales 2061, Australia

Random House New Zealand Limited
18 Poland Road, Glenfield, Auckland 10, New Zealand

Random House (Pty) Limited
Endulini, 5a Jubilee Road, Parktown, 2193, South Africa

The Random House Group Limited Reg. No. 954009

Papers used by Vermilion are natural, recyclable products made from wood grown in sustainable forests.

Printed and bound in Great Britain by William Clowes Ltd, Beccles, Suffolk

A CIP catalogue record for this book is available from the British Library

ISBN 0 09 182562 8

ACKNOWLEDGMENTS

In 1988 I began the first pilot study of the self-esteem training groups, which were based on an early version of this book, at the Shepherd of the Valley Lutheran Church in Phoenix. The Reverend Dick Hamlin, Dr. Dennis Hunter, Jan Robinson, and many other members of the congregation worked extremely hard to make that project a success. Their faith and hard work were invaluable.

My friend and colleague Dr. David Soskis, associate professor of psychiatry at Temple University School of Medicine, suggested additional pilot tests in a wide variety of settings to answer questions such as these: Would the self-esteem training groups be received equally well by other religious groups? Would the groups be helpful in other settings, such as schools, universities, prisons, hospitals, day treatment programs, mental health clinics, nursing homes, and community self-help groups?

Michael Greenwald, Ph.D., a clinical psychologist in Pittsburgh, generously offered to supervise additional pilot studies of the self-esteem training groups so that we could begin to address these questions. Dr. Greenwald encountered outstanding success. This greatly increased my confidence that the self-esteem training groups could help many people from extremely diverse walks of life.

I then discussed the project with Diane Kiddy, M.S.S., vice president of behavioral medicine at the Presbyterian Medical Center of Philadelphia. Since the groups had been so successful on an outpatient basis, we decided to pilot-test them with inpatients. We felt there was a strong need to develop inpatient treatment models that would be more therapeutic, compassionate, and effective.

We decided to test the self-esteem program at The Residence, a short-term, inexpensive residential treatment facility at the Presbyterian Medical Center. This was a challenging test, because many of the patients at The Residence suffer from extremely severe mood disorders, drug addiction, and schizophrenia. In addition, many are unemployed and have very little education. Furthermore, the average length of stay at The Residence is only ten days—due to the new pressures to keep mental health costs low—so we needed a treatment program that would be intensive, upbeat, and fast acting.

My friend and colleague Bruce S. Zahn, M.A., director of psychological services at the Presbyterian Medical Center, worked with me to adapt the self-esteem training groups for The Residence beginning in the fall of 1991. Based in no small measure on Bruce's enthusiasm, warmth, and leadership, that program has been another tremendous success. The patients have been very excited about the groups, and the majority have experienced rapid improvements in their moods and outlook.

I am very greatly indebted to Bruce Zahn and Diane Kiddy for invaluable assistance and collaboration in this effort. The enthusiastic support of Carol Persons, M.D., medical director, and Elizabeth Dean, program administrator of The Residence, has also been crucial to the success of our work. Thank you!

I would also like to thank I. Donald Snook, Jr., president of the Presbyterian Medical Center of Philadelphia, for persistent encouragement and strong leadership. Because of the positive results of our efforts, he has generously offered to support the development of a national training and research program at the Presbyterian Medical Center, so that mental health professionals from around the country can come and learn from what we have developed in order to create similar programs in their own communities.

Many of the ideas in this book were pioneered by two creative and courageous colleagues who have greatly influenced my thinking. During the 1950s, Dr. Albert Ellis, a psychologist in New York, was one of the first to popularize the notion that our thoughts create our moods. During the 1960s, Dr. Aaron Beck, a psychiatrist at the University of Pennsylvania School of Medicine, described the intensely negative thinking patterns of depressed people. He began to develop specific therapeutic strategies, which he called cognitive therapy, to treat this disorder. Since the time of these two great thinkers, there have been important contributions to our understanding and treatment of mood disorders by numerous clinicians and researchers in America and abroad. This has truly been a team effort, and I owe them all a debt of gratitude.

I would like to thank my administrative assistant, Marilyn Cooper, for support in running my office and helping many people from around the country who have called asking for help. People are always telling me, "Marilyn Cooper is *super*. She gave me *so much help* when I called." They're absolutely right! I am fortunate to be working with Marilyn and grateful for her help.

Finally, I would like to thank my wife and colleague, Melanie Burns, M.A., for invaluable consultation in the development of this program and in the preparation of this book.

The expertise and enthusiasm of all of these individuals were crucial in the development of this book. I am deeply grateful to all of you!

CONTENTS

INTRODUCTION

Since *Ten Days to Self-esteem* was first published in 1993, there have been quite a few changes in my life. After more that twenty great years in Philadelphia, my wife and I moved back home to California. Our roots are in this area, and returning home has been a dream come true. I am especially pleased to be associated once again with my old alma mater, Stanford University School of Medicine, where I have abundant opportunities for research, teaching, and program development in the Department of Psychiatry and Behavioral Sciences.

I have had the chance to test the Ten Days to Self-esteem program in a variety of new settings. Right after we arrived, I was invited to teach and consult at the Kaiser mental health clinic in Santa Clara, California, by Dr. Jim Boyers. I hadn't seen Jim since the late 1960s when we were both students at Stanford, and it was great to have the chance to renew our friendship and work together. The Santa Clara clinic is one of the largest outpatient programs in the country—the staff treats the entire spectrum of emotional problems, including depression, anxiety disorders, marital difficulties, schizophrenia, and substance abuse. With Dr. Boyers's help, I implemented a pilot study of the Ten Days to Self-esteem program at the clinic. I have also had the opportunity to adapt the program for the inpatient unit at Stanford University Hospital. There we treat individuals suffering from severe depression, anxiety disorders, eating disorders, and chronic pain. These experiences with patients from so many different walks of life have provided much new data that have made me even more enthusiastic about the program.

I originally developed the Ten Days to Self-esteem program for the Presbyterian/University of Pennsylvania Medical Center in Philadelphia during the late 1980s when I served as acting chief for the Psychiatry Division. Our hospital president, Don Snook, asked if I would be willing to help create a new and different kind of mental health care program for the hospital based on the principles in my book *Feeling Good: The New Mood Therapy*. Because our hospital was an inner-city hospital with limited resources, Mr. Snook emphasized that the program would have to be quite inexpensive, extremely effective, and fast acting.

Ten Days to Self-esteem is the program I created. We initially pilot-tested it in an intensive residential treatment unit that served as an alternative to hospitalization. I called the program Ten Days to Self-esteem because it was originally a ten-day treatment program.

Ten Days to Self-esteem is based on the principles of cognitive behavioral therapy (CBT). A "cognition" is just a fancy name for a thought. Depressed people have a tendency to think about things very negatively and behave in self-defeating ways—they may avoid work, pleasurable activities, and other people, for example. CBT helps depressed and anxious individuals change these negative thinking and behavior patterns.

Between 1988 and 1996, we treated over three thousand patients in this program. Most had multiple psychiatric problems, including severe depression, anxiety, and personality disorders. Approximately half were also substance abusers, typically alcohol along with street drugs. Many were suicidal or hallucinating at the time of admission. Most of our patients also had severe social and economic problems, including unemployment, limited education, and few or no financial resources. The group included a mix of African Americans, Caucasians, and other ethnic groups.

Some colleagues were initially skeptical that a "brainy" treatment like cognitive behavioral therapy would work with such a population. They said our patients were so overwhelmed with real problems of daily living that they would be more concerned with where the next meal was coming from than with learning to develop more positive attitudes. However, our patients took to the cognitive therapy like ducks to water. They actually seemed to respond much more rapidly than the private practice patients I had treated through the years, most of whom were highly educated and living comfortably. The positive impact on the patients was remarkable.

In 1993, *Ten Days to Self-esteem* was published and we gave copies to all the patients to use as their workbooks during the hospitalization. We began to study the depression severity scores of all the patients at intake and at discharge to see how effective the program was. The average scores on the Burns Depression Checklist (BDC) at the time of admission were in the mid- to upper 20s. This is a self-assessment test for depression that you will take beginning in Step 1 and at each step as you read the book so that you can chart your progress. The intake scores indicated that the typical patient in our program was moderately to severely depressed, as one might expect. In contrast, the average depression scores for all the patients at the time of discharge ten days later were 11 or 12. Scores below 10 on the BDC are considered normal, so most patients had improved substantially and many were free of depression by the time of discharge.

Although our patients were clearly not "cured" in such a short period of time, the strong burst of improvement in patients with such profound psychiatric and social difficulties was extremely encouraging. I have seen rapid improvements in a variety of other settings where the Ten Days to Self-esteem program was implemented. While this is positive, these findings do not prove that the program is effective because the placebo effect can be so strong. In other words, if you give a group of depressed patients a sugar pill (a placebo), but the patients believe it is actually a powerful new antidepressant, a significant percent will improve because they expect to improve. Hope alone is a powerful antidepressant. Short-term and long-term controlled outcome studies are necessary before we can accept the validity and effectiveness of any new treatment.

Have there been any studies comparing the cognitive behavioral methods in the Ten Days to Self-esteem program with other established treatments for depression, such as antidepressant medications or other forms of psychotherapy? Actually there have been many. At the time the first edition of this book was published in 1993, CBT had been compared to antidepressant drugs as well as to other forms of psychotherapy in numerous published studies. These studies have demonstrated repeatedly that the methods are fast acting, safe, and effective for the majority of people suffering from depression and low self-esteem, including those with severe, biological depressions.[1] What is even more impressive is that several long-term follow-up studies have shown that people treated with CBT appear to stay undepressed and have fewer relapses of depression following recovery than people treated with antidepressant medications alone.

Since 1993, there have been even more published studies comparing CBT with other treatments for depression. In 1995, Drs. David Antonuccio and William Danton, from the University of Nevada, and Garland DeNelsky, from the Cleveland Clinic Foundation, reviewed these studies and published a landmark article entitled "Antidepressants vs. Psychotherapy in the Treatment of Depression: Challenging the Conventional Wisdom with Data."[2] The authors concluded that cognitive behavior therapy is at least as good as, and probably better than, antidepressant drugs for adults with severe or mild depression. At least one other new form of short-term psychotherapy, called interpersonal therapy, also appears to be effective for depression. The authors also found that patients treated with CBT do better in the long run than patients treated with medications or other forms of psychotherapy—in other words, they remain undepressed longer and have fewer relapses following recovery.

Dr. Antonuccio and his colleagues emphasized that these findings have largely been ignored by the media and the general public. This is because of a strong cultural bias that depression is a biological and genetic disorder and that antidepressant drugs represent the most powerful form of treatment—impressions that are not solidly grounded in fact.

In all these studies, trained professionals administered the cognitive therapy. Is there any evidence that a cognitive therapy self-help book alone can have antidepressant effects? Self-help books have been quite controversial, and many people feel skeptical about the motives of the individuals who write them. When I look through the self-help sections of popular bookstores, the superficial jargon and quick fixes that are promised in the books often turn me off as well. (Of course, my own books are noteworthy exceptions!)

However, academic researchers have begun to take a serious look at the value of self-help books as a new form of therapy. This type of treatment is called bibliotherapy, or reading therapy. Bibliotherapy can be administered in one of two ways. You can read a self-help book between therapy sessions to increase the speed of recovery, or you can read a self-help book on your own without any other therapy as a treatment for depression or other problems as well.

Five well-designed studies have evaluated the effectiveness of my first book, *Feeling Good: The New Mood Therapy*, as a bibliotherapy "treatment" for depression without any other medications or psychotherapy.[3-7] A team of investigators headed by Dr. Forrest Scogin at the University of Alabama has conducted these studies over the past decade. To make a long story short, the investigators have concluded that *Feeling Good* bibliotherapy appears to be as effective as a course of psychotherapy or treatment with the best antidepressant drugs.

For example, in a study published in the prestigious *Journal of Consulting and Clinical Psychology* in 1995, Drs. Christine Jamison and Forrest Scogin reported on the effects of *Feeling Good* bibliotherapy in eighty depressed individuals suffering from major depressive episodes.[6] This is the type of depression normally treated by psychiatrists in outpatient and inpatient settings. The investigators randomly assigned the patients to one of two groups. They gave the patients in the first group a copy of *Feeling Good* and encouraged them to read it within four weeks. This group was called the Immediate Bibliotherapy Group. They also gave these patients a booklet containing blank copies of the self-help forms in the book in case they decided to do some of the suggested exercises.

The researchers told the patients in the second group that they would be placed on a four-week waiting list before beginning treatment. This was called the Delayed Bibliotherapy Group because these patients were not given a copy of *Feeling Good* until the second four weeks of the study. The Delayed Bibliotherapy Group served as a control group to make sure that any improvement in the Immediate Bibliotherapy Group was not just due to the passage of time.

At the initial evaluation, the researchers gave all the patients two depression-severity tests. There was no difference in the depression levels in the two groups—patients in both groups were moderately to severely depressed. At the end of the first four weeks, the researchers gave all the patients the same two depression tests. The patients in the Immediate Bibliotherapy Group improved considerably. In fact, the average scores on both depression tests were in the range considered normal. In contrast, the patients in the Delayed Bibliotherapy Group did not improve. This showed that the improvement from *Feeling Good* was not just due to the passage of time.

Then Drs. Jamison and Scogin gave the patients in the Delayed Bibliotherapy Group a copy of *Feeling Good* and asked them to read it during the second four weeks of the study. These patients improved during the next four weeks, just as the patients in the Immediate Bibliotherapy Group had improved during the first four weeks of the study.

Finally, the researchers did a three-month follow-up evaluation to see if the effects of the *Feeling Good* bibliotherapy would last. The patients did not relapse but maintained their gains during this time. In fact, there was a tendency for continued improvement following the completion of the treatment.

The results of this study indicated that *Feeling Good* definitely had antidepressant effects. In fact, at the end of the four weeks of bibliotherapy treatment, more than 70% of the patients no longer met the criteria for a major depressive episode. This meant they recovered according to the criteria in the American Psychiatric Association's *Diagnostic and Statistical Manual* (*DSM*). At the three-month evaluation, 75% of the patients in the Immediate Bibliotherapy Group and 73% of the patients in the Delayed Bibliotherapy Group were no longer depressed according to the official diagnostic critieria.

There were several additional findings. First, the treatment seemed to work faster than professional therapy. Research studies with antidepressant medications or psychotherapy typically last twelve weeks or more. Second, the magnitude of the improvement was as great as the improvement in most published studies using antidepressant medications, psychotherapy, or both. Third, the percentage of patients who dropped out of the study was only around 10%. This is less than most published treatment studies using medication or psychotherapy, which typically have dropout rates from 15% to over 50%. Fourth, the patients who improved developed more positive attitudes and thinking patterns on two psychological tests after reading *Feeling Good*. This was consistent with the premise of the cognitive behavioral therapy: You can defeat depression by changing the negative thinking patterns that cause it. Finally, the cost of this new "treatment" was quite small, since a paperback copy of *Feeling Good* costs less than one day of antidepressant drug treatment—and is presumably free of any troublesome side effects as well! Given the tremendous pressures to cut health-care costs, this finding is of considerable interest.

While the results of this study were encouraging, the three-month follow-up evaluation was not really long enough to determine whether the beneficial effects would last. Motivational speakers can get a crowd of people fired up and feeling optimistic for brief periods of time—but these brief mood-elevating effects often don't persist. Would the effects of the bibliotherapy last beyond three months?

In a study published in the summer of 1997, Drs. Nancy Smith, Mark Floyd, and Forrest Scogin, from the University of Alabama, and Dr. Christine Jamison, from the Tuskegee Veterans Affairs Medical Center, reported the results of a three-year follow-up study of the patients in the bibliotherapy study.[7] The researchers discovered that the patients did not relapse but maintained their gains during the three-year period. Scores on the two depression tests at the three-year evaluation were actually slightly better than the scores at the completion of the bibliotherapy treatment. The diagnostic findings at the three-year evaluation confirmed the same thing—72% of the patients still did not meet the criteria for a major depressive episode.

The researchers also learned that 70% of the patients in the study did not seek or receive any further treatment with medications or psychotherapy during the follow-up period. Approximately half indicated that when they were upset, they opened up *Feeling Good* and reread the most helpful sections. The researchers speculated that these self-administered "booster sessions" may have been important in maintaining a positive outlook following recovery. Forty percent of the patients said that the best part of the book was that it helped them change their negative thinking patterns, such as learning to be less perfectionistic and to give up all-or-nothing thinking. The researchers speculated that bibliotherapy could have a significant role in public education and might help prevent serious episodes of depression among individuals with a tendency toward negative thinking.

These studies inspired the creation of *Ten Days to Self-esteem*. I reasoned that if just reading *Feeling Good* could have antidepressant effects, a systematic self-treatment program might be even more useful. You will notice that the book is divided into ten steps. At each step, you will learn specific ideas and techniques to help you overcome negative feelings such as loneliness, depression, guilt, and inferiority. You will see as you read this book that I repeatedly urge you to pick up a pen or pencil and TAKE THE TESTS and DO THE EXERCISES while you are reading. This personal effort and involvement can make all the difference in the world. The written exercises will be crucial to your personal growth.

You can use this book in four different ways. First, you can use it as a self-treatment for depression, just as in Dr. Scogin's bibliotherapy studies. On any given day, probably twenty-five million Americans feel down in the dumps with some of the symptoms of depression. Clearly they don't all need to go to a psychiatrist or a psychologist for help. A little mental tune-up with these methods may be sufficient for many people.

Remember, however, that there are times when professional treatment is indicated. You should consider a consultation with a mental health professional if:

- you feel hopeless or suicidal;

- you have been quite depressed for at least four weeks and you have not improved in spite of your own efforts;

- you feel so overwhelmed or discouraged that you cannot function effectively at school or at work;

- you cannot relate to other people in a positive and satisfying way;

- you hear voices or have hallucinations or unusual experiences that others cannot readily understand;

- you have aggressive sexual or violent impulses you cannot control;

- you are abusing drugs or alcohol.

A second way you can use this book is as a supplement to individual therapy sessions. Dr. Jim Boyers has told me that he often uses the book in this way with good success. In fact, when I first wrote *Feeling Good*, this is how I imagined the book would be used. I intended it to be a tool my patients could use between therapy sessions to speed up the treatment, and I never dreamed that it might someday be used alone as a treatment for depression.

It appears that more and more therapists are beginning to recommend self-help books for patients to read between therapy sessions. In 1994, the results of a nationwide survey about the use of bibliotherapy by mental health professionals were published in *The Authoritative Guide to Self-help Books*.[8] Drs. John W. Santrock and Ann M. Minnet and Barbara D. Campbell, a research associate, from the University of Texas in Dallas, conducted this study. They surveyed five hundred American mental health professionals from all fifty states and asked whether they "prescribed" books for patients to read between sessions to speed recovery. Seventy percent of the therapists polled indicated that they had recommended at least three self-help books to their patients during the previous year, and 86% reported that these books provided a positive benefit to their patients. The therapists were also asked which self-help books, from a list of a thousand, they most frequently recommended for their patients. My *Feeling Good: The New Mood Therapy* was the number-one-rated book for depressed patients, and my *Feeling Good Handbook* was rated number two. I am hopeful that *Ten Days to Self-esteem* will be as helpful to depressed individuals as those two books have been.

A third way you can use this book is in conjunction with a cognitive therapy group program in a variety of settings, such as outpatient clinics, hospitals, day-treatment programs, and so forth. I have developed a companion book called *Ten Days to Self-esteem: The Leader's Manual* for therapists and administrators who wish to set up programs along these lines.

Finally, the program can be used for education and prevention in school settings. *Ten Days to Self-esteem* should be suitable for individuals in the eighth grade or older. I hope that learning about these concepts might help to prevent serious depressions in children and adolescents with a tendency toward negative thinking.

Of course, no treatment is a panacea. It is highly encouraging that so many patients with mild to moderate depressions seem to respond to self-help therapy alone, but it is also clear that some patients with more severe or chronic depressions will need the help of a therapist and possibly an antidepressant medication as well. Many patients have received antidepressants or other medicines at the same time they received the cognitive therapy. The combination can often be very helpful, especially for patients with severe or long-standing mood problems.

If the book is helpful for you, that's great. But if you find that your mood does not improve when you read it, that is not unusual either. I have treated large numbers of patients who could not turn their negative thinking around without some additional help. This is common, and it is nothing to be ashamed of. Remember that 70% of the patients who read *Feeling Good* improved—but 30% did not. Different people require different approaches; fortunately, we now have many effective treatments for depression. But MAKE SURE YOU HAVE DONE THE EXERCISES before you conclude that the methods are not working!

Negative thinking patterns can be immensely deceptive and persuasive, and change is rarely easy. But with patience and persistence, I believe that nearly all individuals suffering from depression can improve and experience a sense of joy and self-esteem once again. Observing this has always given me tremendous satisfaction, and I hope it is something you will experience as you begin to understand and apply the ideas in this book.

—David D. Burns, M.D.
Clinical Associate Professor of Psychiatry and Behavioral Sciences
Stanford University School of Medicine

References

[1] Antonuccio, D. O.; Danton, W. G.; and DeNelsky, G. Y. (1995). Psychotherapy versus medication for depression: Challenging the conventional wisdom with data. *Professional Psychology: Research and Practice,* 26:574–585.

[2] Ibid.

[3] Scogin, F.; Hamblin, D.; and Beutler, L. (1987). Bibliotherapy for depressed older adults: A self-help alternative. *The Gerontologist,* 27:383–387.

[4] Scogin, F.; Jamison, C.; and Gochneaut, K. (1989). The comparative efficacy of cognitive and behavioral bibliotherapy for mildly and moderately depressed older adults. *Journal of Consulting and Clinical Psychology,* 57:403–407.

[5] Scogin, F.; Jamison, C.; and Davis, N. (1990). A two-year follow-up of the effects of bibliotherapy for depressed older adults. *Journal of Consulting and Clinical Psychology,* 58:665–667.

[6] Jamison, C.; and Scogin, F. (1995). Outcome of cognitive bibliotherapy with depressed adults. *Journal of Consulting and Clinical Psychology,* 63:644–650.

[7] Smith, N. M.; Floyd, M. R.; Jamison, C.; and Scogin, F. (1997). Three-year follow-up of bibliotherapy for depression. *Journal of Consulting and Clinical Psychology,* 65(2):324–327.

[8] Santrock, J. W.; Minnett, A. M.; and Campbell, B. D. (1994). *The Authoritative Guide to Self-help Books.* New York: Guilford Press.

ABBREVIATIONS OFTEN USED IN THIS MANUAL

Abbr.	Meaning	Definition
BAI	Burns Anxiety Inventory	A test measuring how anxious you feel
BDC	Burns Depression Checklist	A test measuring how depressed you feel
CBA	Cost-Benefit Analysis	A form on which you list the advantages and disadvantages of a negative thought, feeling, or belief
DML	Daily Mood Log	A form for recording upsetting events, feelings, and thoughts
NT	Negative Thought	A negative thought that goes through your mind when you feel upset
PT	Positive Thought	A more positive and realistic thought
RSAT	Relationship Satisfaction Scale	A test measuring your satisfaction with your personal relationships

THE TEN STEPS
—— TO ——
SELF-ESTEEM

STEP 1

THE PRICE OF HAPPINESS

GOALS FOR STEP 1

1. You will learn how to measure your moods as well as your satisfaction in your relationships with others using three self-assessment tests. You will take all three tests at least once per week to chart how much you have improved as you progress from step to step.

2. You will identify your personal goals for this experience. What do you hope to learn and accomplish as you read this book? If you had a magic wand and could solve all of your problems, how would things change in your life? Would you like to be happier and more optimistic? Would you like to enjoy greater self-confidence and a positive self-image? What's on your wish list?

3. You will learn about the price of happiness. I will ask you to decide whether you are willing to pay the price.

HOW TO MEASURE YOUR MOODS

I want you to complete three self-assessment tests now. They are called the Burns Depression Checklist (page 21), the Burns Anxiety Inventory (pages 23–24), and the Relationship Satisfaction Scale (page 27). The Burns Depression Checklist measures feelings of sadness, discouragement, and inferiority. The Burns Anxiety Inventory measures feelings of worry and nervousness. The Relationship Satisfaction Scale measures how close you feel to others. The scoring instructions accompanying the tests will help you interpret your scores.

I will ask you to repeat these three tests each time you progress from one step to the next, so you can chart your progress. This will not be time-consuming. Once you are used to these tests, you will be able to complete them in just a few minutes. You should take the tests at least once per week, but you may take them more often if you are moving more rapidly through the book.

The tests are extremely accurate and can measure very small fluctuations in your moods in much the same way that a thermometer measures your temperature. If you have had a sudden change in your moods for better or for worse, you can note this at the bottom after you take each test. For example, you could write "When I felt unusually good" or "When

I was in a really bad mood." You might also want to note what made you upset, such as "I got criticized by my boss."

THE BURNS DEPRESSION CHECKLIST

On page 20 you will find an example of a completed Burns Depression Checklist. (The name of this test will be abbreviated BDC. If you find any abbreviations you do not understand while you are reading this book, turn to the list on page 14.) You can see that the woman who completed the BDC on this page indicated that she felt somewhat sad, discouraged, and guilty. She also felt moderately inferior, low on self-esteem, and irritable. She indicated a loss of interest in life and a tendency to procrastinate at doing things. She felt a decreased interest in sex and thought that she was looking old and unattractive. Finally, she indicated that at times she felt life was not worth living, even though she had no real intention of making a suicide attempt.

After completing the fifteen questions, she added up her total score and recorded it at the bottom. The score of 17 indicated that she was feeling a mild depression. This score would be comparable to a fever of 100.5 degrees Fahrenheit. It's not exceptionally severe, but it's certainly enough to drain your energy and take all the joy out of life!

After you review the sample BDC on page 20, complete the blank one on page 21 and put your score on the bottom. Answer the questions according to the way you have been feeling over the last several days.

The scoring on the BDC can range between 0 (if you answered 0 on all fifteen questions) and 45 (if you answered 3 on all fifteen questions). Higher scores indicate more severe depression. You can interpret your score on the test with the scoring key on page 22. As you can see, lower scores are better and higher scores indicate greater depression.

Scores between 0 and 4 are the very best. Most people with scores in this range are quite happy and have no symptoms of depression at all. Although no one can be happy all the time, this is where I would like your scores to be *most* of the time. Even if you feel quite depressed and pessimistic right now, this is our ultimate goal. At first, of course, we will be very pleased with any reduction in your score. Even a small change of a few points will show that you are starting to feel better.

Scores from 5 to 10 are normal but could stand improvement. If you score in this range you are not considered clinically depressed, but you are not as happy as you would like to be. You may need a little tune-up to brighten your outlook on life.

Scores above 10 indicate increasingly severe depression and may indicate the need for treatment. Unfortunately, many people with elevated scores on the BDC do not seek therapy. They often feel hopeless or worthless and do not recognize they have a very treatable problem.

The loss of self-esteem and feelings of hopelessness are the worst aspects of depression. You may tell yourself that you're no good and feel absolutely convinced that there is no solution for your problems. It's not like having a cold, which is an illness that you know will go away after a period of time. In one sense, depression can feel even worse than cancer, because most cancer patients feel hope as well as self-esteem.

I want you to know that even though depression can be extraordinarily painful and demoralizing, the prognosis for a full recovery is nearly always quite positive—no matter how bad you feel, and no matter how long you have felt that way. My clinical experience and numerous research studies have documented that people who try persistently can experience joy and self-esteem again.

I once treated a divorced schoolteacher named Joshua, with a life of chronic severe depression and loneliness, who told me that he was "defective at the core." He felt miserable and criticized himself relentlessly. I tried for months to persuade Joshua to stop beating himself up so mercilessly, but he fought me tooth and nail. He argued that he really was worthless and claimed that I just didn't understand. Joshua had a long list of evidence to support his negative self-image: lousy work performance, failed relationships with women, a lack of any real hobbies or interests in life, and unrelenting depression since childhood. He stubbornly insisted he was a hopeless case and appeared stuck.

One night when jogging I remembered a technique I had developed called the Cost-Benefit Analysis. I called Joshua at home at 7 A.M., so I could catch him before he left for school, and asked him to do two pages of written homework on his own before his psychotherapy session later that day. First, he was to draw a line down the middle of a piece of paper from top to bottom. In the left-hand column he was to list the advantages of thinking of himself as a "defective human being." In the right-hand column he was to list the disadvantages. I asked him to think carefully about the costs as well as the benefits of this mind-set.

Next, he was to perform a similar analysis on a second piece of paper. He was to draw a line down the middle once again. This time he was to list the advantages and disadvantages of thinking of himself as a "human being with defects" in the left- and right-hand columns. What were the costs and benefits of this mind-set? Joshua was a bit taken aback that I had called so early in the morning, but agreed to complete the two Cost-Benefit Analyses and bring them to his session later that afternoon.

When I saw Joshua that afternoon, he had a different attitude. He explained that since completing the lists, he'd begun to feel a whole lot better, because he'd started to think about himself in an entirely new light. He said that even though the *facts* of his life hadn't yet changed—he was still a lousy teacher and still didn't have any good relationships with women—his depression had vanished. He said it had dawned on him that if he thought of himself as a "human being with defects," he could be completely honest about his many deficiencies, without feeling worthless or "defective at the core." He explained that he could begin to develop some hobbies and he could *work* on his teaching in order to become an average or even a good teacher. By the same token, he could begin to date and improve his personal relationships. Joshua's subtle change in coming to see himself as a "human being with defects" clearly worked a transformation in the way he felt about himself and his life.

So you see, even people who have suffered from decades of severe depression—people who feel hopeless and profoundly mistrustful that anyone or anything could ever help them—can recover. I am confident that as you learn to think about yourself and your life more hopefully and realistically, you, like Joshua, can also experience greater self-esteem and wake up thinking, "Hey, it's a great day! It's great to be alive!"

THE BURNS DEPRESSION CHECKLIST*

Place a check (√) in the box to the right of each category to indicate how much this type of feeling has bothered you in the past several days.

	0 Not at All	1 Somewhat	2 Moderately	3 A Lot
1. **Sadness:** Do you feel sad or down in the dumps?		√		
2. **Discouragement:** Does the future look hopeless?		√		
3. **Low self-esteem:** Do you feel worthless?			√	
4. **Inferiority:** Do you feel inadequate or inferior to others?			√	
5. **Guilt:** Do you get self-critical and blame yourself?		√		
6. **Indecisiveness:** Is it hard to make decisions?	√			
7. **Irritability:** Do you frequently feel angry or resentful?			√	
8. **Loss of interest in life:** Have you lost interest in your career, hobbies, family, or friends?			√	
9. **Loss of motivation:** Do you have to push yourself hard to do things?			√	
10. **Poor self-image:** Do you feel old or unattractive?			√	
11. **Appetite changes:** Have you lost your appetite? Do you overeat or binge compulsively?	√			
12. **Sleep changes:** Is it hard to get a good night's sleep? Are you excessively tired and sleeping too much?	√			
13. **Loss of sex drive:** Have you lost your interest in sex?		√		
14. **Concerns about health:** Do you worry excessively about your health?	√			
15. **Suicidal impulses:** Do you have thoughts that life is not worth living or think you'd be better off dead?†		√		
Total score on items 1–15 →				17

†Anyone with suicidal urges should seek immediate help from a mental health professional.

THE BURNS DEPRESSION CHECKLIST*

Place a check (√) in the box to the right of each category to indicate how much this type of feeling has bothered you in the past several days.

	0 Not at All	1 Somewhat	2 Moderately	3 A Lot
1. **Sadness:** Do you feel sad or down in the dumps?				
2. **Discouragement:** Does the future look hopeless?				
3. **Low self-esteem:** Do you feel worthless?				
4. **Inferiority:** Do you feel inadequate or inferior to others?				
5. **Guilt:** Do you get self-critical and blame yourself?				
6. **Indecisiveness:** Is it hard to make decisions?				
7. **Irritability:** Do you frequently feel angry or resentful?				
8. **Loss of interest in life:** Have you lost interest in your career, hobbies, family, or friends?				
9. **Loss of motivation:** Do you have to push yourself hard to do things?				
10. **Poor self-image:** Do you feel old or unattractive?				
11. **Appetite changes:** Have you lost your appetite? Do you overeat or binge compulsively?				
12. **Sleep changes:** Is it hard to get a good night's sleep? Are you excessively tired and sleeping too much?				
13. **Loss of sex drive:** Have you lost your interest in sex?				
14. **Concerns about health:** Do you worry excessively about your health?				
15. **Suicidal impulses:** Do you have thoughts that life is not worth living or think you'd be better off dead?†				
Total score on items 1–15 →				

*Copyright © 1984 by David D. Burns, M.D., from *Ten Days to Self-esteem*, copyright © 1993.
†Anyone with suicidal urges should seek immediate help from a mental health professional.

SCORING KEY FOR THE BURNS DEPRESSION CHECKLIST

Total Score	Degree of Depression
0 – 4	minimal or no depression
5 – 10	normal but unhappy
11 – 20	borderline to mild depression
21 – 30	moderate depression
31 – 45	severe depression

THE BURNS ANXIETY INVENTORY

On page 23 you will find the Burns Anxiety Inventory (BAI). The thirty-three items on the BAI evaluate the symptoms of anxiety, such as worry, nervousness or feelings of panic, fears of dying, or a racing heart. You can answer this test in the same way that you answered the Burns Depression Checklist. For each symptom, ask yourself how strongly you have been feeling this way in the past few days on a scale from "not at all" (scored 0) to "a lot" (scored 3). Please put a check in the space to the right of each item that best indicates how you have been feeling, as in this example:

	0 Not at All	1 Somewhat	2 Moderately	3 A Lot
1. Anxiety, nervousness, worry, or fear			√	

You can see that the man who completed item 1 indicated he had been feeling moderately worried. Once you complete all thirty-three questions, add up your total score and put the total at the bottom, along with today's date.

Your total score on the BAI can range between 0 (indicating no anxiety) and 99 (the most intense anxiety). As with the BDC, low scores are the best. Higher scores indicate more severe levels of anxiety. The scoring key on page 25 will help you interpret scores on this test.

THE BURNS ANXIETY INVENTORY*

Place a check (√) in the box to the right of each category to indicate how much this type of feeling has bothered you in the past several days.

Category I: Anxious Feelings	0 Not at All	1 Somewhat	2 Moderately	3 A Lot
1. Anxiety, nervousness, worry, or fear				
2. Feeling that things around you are strange or unreal				
3. Feeling detached from all or part of your body				
4. Sudden unexpected panic spells				
5. Apprehension or a sense of impending doom				
6. Feeling tense, stressed, "uptight," or on edge				
Category II: Anxious Thoughts	0 Not at All	1 Somewhat	2 Moderately	3 A Lot
7. Difficulty concentrating				
8. Racing thoughts				
9. Frightening fantasies or daydreams				
10. Feeling that you're on the verge of losing control				
11. Fears of cracking up or going crazy				
12. Fears of fainting or passing out				
13. Fears of physical illnesses or heart attacks or dying				
14. Concerns about looking foolish or inadequate				
15. Fears of being alone, isolated, or abandoned				
16. Fears of criticism or disapproval				
17. Fears that something terrible is about to happen				

*Copyright © 1984 by David D. Burns, M.D., from *Ten Days to Self-esteem*, copyright © 1993.

THE BURNS ANXIETY INVENTORY (Continued)

Category III: Physical Symptoms	0 Not at All	1 Somewhat	2 Moderately	3 A Lot
18. Skipping, racing, or pounding of the heart (palpitations)				
19. Pain, pressure, or tightness in the chest				
20. Tingling or numbness in the toes or fingers				
21. Butterflies or discomfort in the stomach				
22. Constipation or diarrhea				
23. Restlessness or jumpiness				
24. Tight, tense muscles				
25. Sweating not brought on by heat				
26. A lump in the throat				
27. Trembling or shaking				
28. Rubbery or "jelly" legs				
29. Feeling dizzy, lightheaded, or off balance				
30. Choking or smothering sensations or difficulty breathing				
31. Headaches or pains in the neck or back				
32. Hot flashes or cold chills				
33. Feeling tired, weak, or easily exhausted				
Total score on items 1–33 $\longrightarrow$				

SCORING KEY FOR THE BURNS ANXIETY INVENTORY

Total Score	Degree of Anxiety
0 – 4	minimal or no anxiety
5 – 10	borderline anxiety
11 – 20	mild anxiety
21 – 30	moderate anxiety
31 – 50	severe anxiety
51 – 99	extreme anxiety or panic

RELATIONSHIP SATISFACTION SCALE

The Relationship Satisfaction Scale (RSAT) on page 27 evaluates how satisfied you feel about your most intimate relationship. It is suitable for both heterosexual and same-sex relationships. Although this test was designed to measure marital satisfaction, you can also use it to evaluate a relationship with a friend, lover, family member, or colleague. If you do not have any close relationships at this time, you can simply think of people in general when taking the test.

This book will not focus directly on intimate relationships. Nevertheless, depression and low self-esteem often result from troubled marriages and from tensions in family and professional relationships. Many of us base our self-esteem on being cared about and valued by others. If you feel lonely or unloved, it is natural to feel sad. It will be interesting to see if your feelings of intimacy and satisfaction in personal relationships increase as your self-esteem improves.

The seven items on the RSAT ask about communication and openness, resolving conflicts and arguments, and the degree of affection and caring. For each item on the scale, indicate how satisfied you have recently been feeling between "very dissatisfied" (scored 0) and "very satisfied" (scored 6).

After you have completed the Relationship Satisfaction Scale, add up your total score. Put the total in the box at the bottom. Your score will be between 0 (if you answered "very dissatisfied" for all seven relationship areas) and 42 (if you answered "very satisfied" for all seven relationship areas). Use the scoring key on page 28 to interpret your score.

How to use the scoring key: First, locate your score in the left-hand column, which is labeled "Total score." Let's assume that your score was less than 10. Now look in the second column, labeled "Level of satisfaction." This column indicates that you probably feel extremely dissatisfied with your relationship. The third column of the scoring key indicates that at least 75% of people with troubled relationships will score higher than this. This means that most of them feel more satisfied with their partners than you do. The fourth column indicates that 100% of the people with successful relationships will score higher than you. The bottom line is that you are extremely unhappy with your partner. You are not a happy camper!

Caution: This does *not* mean you necessarily have a *bad* relationship, and the test does not say who is to blame for the difficulties. It simply means that you are exceedingly dissatisfied and that there is much room for improvement.

In contrast, let's assume that you scored between 31 and 35 on the RSAT. The second column indicates that you probably feel somewhat satisfied with your relationship. You can see in the third column that only about 5% of people with troubled relationships will score higher. This means you feel better about your relationship than 95% of the people with troubled ones. That's good. The far right column indicates that 50% of people with successful relationships will score higher. This means you are doing reasonably well, but there is considerable room for improvement to make your relationship even better.

It's important to remember that the RSAT does not measure how "good" or "adequate" any marriage or relationship is. It simply measures how satisfied or dissatisfied you feel. How good is a good relationship? How bad is a bad one?

To find out, I recently asked over eleven hundred individuals to take the Relationship Satisfaction Scale, based on their marriages or most intimate relationships. Most of them attended lectures and workshops that I was conducting throughout the United States. Approximately one third (32.5%) indicated their marriages were "troubled" and two thirds (67.5%) indicated their marriages were "successful overall." The scoring key is based on a statistical analysis of the data from these two groups.

RELATIONSHIP SATISFACTION SCALE*

Place a check (√) in the box to the right of each category that best describes the amount of satisfaction you feel in your closest relationship.

	0 Very Dissatisfied	1 Moderately Dissatisfied	2 Slightly Dissatisfied	3 Neutral	4 Slightly Satisfied	5 Moderately Satisfied	6 Very Satisfied
1. Communication and openness							
2. Resolving conflicts and arguments							
3. Degree of affection and caring							
4. Intimacy and closeness							
5. Satisfaction with your role in the relationship							
6. Satisfaction with the other person's role							
7. Overall satisfaction with your relationship							
Total score on items 1–7 →							

Note: Although this test assesses your marriage or most intimate relationship, you can also use it to evaluate your relationship with a friend, family member, or colleague. If you do not have any intimate relationships at this time, you can simply think of people in general when you take the test.

*Copyright © 1983 by David D. Burns, M.D., from *Ten Days to Self-esteem*, copyright © 1993.

SCORING KEY FOR THE RELATIONSHIP SATISFACTION SCALE

Total Score	Level of Satisfaction	Percentage of People with Troubled Relationships Who Score Higher	Percentage of People with Successful Relationships Who Score Higher
0 – 10	extremely dissatisfied	75%	100%
11 – 20	very dissatisfied	35%	95%
21 – 25	moderately dissatisfied	25%	90%
26 – 30	somewhat dissatisfied	15%	75%
31 – 35	somewhat satisfied	5%	50%
36 – 40	moderately satisfied	1%	10%
41 – 42	very satisfied	less than 1%	less than 1%

PERSONAL GOALS FOR
THE SELF-ESTEEM TRAINING GROUPS

Now that we've evaluated your moods and personal relationship satisfaction, let's define some of your goals. If you had a magic wand and could solve all of your problems, what would be on your wish list? How would your life change? Would you overcome depression? Would you develop greater self-esteem? Would you feel closer to other people? Would you become more productive and successful? Please list at least three personal goals you would like to accomplish as you read *Ten Days to Self-esteem:*

1. _____

_____

2. _____

_____

3. _____

_____

THE PRICE OF HAPPINESS

What do you think it will take for you to achieve your goals and make some significant changes in your life? What is the key to self-esteem and happiness?

In my clinical practice during the past twenty years, I have had the opportunity to work with many men and women from all walks of life with a wide variety of problems. I have seen people who responded to treatment quickly and others who required a long, persistent effort to recover. I have discovered that one of the most important keys to recovery, regardless of your age, sex, or race, is the willingness to help yourself.

Some people do not seem to understand or accept this simple idea. They are quite happy to complain endlessly about how bad things are as long as they don't have to *do* anything to solve their problems. They see themselves as victims of unfair circumstances and wait passively for someone or something to fix things for them. Sadly, that usually doesn't happen. Years later they are still feeling miserable, waiting for justice or magic to make their lives better.

Of course, this passive approach to personal growth has sometimes been reinforced by mental health professionals and the media. The stereotype of psychotherapy portrayed in popular books and movies is lying on the couch and saying whatever comes into your mind, while a kindly psychoanalyst listens and nods knowingly from time to time. After years and years, something wonderful is supposed to happen.

Although a warm and caring relationship with someone you trust can often make you *feel* much better, I want you to *get* better. That means working hard to make real changes in your life—now and in the future.

I have had the pleasure of treating many people through the years who did understand this. They worked hard during sessions and between sessions to develop greater self-esteem. They did not blame the world but assumed personal responsibility for changing their lives. Their hard efforts paid off handsomely, because they recovered the most rapidly. As I mentioned in the Introduction, research studies have demonstrated that self-help does work.

This is why I want to ask you right now: Are you willing to pay the price of happiness? Are you willing to do something active to change your life in addition to reading this? Put a check in one of these boxes to indicate whether you are willing to do the written exercises and other self-help assignments while you read this book:

1.	Yes, I *will* do the self-help assignments.	☐
2.	No, I *won't* do them.	☐
3.	I *haven't decided* yet.	☐

Did you put a check in one of the boxes? Or did you just read it? I'll bet I know the answer! You didn't do it, did you? You see, that's just the attitude we've got to defeat. Let me make a suggestion that could be quite helpful to you—

Grab a pen or pencil and put a $\sqrt{}$ in one of those three boxes now!

Did I make my point? I know you may have lots of good excuses for not doing the written exercises while you are reading. Now read the list titled Fifteen GOOD Reasons for NOT Doing the Self-help Exercises on page 31 and check off all the reasons that apply to you.

You can see that there are *many* reasons not to do the self-help assignments! These are all *powerful* forces that can interfere with your motivation to help yourself. Did you find that some of these reasons for not doing the written exercises are similar to the way you are thinking?

A lot of the people I have seen in therapy through the years think this way also. At first they have lots of good reasons why they *can't* or *shouldn't have to* do the self-help assignments between sessions. I tell all my new clients that the self-help assignments are required, not optional. If they don't feel comfortable with this arrangement, I am always happy to refer them to more traditional colleagues who would not require them to do things to help themselves between sessions. Fortunately, very few people drop out when I give them this option.

I believe that you, too, will have to apply what you are learning through active effort and practice to change your life, just like the patients I see privately. Are you willing to do this?

If so, grab a pen or pencil *now,* and complete the BDC test on page 21 if you did not already do so. It will only take about 30 seconds, and you'll get a precise reading on how you feel. Once you're done, complete the BAI on pages 23–24 and the RSAT on page 27.

Did you complete the tests? If so, I'm proud of you! You've taken your first (and most difficult) step on the path to self-esteem.

Here's what it will take. The self-help assignments at each step will include the following:

- **Self-assessment:** I will ask you to take the three mood tests at the beginning of each step to track your progress.

- **Bibliotherapy:** I will suggest supplemental reading from my *Feeling Good Handbook* as well as other self-help books to enhance your understanding of each step.

- **Writing assignments:** I will ask you to do a variety of written exercises while you read each step, just as I did above. I will also ask you to keep a daily journal of your negative thoughts on a form called the Daily Mood Log.

- **Behavioral assignments:** I may ask you to do something you've been putting off or to schedule your time more productively.

- **Interpersonal assignments:** Although the main focus of *Ten Days to Self-esteem* is on self-esteem, I may also ask you to practice some new communication skills that can help

FIFTEEN *GOOD* REASONS FOR *NOT* DOING THE SELF-HELP EXERCISES

	Check (√) All That Apply
1. I don't really trust Dr. Burns. Who is this guy, and what makes him such an expert?	
2. I'm not convinced that the exercises will make a difference in my life.	
3. I'm not in the mood to do any assignments right now. Maybe later.	
4. This seems too much like being in school and doing homework. Ugh!	
5. I'm not used to writing in a book. I usually just read a book.	
6. I feel so hopeless or worthless that I don't think anything or anyone could ever help me.	
7. I'm afraid I'm not smart enough to do a good job at this.	
8. I don't like being bossed around or told what to do.	
9. I think others are to blame for my problems. Why should I have to change?	
10. I believe my bad moods result from a chemical imbalance, a nutrition problem, or an allergy, and so these written exercises couldn't really help.	
11. I want to read and see if this makes good sense before I get involved.	
12. I'm afraid of what might happen if I do change. My life may be miserable but at least it's familiar.	
13. I'm afraid that other people may read what I write down and get upset or look down on me.	
14. I believe that my moods are governed by forces beyond my control. There's really nothing I could do to change the way I feel.	
15. I believe that I'm too seriously depressed to be helped by this sort of thing.	

you develop more satisfying personal relationships with friends, family members, and colleagues at work.

These self-help assignments will be crucial to your success. Do not neglect them!

Although you may have the highest intentions to do the self-help assignments, you will feel tempted not to do them. In fact, I'll bet you a hundred dollars to a dime that you have already been strongly tempted not to do the written assignments in this book while you were reading. Please resist this temptation! *Make these self-help assignments your highest priority!*

Please answer the questions in the Self-help Contract in the box on page 33.

That was a written self-help assignment. I just asked you to fill out the contract on page 33. Did you do it? If you did, I congratulate you! But I'll bet that you didn't! Do you see what I mean? There's a *tremendous* temptation *not* to do the self-help assignments, and this urge can be very difficult to resist!

I have a hunch that you may be thinking: "I can just read this. I don't actually have to write anything in this book. It's not really important. It's too much work. Why does Burns keep harping away at this? He's getting on my nerves. Other people may need to do the writing, but I don't need to do it. I'm different."

Resist these thoughts! Right now, before you read another word, grab a pen or pencil and complete the Self-help Contract on page 33. It asks how many minutes per day you are willing to spend doing the self-help assignments. The Self-help Contract also asks how many days per week you are willing to do the assignments, and how many weeks you will keep it up.

Many of my new patients ask for guidelines on this. I would suggest that you budget at least fifteen minutes per day, six days per week. If you get very involved in a particular exercise, as often happens, you may spend more time. However, if you know that you are obligated to do only fifteen minutes of self-help exercises, they won't seem overwhelming.

I would also recommend that if you are reading this book on your own, you should not attempt more than one step per day as a maximum. Take time to do the written exercises and digest the ideas. Don't try to sit down on a weekend and read this book from cover to cover all at once. You need to think about the ideas and techniques in each step. If you get restless and feel that one step is not enough in a day, then do the supplementary reading I suggest at the end of each step. This will give you a deeper understanding of the material.

This book contains ideas that I have distilled out of more than fifteen years of clinical experience. Give yourself time and don't try to learn it all at once. It's just like jogging. It will take a little time to get in shape. The effort you put out to help yourself will reap handsome dividends!

I have a personal as well as a clinical understanding of the importance of self-help as well as patience in recovery. I am currently being treated for a hand injury resulting from a minor fall that I took while playing tennis with my wife. I didn't think the injury was serious and went to a local orthopedic surgeon whom I chose at random out of the phone book. Unfortunately, he misdiagnosed a fracture. Thinking my hand was broken (it wasn't), he put me in a cast for four months. During that time there was increasing swelling and pain, which I called to his attention, but he didn't seem overly concerned.

SELF-HELP CONTRACT

1. I understand that the self-help assignments, such as writing in this book, are not optional but are a necessary part of this program.

    yes ☐   no ☐

2. I am willing to do the self-help assignments.

    yes ☐   no ☐   undecided ☐

3. I am willing to do the self-help assignments consistently even if I feel skeptical, resentful, bored, anxious, frustrated, or discouraged at times.

    yes ☐   no ☐   undecided ☐

4. I am willing to spent at least ☐ minutes per day (please fill in a number) doing the self-help assignments, ☐ days per week (please fill in a number), and I will continue doing the self-help assignments for ☐ weeks (please fill in a number).

Although there was no real fracture, I developed a severe complication from being in the cast called reflex sympathetic dystrophy. It's a fancy name for a poorly understood disease, but the bottom line is that you get severe pain along with a loss of muscle, bone, and nerve function in your hand. When the doctor finally took my hand out of the cast, it was red, swollen, and grotesque. I was almost totally paralyzed in my wrist, thumb, and fingers.

The doctor appeared upset, and I was frightened. I am right-handed, and this is the hand I use in my daily office practice when taking notes on patients, when writing books, and when playing my favorite sport, table tennis. Needless to say, I got a new doctor immediately!

I was fortunate to get a consultation with a colleague at the University of Pennsylvania, Dr. A. Lee Osterman. Dr. Osterman is one of the country's most renowned hand surgeons. He made the correct diagnosis and referred me to Terri Skirven, the director of occupational therapy for his unit. Dr. Osterman and Terri Skirven advised me that the best hope for recovery from this disorder is *intense*, aggressive hand therapy.

This means that I have to exercise my hand almost constantly while I am awake and I have to wear splints when I am sleeping. The treatment literally requires six to eight hours per day of hard work. Even when I'm seeing my own psychiatric patients, I squeeze balls, lift weights, and wear various splints to stretch the frozen joints. I also do these exercises constantly while I'm lecturing or conducting workshops for mental health professionals.

At first, even fifteen to thirty minutes of these painful and boring exercises seemed burdensome. Once I got into the swing of things, however, they became a habit, and now I do them automatically. I will continue to do them for many months until I have recovered. It's well worth the effort if I can get my right hand back! You don't realize what a miracle a hand can be until you nearly lose one.

Of course, self-esteem and happiness are an even greater miracle. Are they also worth some work?

EVALUATION OF STEP 1

At the end of each step you will find an evaluation form. This form encourages you to summarize the most important ideas and techniques that were discussed and to describe your negative and positive reactions to what you learned. Please fill it out after each step. If you are participating in a self-esteem training group, be prepared to discuss your feelings at the beginning of the next session. Even if you are working on your own without a group, it will be helpful to reflect on what you have read as you fill out this form.

You have now completed the first step. What did you learn? Put a brief summary of several of the most important ideas we discussed here:

1. _____

_____

2. _____

_____

3. _____

_____

What did you like the least about what you have read so far? Were there things that were confusing, that you didn't understand? Were there things that you didn't agree with? Was there anything that I said that turned you off? I would especially urge you to write down any negative reactions if you are attending one of the self-esteem training groups based on this book. Was there anything your group leader or the other participants said that irritated you or rubbed you the wrong way? Although it can be embarrassing to express negative feelings, it can help the leader make necessary modifications to improve the sessions.

Please write down three things you *didn't* like about Step 1. If there is nothing, then make something up!

1. _____

_____

2. _____

_____

3. _____

_____

Now write down three things you *did* like about what you have been reading. What were some of the most positive aspects of the experience? Was there anything that was particularly helpful, interesting, or useful? Describe any positive reactions you had:

1. _____

_____

2. _____

_____

3. _____

_____

SELF-HELP ASSIGNMENTS FOR STEP 2

If you are participating in a Ten Days to Self-esteem group, your leader may give you self-help assignments to complete before the next session.

Assignments	Check (√) If Assigned	Check (√) When Finished
1. Complete the evaluation form for Step 1. Be prepared to discuss your positive and negative reactions at the next session.		
2. Take the three mood tests again. They are located at the beginning of the next step.		
3. Read the next step in this book and do as many of the written exercises as possible.		
4. Bring your copy of this book to the next session.		
5. Bring any written homework to the next session.		
6. Bibliotherapy (was any reading assigned?)		
7.*		
8.		
9.		
10.		

*Use these spaces for any additional assignments.

SUPPLEMENTARY READING FOR STEP 1

1. Complete Chapter 1 of *The Feeling Good Handbook* (see Recommended Reading on page 317).
2. Pay particular attention to the Self-awareness Exercise in Chapter 1 of *The Feeling Good Handbook*.

STEP 2

YOU <u>FEEL</u> THE WAY YOU <u>THINK</u>

GOALS FOR STEP 2

In this step you will learn about several simple but revolutionary ideas that can change your life:

1. You FEEL the way you THINK. You will discover that negative feelings like depression, anxiety, and anger do not actually result from the bad things that happen to you but from the way you think about these events.
2. Most BAD feelings come from ILLOGICAL thoughts ("distorted thinking").
3. You can CHANGE the way you FEEL!

MOOD TESTING

You already took three mood tests at the beginning of Step 1. I would like you to take the three tests again at the beginning of each step to chart your progress. If you need help, you can review the instructions for these tests in Step 1 beginning on page 18.

THE BURNS DEPRESSION CHECKLIST*

Place a check (√) in the box to the right of each category to indicate how much this type of feeling has bothered you in the past several days.

	0 Not at All	1 Somewhat	2 Moderately	3 A Lot
1. **Sadness:** Do you feel sad or down in the dumps?				
2. **Discouragement:** Does the future look hopeless?				
3. **Low self-esteem:** Do you feel worthless?				
4. **Inferiority:** Do you feel inadequate or inferior to others?				
5. **Guilt:** Do you get self-critical and blame yourself?				
6. **Indecisiveness:** Is it hard to make decisions?				
7. **Irritability:** Do you frequently feel angry or resentful?				
8. **Loss of interest in life:** Have you lost interest in your career, hobbies, family, or friends?				
9. **Loss of motivation:** Do you have to push yourself hard to do things?				
10. **Poor self-image:** Do you feel old or unattractive?				
11. **Appetite changes:** Have you lost your appetite? Do you overeat or binge compulsively?				
12. **Sleep changes:** Is it hard to get a good night's sleep? Are you excessively tired and sleeping too much?				
13. **Loss of sex drive:** Have you lost your interest in sex?				
14. **Concerns about health:** Do you worry excessively about your health?				
15. **Suicidal impulses:** Do you have thoughts that life is not worth living or think you'd be better off dead?†				
Total score on items 1–15 →				

†Anyone with suicidal urges should seek immediate help from a mental health professional.

THE BURNS ANXIETY INVENTORY*

Place a check (√) in the box to the right of each category to indicate how much this type of feeling has bothered you in the past several days.

Category I: Anxious Feelings	0 Not at All	1 Somewhat	2 Moderately	3 A Lot
1. Anxiety, nervousness, worry, or fear				
2. Feeling that things around you are strange or unreal				
3. Feeling detached from all or part of your body				
4. Sudden unexpected panic spells				
5. Apprehension or a sense of impending doom				
6. Feeling tense, stressed, "uptight," or on edge				
Category II: Anxious Thoughts	0 Not at All	1 Somewhat	2 Moderately	3 A Lot
7. Difficulty concentrating				
8. Racing thoughts				
9. Frightening fantasies or daydreams				
10. Feeling that you're on the verge of losing control				
11. Fears of cracking up or going crazy				
12. Fears of fainting or passing out				
13. Fears of physical illnesses or heart attacks or dying				
14. Concerns about looking foolish or inadequate				
15. Fears of being alone, isolated, or abandoned				
16. Fears of criticism or disapproval				
17. Fears that something terrible is about to happen				

*Copyright © 1984 by David D. Burns, M.D., from *Ten Days to Self-esteem*, copyright © 1993.

THE BURNS ANXIETY INVENTORY (Continued)

Category III: Physical Symptoms	0 Not at All	1 Somewhat	2 Moderately	3 A Lot
18. Skipping, racing, or pounding of the heart (palpitations)				
19. Pain, pressure, or tightness in the chest				
20. Tingling or numbness in the toes or fingers				
21. Butterflies or discomfort in the stomach				
22. Constipation or diarrhea				
23. Restlessness or jumpiness				
24. Tight, tense muscles				
25. Sweating not brought on by heat				
26. A lump in the throat				
27. Trembling or shaking				
28. Rubbery or "jelly" legs				
29. Feeling dizzy, lightheaded, or off balance				
30. Choking or smothering sensations or difficulty breathing				
31. Headaches or pains in the neck or back				
32. Hot flashes or cold chills				
33. Feeling tired, weak, or easily exhausted				
Total score on items 1–33 →				

RELATIONSHIP SATISFACTION SCALE*

Place a check (√) in the box to the right of each category that best describes the amount of satisfaction you feel in your closest relationship.

	0 Very Dissatisfied	1 Moderately Dissatisfied	2 Slightly Dissatisfied	3 Neutral	4 Slightly Satisfied	5 Moderately Satisfied	6 Very Satisfied
1. Communication and openness							
2. Resolving conflicts and arguments							
3. Degree of affection and caring							
4. Intimacy and closeness							
5. Satisfaction with your role in the relationship							
6. Satisfaction with the other person's role							
7. Overall satisfaction with your relationship							
Total score on items 1–7 ⟶							

Note: Although this test assesses your marriage or most intimate relationship, you can also use it to evaluate your relationship with a friend, family member, or colleague. If you do not have any intimate relationships at this time, you can simply think of people in general when you take the test.

*Copyright © 1983 by David D. Burns, M.D., from *Ten Days to Self-esteem*, copyright © 1993.

IDEA 1: YOU <u>FEEL</u> THE WAY YOU <u>THINK</u>

When you are upset, you probably think about something bad that has happened to you. You may feel angry or discouraged because you lost your job, because you were criticized or rejected by someone you loved, or because you had to be hospitalized for emotional problems. It's natural to feel unhappy when bad things happen.

What are some of the things that make you feel bad? Picture in your mind's eye a time when you felt sad and discouraged or worried or angry. It may have been recently or at any time in your life. Describe what happened to you here. Try to be specific: *Who* were you with? *What* happened? *When* was it? *Where* were you?

_____

_____

_____

_____

Now describe how you felt. Some people have difficulty describing their feelings, but it's really quite easy. The Feeling Words table that follows will make it a little clearer. Look at the major categories of negative feelings in the left-hand column. Then choose the words that best describe your bad feelings. List several of your bad feelings here:

1. _____   3. _____

2. _____   4. _____

Do you know what causes these bad feelings? Scientists and philosophers have been speculating about this for centuries. Some people believe their bad moods result from their hormones or body chemistry. They may think they have a medical condition, hormone problems, a chemical imbalance, an allergy, or a vitamin deficiency that makes them feel gloomy and irritable.

Certainly there is some truth to this idea. Medications such as lithium and antidepressants can be quite helpful for certain kinds of emotional problems, and this suggests that brain chemistry does play an important role in the way we think, feel, and behave.

Other people think they get upset because of the bad things that happen to them. You may have been treated badly by a loved one or betrayed by a friend or colleague. Reports of child abuse and domestic violence suggest that these tragic problems may be far more common than we once believed. It's certainly normal to feel intense hurt and anger when someone you trusted has taken advantage of you. It can sometimes be quite difficult to develop feelings of optimism and self-respect again. Has this ever happened to you? Were you ever betrayed by a friend or abused by another person?

FEELING WORDS

Feeling	Words That Express This Feeling		
angry	mad resentful upset	p.o.'d irritated furious	ticked off incensed enraged
anxious	worried panicky nervous	afraid fearful concerned	scared frightened uneasy
embarrassed	foolish	self-conscious	flustered
guilty	ashamed	at fault	bad
hopeless	discouraged	pessimistic	desperate
lonely	abandoned	alone	rejected
sad	bummed out depressed	down disappointed	unhappy hurt
stressed	overwhelmed pressured	burned out overworked	tense uptight

Some people believe they get depressed for yet another reason: They feel defective and inferior and believe that there is something deeply wrong with them. They tell themselves they aren't confident, charming, pretty, or smart enough to feel happy and worthwhile. They compare themselves to others who appear to be more confident and successful. Then they decide, "I'm not like that. How could I ever be happy? I'm just a second-rate human being, a born loser." Do you ever think like that? Does this sound at all like you?

Finally, some people get depressed because of difficulties in their careers or personal relationships. Many of us base our self-esteem on being successful at work, at school, and in our relationships with others. Then when we lose our jobs or get rejected by someone we love, we may feel devastated. Did you ever have this experience?

All of these ideas have some degree of truth. Certainly your moods are influenced by your body chemistry and by the good and bad things that happen to you. But all of these theories have one big disadvantage—they all have a tendency to make you a victim of circumstances beyond your control. This is because you can't ordinarily change your body chemistry unless you take a pill, and you certainly can't change the world or prevent bad things from happening to you from time to time. There are very few of us—including famous and successful people—who can escape from tragedy and disappointment during our lives.

In this step you will learn about a simple but revolutionary idea that can give you much greater control over the way you feel. The idea is not new. In fact, it goes all the way back to a Greek philosopher named Epictetus. Epictetus said, "Men are not disturbed by things, but by the views they take of them." This means that your thoughts—not actual events—create your moods. In other words, the bad things that happen do not really cause us to become upset. We get upset because of the way we *think* about these events.

Only one person in this world can ever make you feel depressed, worried, or angry—and that person is you! This idea can change your life.

If you are rejected or lose your job, you may feel sad and self-critical because you tell yourself, "I'm no good. There must be something wrong with me." You may also feel angry and frustrated because you tell yourself, "Life is unfair. Why is this always happening to me?" These Negative Thoughts are quite natural. Nearly all of us think this way from time to time. When you learn to change these thoughts, you can CHANGE the way you FEEL.

For example, Tyrone was laid off from work along with several other employees of his company because of a business slowdown. He felt bummed out, worried, angry, and guilty. What do you think his Negative Thoughts were? What would you be thinking if you were Tyrone? You will find his Negative Thoughts in the balloon above the head of the Stick Figure on page 45.

The Stick Figure can help you figure out the bad thoughts that upset you. Think of a time when you felt really bad. If you like, you can use the upsetting event you described on page 42. Ask yourself, "What was I thinking when I felt upset? What did I tell myself when I felt sad (or angry or worried)?" Write down your Negative Thoughts in the balloon above the head of the second Stick Figure, the one on page 46.

So far you have learned that your feelings result more from the way you think about things than from what actually happens. What accounts for the fact that we can have so many different kinds of feelings? It's because specific kinds of feelings result from specific kinds of thoughts.

To take a trivial example, you might feel angry if you caught the flu and told yourself, "This is unfair! I'm too busy for this nonsense. Why does this always have to happen when I have an important deadline?" In contrast, you might feel relieved if you thought about it like this: "I've been working too hard. Now I have a good excuse to crawl into bed with a trashy novel and pamper myself for a few days. The world won't come to an end!" In both cases the actual event is the same, and the different feelings are created by the different ways of thinking about it.

This basic idea is exceedingly important, but I know you may not yet entirely agree with me. You may still think that other people or lousy circumstances can upset you no matter what you're thinking. I understand your point of view very well.

Let me ask you a question. How are you feeling *right now* as you read this? Do you feel skeptical? If so, you are probably telling yourself that you aren't convinced by my argument.

The Stick Figure Technique: When you feel upset, draw an unhappy Stick Figure with a balloon above his or her head. Then write your Negative Thoughts in the balloon. This will show why the Stick Figure is unhappy.

The Stick Figure Technique: Your turn! Make up some Negative Thoughts that explain why this Stick Figure is feeling unhappy. Write them in the balloon above his or her head.

Do you feel angry? If so, you may be telling yourself that Dr. Burns is a rip-off artist who writes simplistic books for personal profit. Do you feel sad and discouraged? If so, you are likely to be thinking that these methods couldn't help you. Do you feel excited and hopeful? If so, you are probably telling yourself that this book could be very interesting and helpful to you.

Every reader reads exactly the same words on this page, and yet each of you will have different feelings about what I am telling you. Do you know why? The same written words can't possibly cause ten different people to have ten different kinds of emotions! If the words on the page aren't creating your emotions, then *you* must be creating your own feelings. Do you see what I mean? Your thoughts, not external events, create your moods.

Look at the table on page 48 entitled Your Thoughts and Your Feelings. A number of different kinds of feelings are listed in the left-hand column. In the middle column, I want you to write down the types of events that might trigger each kind of feeling. Then, in the right-hand column, I want you to write down the kinds of thoughts that would be associated with each type of feeling.

The first emotion on the chart is sadness or depression. Can you think of a time when you were sad or depressed? What happened to you? What were you thinking? You can see on page 48 that I have completed the first part of the exercise for you. If you are feeling sad or depressed, you are probably thinking about something that you have lost. Usually you have lost something that is important to your feelings of self-esteem and happiness, such as an important relationship through death or divorce.

See if you can fill in the blank spaces for the rest of the feelings on the table. When you do the exercise, it will be easier if you can think of a time when you had each of these feelings. Can you think of a time when you were mad? What were you thinking? Can you think of a time when you felt worried or frightened? What were you thinking? Can you think of a time when you felt guilty or ashamed? What were you thinking?

When you are done, you can compare your answers with the ones I have written on page 60. Please do not look at the answers until you have done as many as you can!

YOUR THOUGHTS AND YOUR FEELINGS

Emotion	Describe the Events That Trigger This Emotion	What Kinds of Thoughts Lead to This Emotion?
sadness or depression	*Events that involve a loss: a romantic rejection, the death of a loved one, job or money problems, aging, poor health, the failure to reach a personal goal.*	*You may tell yourself you can never be happy without the thing you have lost, or that person whom you loved so much. You may feel a loss of self-esteem because you tell yourself you're inferior or unlovable.*
guilt or shame		
frustration		
anger		
anxiety, worry, fear, or panic		
loneliness		
hopelessness or discouragement		

IDEA 2: MOST BAD FEELINGS COME FROM ILLOGICAL THOUGHTS ("DISTORTED THINKING")

So far you have learned that only your thoughts can upset you, and that specific kinds of thoughts create specific kinds of feelings.

Now we come to another idea that is extraordinarily interesting and quite controversial. When you feel upset, the thoughts that make you feel bad are often illogical and distorted, even though these thoughts may seem as real as the skin on your hand! In other words, when you feel lousy, you are nearly always fooling yourself about something, even though you aren't aware of this. It's as if you are wearing a strong pair of eyeglasses that distort your view of the world, or looking into the trick mirrors at the amusement park that make you look too fat, too short, or too skinny.

Let me repeat this: Bad feelings like depression, anxiety, guilt, hopelessness, frustration, and anger are often caused by *distorted* thoughts. When you put the lie to these *distorted* thoughts, you can CHANGE the way you FEEL.

The chart on page 50 lists the ten forms of twisted thinking that lead to most bad feelings. Review the chart now. Can you think of times when you were involved in some of these distortions? Think of a time when you were upset or look at the thoughts you wrote down in the balloon above the Stick Figure's head on page 46. Were you involved in all-or-nothing thinking? Labeling? "Should" statements?

I want you to do an exercise to test this idea that distorted thoughts make us depressed and anxious. Remember Tyrone, the Stick Figure man who got depressed after he lost his job? His Negative Thoughts were "I'm a born loser. I'll never get another job. I'm letting my family down." I have written his thoughts in the left-hand column of the Daily Mood Log on page 52. Can you find any of the distortions in Tyrone's thoughts? Study the Distorted Thinking chart on page 50 and look for the distortions in each of Tyrone's Negative Thoughts. Record the distortions in the middle column of the Daily Mood Log on page 52. You will probably find several distortions in each of his thoughts.

I have completed the first one to give you an idea of how to do it. I want you to identify the distortions in Tyrone's second and third thoughts. I want you to *write* in the book on page 52. Don't just do this exercise in your head. This exercise is quite powerful, but it will only work on paper. You will discover how important this is later on, when we work with

DISTORTED THINKING*

1. **All-or-nothing thinking:** You look at things in absolute, black-and-white categories.
2. **Overgeneralization:** You view a negative event as a never-ending pattern of defeat.
3. **Mental filter:** You dwell on the negatives and ignore the positives.
4. **Discounting the positives:** You insist that your accomplishments or positive qualities don't count.
5. **Jumping to conclusions:** You conclude things are bad without any definite evidence.
    (a) **Mind reading:** You assume that people are reacting negatively to you.
    (b) **Fortune-telling:** You predict that things will turn out badly.
6. **Magnification or minimization:** You blow things way out of proportion or you shrink their importance.
7. **Emotional reasoning:** You reason from how you feel: "I feel like an idiot, so I must be one."
8. **"Should" statements:** You criticize yourself or other people with "shoulds," "shouldn'ts," "musts," "oughts," and "have-tos."
9. **Labeling:** Instead of saying, "I made a mistake," you tell yourself, "I'm a jerk" or "a loser."
10. **Blame:** You blame yourself for something you weren't entirely responsible for, or you blame other people and overlook ways that you contributed to a problem.

*Copyright © 1980 by David D. Burns, M.D. Adapted from *Feeling Good: The New Mood Therapy* (New York: William Morrow & Company, 1980; Avon, 1992).

your Negative Thoughts. I want you to get into the habit *now* of doing this exercise with pen and paper.

Okay, here's my analysis of Tyrone's first thought, "I'm a born loser."

- All-or-nothing thinking: He's looking at himself in black-and-white categories, because he sees himself as a *total* loser.

- Overgeneralization: He lost his job, but he's generalizing to his entire self.

- Mental filter: He's dwelling on this bad event and letting it discolor his entire view of life, much like the drop of ink that discolors a beaker of water.

- Discounting the positives: He's overlooking his many good qualities.

- Magnification or minimization: He's blowing this negative event out of proportion.

- Emotional reasoning: Tyrone reasons from how he feels. He *feels* like "a born loser," so he believes he really *is* one!

- "Should" statements: He may have the belief that he should always be successful at things and never fail. He may also believe that if he is a good person and tries hard, life should always go smoothly.

- Labeling: He's labeling himself as "a born loser" instead of trying to learn from the situation or thinking about the best way to find a new job.

- Blame: He's automatically blaming himself for getting laid off. In point of fact, lots of people at his plant were laid off due to a slowdown in the economy. Tyrone's employment record has been excellent.

After you have identified the distortions in Tyrone's second and third thoughts, I would like you to work on your own Negative Thoughts. Study the thoughts that you wrote down in the balloon above the Stick Figure's head on page 46. See if you can find any distortions in your thoughts, using the Distorted Thinking chart on page 50. Write down as many distortions as you can here.

1. _____   5. _____

2. _____   6. _____

3. _____   7. _____

4. _____   8. _____

DAILY MOOD LOG

Negative Thoughts Write down the thoughts that make you upset.	Distortions Use the Distorted Thinking chart on page 50.	Positive Thoughts Substitute other thoughts that are more positive and realistic.
1. I'm a born loser.	1. all-or-nothing thinking, overgeneralization, mental filter, discounting the positives, magnification, emotional reasoning, "should" statements, labeling, blame.	1.
2. I'll never get another job.	2.	2.
3. I'm letting my family down.	3.	3.

52

IDEA 3: YOU CAN **CHANGE** THE WAY YOU **FEEL**

Now we've come to crunch time. How can you put these ideas to practical use to make you feel better? The final and most important idea is that when you CHANGE those illogical, self-critical thoughts, you can CHANGE the way you FEEL. Let's use this idea to help Tyrone. Once you've had some practice changing other people's thoughts, we can begin to work on your Negative Thoughts and feelings. It's a bit more difficult to change your own thoughts because they seem so real. You will need a little more practice first.

So let's see what we can do to help poor Tyrone. Put yourself in his shoes. Imagine that you lost your job. You are thinking, "I'm a born loser." What could you tell yourself in place of this Negative Thought? Can you think of a more positive and realistic thought to substitute for it?

See if you can write a Positive Thought in the right-hand column of the Daily Mood Log on page 52. The Positive Thought should have these characteristics:

- It should be affirming.

- It should be absolutely valid and realistic.

- It should put the lie to the Negative Thought.

Write a more positive and realistic thought in the right-hand column now.

Did you do it? No? You say you just thought about it in your head? Let's have a friendly little chat, you and me. Here's what I would gently like to suggest—

Pick up a pen or pencil and do the written exercise NOW! This is VERY IMPORTANT. Do you want to change your life? Then do the self-help assignments!

Here's a Positive Thought that you could write in the right-hand column: "I'm a human being who's out of work. Lots of people are in my predicament these days. I lost my job, and that's a pain in the ass, but it doesn't make me a loser. Several of my buddies are out of work, and they're not losers."

Now repeat this process with Tyrone's other two thoughts: "I'll never get another job" and "I'm letting my family down." Remember to identify the distortions in the middle column first. Then substitute more positive and realistic thoughts in the right-hand column.

After you are done, put a big X through that unhappy Stick Figure on page 45 as you chase those bad thoughts and feelings away!

Complete the new Stick Figure on page 55. Write the Positive Thoughts from your Daily

Mood Log in the balloon above the smiling Stick Figure's head to show how Tyrone is now thinking and feeling.

I want to erase one possible misconception at this point. It's natural to feel disappointed when something bad happens, like getting laid off when you need work. Tyrone has a right to feel sad. However, he's going too far when he calls himself a loser who will never get another job. Those exaggerated thoughts double his trouble, because now he's got two problems for the price of one. He's not only lost his job, he's lost his sense of self-esteem.

The purpose of this exercise is not to make Tyrone feel happy and delighted because he's been laid off. That would be ridiculous. No one can feel happy all the time. We simply want Tyrone to think about the situation more realistically, so that he will have a sense of self-respect while he's looking for a new job. Doesn't that make good sense?

DISTORTED THINKING EXERCISE 1

Lyle is a single musician who is recovering from alcoholism and severe depression. At night he often feels discouraged, alone, and sorely tempted to drink instead of going to an AA meeting. As part of the homework for his self-esteem training group, he recorded his negative feelings and thoughts on the Daily Mood Log. First, he wrote a brief description of the situation:

Step One: Describe the Upsetting Event. *I'm sitting home alone Monday night with nothing to do. I'd really like a drink.*

Step Two: Record Your Negative Feelings. The next step is to identify your negative emotions and to rate how intense each one is, on a scale from 0% (the least) to 100% (the most). Use words like *sad, anxious, angry, guilty, lonely, hopeless, frustrated, inferior,* and so on. Here's what Lyle wrote down:

Emotion	Rating (0%–100%)	Emotion	Rating (0%–100%)
1. Inadequate	50%	4. Angry	60%
2. Frustrated	50%	5. Sad	75%
3. Afraid	50%	6. Discouraged	90%

Step Three: Record Your Negative Thoughts. Lyle wrote his thoughts in the Negative Thoughts column on the form on page 56. Notice that he put how strongly he believed each one, on a scale from 0% to 100%. Choose one or two of his Negative Thoughts and try to identify the distortions in them, using the checklist on page 50.

The Happy Stick Figure: Write down Tyrone's Positive Thoughts in the balloon above the Stick Figure's head.

LYLE'S DAILY MOOD LOG

Negative Thoughts Write down the thoughts that make you upset and estimate your belief in each one (0%–100%).	Distortions Use the Distorted Thinking chart on page 50.
1. I'll get fewer jobs to play than I had last year. 70%	
2. I'll never be able to make enough money to buy a new car. 70%	
3. Life is passing me by. I'm getting old. 50%	
4. I'm a failure. 60%	
5. I'm not getting what I deserve out of life. 70%	
6. Life won't be enjoyable unless I get what I want. 70%	

DISTORTED THINKING EXERCISE 2

It's important to do this exercise in a systematic, step-by-step manner. If you feel awkward about working on your own personal problems, you can pretend to be someone else such as a friend or family member who often gets upset.

Step One: Describe the Upsetting Event. Think of something that upset you at any time in your life. It can be a situation that happened recently or a long time ago. It can be something minor like getting turned down for a date, or worrying because you haven't heard from your son or daughter who is out late with friends. It can also be something major like discovering that your elderly parents need to go into a nursing home. Briefly describe the situation. Be specific as to *what* happened, *when* it was, *where* you were, and *whom* you were with.

_____

_____

_____

_____

_____

_____

_____

_____

Step Two: Record Your Negative Feelings and rate how intense each one was, on a scale from 0% (the least) to 100% (the most). Use words like _sad, angry, anxious, frustrated, discouraged, inadequate,_ and so on.

Emotion	Rating (0%–100%)	Emotion	Rating (0%–100%)
1.		4.	
2.		5.	
3.		6.	

Step Three: Record Your Negative Thoughts in the left-hand column of the DML on page 58. Ask yourself, "What was I thinking when I felt upset? What was I telling myself?" You might have been thinking, "I'm always failing in relationships," or "Maybe my son has been in a terrible accident." Estimate how strongly you believed each Negative Thought when it first went through your mind on a scale from 0% (not at all) to 100% (completely). Put your estimate at the end of each Negative Thought, just as in the example on page 56. Now identify the distortions in your thoughts using the Distorted Thinking chart on page 50.

In the next several sessions, you will learn about many techniques that can help you CHANGE the way you FEEL.

Negative Thoughts	Distortions
Write down the thoughts that make you upset and estimate your belief in each one (0%–100%).	Use the Distorted Thinking chart on page 50.

SUMMARY OF STEP 2

THE STEPS TO FEELING GOOD

1. Write down a brief description of what happened when you got upset.
2. Identify your bad feelings about that event. Use the Feeling Words chart on page 43.
3. Use the Triple-Column Technique:
   - Write down the Negative Thoughts that make you feel bad about yourself.
   - Find the distortions in those thoughts using the Distorted Thinking chart on page 50.
   - Write down more positive and realistic thoughts that will make you feel better.

When you are done, *congratulate* yourself for doing a *great job*!

ANSWER TO THE EXERCISE ON PAGE 48
YOUR THOUGHTS AND YOUR FEELINGS

Emotion	Describe the Events That Trigger This Emotion	What Kinds of Thoughts Lead to This Emotion?
sadness or depression	Events that involve a loss: a romantic rejection, the death of a loved one, job or money problems, aging, poor health, the failure to reach a personal goal.	You may tell yourself you can never be happy without the thing you have lost, or that person whom you loved so much. You may feel a loss of self-esteem because you tell yourself you're inferior or unlovable.
guilt or shame	You believe that you've hurt someone's feelings or failed to live up to your own personal or moral standards.	When you feel guilty you judge yourself and label yourself as bad: "It's my fault. I shouldn't have done that." When you feel ashamed you are worried that others will find out what you're really like and judge you. You feel you must hide your inadequacy.
frustration	Things don't go as well as you expected: the train is late, your diet isn't working, or friends don't keep their commitments.	You insist that things _should_ be the way you expected.
anger	Someone is treating you unfairly, abusing you, rejecting you, or taking advantage of you.	You tell yourself the other person is a jerk who _should_ be different. You see yourself as the innocent victim. You tell yourself that the other person is selfish and unreasonable and entirely to blame. You feel entitled to better treatment.
anxiety, worry, fear, or panic	You may worry about your health, your career, your performance, your grades, or how others will view you. You may have irrational fears and phobias, such as the fear of heights, germs, airplanes, etc.	You have thoughts of danger and tell yourself that something bad is about to happen — "What if this pain in my chest is the 'big one'?" "What if my mind goes blank when I have to talk in front of all those people?"
loneliness	You have few friends or you've just broken up with someone you cared about. You may also feel lonely in a crowd because you find it hard to open up and get close to people.	You tell yourself that you're bound to feel unhappy because you're not getting enough love and attention from others. You think there's something wrong with you or that you are basically "different" from other people.
hopelessness or discouragement	You aren't doing well with an emotional problem such as depression or anxiety, or a personal relationship problem such as an unhappy marriage. You may feel stuck in your career or in	You tell yourself that things aren't going to get any better. You believe that your problems will never go away and that you'll feel miserable forever.

EVALUATION OF STEP 2

What did you learn in Step 2? Put a brief summary of several of the most important ideas we discussed here:

1. _____

_____

2. _____

_____

3. _____

_____

Was there anything in today's step that bothered you or rubbed you the wrong way? If you are in a group, was there anything the leader or other members said that turned you off? Describe any negative feelings you had:

_____

_____

_____

_____

Was there anything in today's step that was particularly helpful, interesting, or useful? Did the leader or other participants say anything during today's session that you liked? Describe any positive reactions you had:

_____

_____

_____

_____

SELF-HELP ASSIGNMENTS FOR STEP 3

If you are participating in a Ten Days to Self-esteem group, your leader may give you self-help assignments to complete before the next session.

Assignments	Check (√) If Assigned	Check (√) When Finished
1. Complete the evaluation form for Step 2. Be prepared to discuss your positive and negative reactions at the next session.		
2. Take the three mood tests again. They are located at the beginning of the next step.		
3. Read the next step in this book and do as many of the written exercises as possible.		
4. Bring your copy of this book to the next session.		
5. Work with the Daily Mood Log for ten minutes per day. (Extra copies begin on page 290.)		
6. Bring any written homework to the next session.		
7. Bibliotherapy (was any reading assigned?)		
8.*		
9.		
10.		

*Use these spaces for any additional assignments.

SUPPLEMENTARY READING FOR STEP 2

1. Complete Chapter 1 of *The Feeling Good Handbook* if you didn't already.
2. Read Chapter 5 of *The Feeling Good Handbook.*

STEP 3

YOU CAN <u>CHANGE</u> THE WAY YOU <u>FEEL</u>

GOALS FOR STEP 3

1. In this step you will learn the difference between healthy and unhealthy feelings. Is anger good or bad? What's the difference between healthy sadness and clinical depression?
2. You will learn how to break out of a bad mood.
3. You will learn what to do when you're stuck in a bad mood.

MOOD TESTING

You have already taken three mood tests at the beginning of Steps 1 and 2. I would like you to take the three tests again at the beginning of this step to chart your progress. If you need help, you can review the instructions for these tests in Step 1 beginning on page 18.

THE BURNS DEPRESSION CHECKLIST*

Place a check (√) in the box to the right of each category to indicate how much this type of feeling has bothered you in the past several days.

	0 Not at All	1 Somewhat	2 Moderately	3 A Lot
1. **Sadness:** Do you feel sad or down in the dumps?				
2. **Discouragement:** Does the future look hopeless?				
3. **Low self-esteem:** Do you feel worthless?				
4. **Inferiority:** Do you feel inadequate or inferior to others?				
5. **Guilt:** Do you get self-critical and blame yourself?				
6. **Indecisiveness:** Is it hard to make decisions?				
7. **Irritability:** Do you frequently feel angry or resentful?				
8. **Loss of interest in life:** Have you lost interest in your career, hobbies, family, or friends?				
9. **Loss of motivation:** Do you have to push yourself hard to do things?				
10. **Poor self-image:** Do you feel old or unattractive?				
11. **Appetite changes:** Have you lost your appetite? Do you overeat or binge compulsively?				
12. **Sleep changes:** Is it hard to get a good night's sleep? Are you excessively tired and sleeping too much?				
13. **Loss of sex drive:** Have you lost your interest in sex?				
14. **Concerns about health:** Do you worry excessively about your health?				
15. **Suicidal impulses:** Do you have thoughts that life is not worth living or think you'd be better off dead?†				
Total score on items 1–15 →				

†Anyone with suicidal urges should seek immediate help from a mental health professional.

THE BURNS ANXIETY INVENTORY*

Place a check (√) in the box to the right of each category to indicate how much this type of feeling has bothered you in the past several days.

Category I: Anxious Feelings	0 Not at All	1 Somewhat	2 Moderately	3 A Lot
1. Anxiety, nervousness, worry, or fear				
2. Feeling that things around you are strange or unreal				
3. Feeling detached from all or part of your body				
4. Sudden unexpected panic spells				
5. Apprehension or a sense of impending doom				
6. Feeling tense, stressed, "uptight," or on edge				
Category II: Anxious Thoughts	0 Not at All	1 Somewhat	2 Moderately	3 A Lot
7. Difficulty concentrating				
8. Racing thoughts				
9. Frightening fantasies or daydreams				
10. Feeling that you're on the verge of losing control				
11. Fears of cracking up or going crazy				
12. Fears of fainting or passing out				
13. Fears of physical illnesses or heart attacks or dying				
14. Concerns about looking foolish or inadequate				
15. Fears of being alone, isolated, or abandoned				
16. Fears of criticism or disapproval				
17. Fears that something terrible is about to happen				

*Copyright © 1984 by David D. Burns, M.D., from *Ten Days to Self-esteem*, copyright © 1993.

THE BURNS ANXIETY INVENTORY (Continued)

Category III: Physical Symptoms	0 Not at All	1 Somewhat	2 Moderately	3 A Lot
18. Skipping, racing, or pounding of the heart (palpitations)				
19. Pain, pressure, or tightness in the chest				
20. Tingling or numbness in the toes or fingers				
21. Butterflies or discomfort in the stomach				
22. Constipation or diarrhea				
23. Restlessness or jumpiness				
24. Tight, tense muscles				
25. Sweating not brought on by heat				
26. A lump in the throat				
27. Trembling or shaking				
28. Rubbery or "jelly" legs				
29. Feeling dizzy, lightheaded, or off balance				
30. Choking or smothering sensations or difficulty breathing				
31. Headaches or pains in the neck or back				
32. Hot flashes or cold chills				
33. Feeling tired, weak, or easily exhausted				
Total score on items 1–33 $\longrightarrow$				

RELATIONSHIP SATISFACTION SCALE*

Place a check (√) in the box to the right of each category that best describes the amount of satisfaction you feel in your closest relationship.

	0 Very Dissatisfied	1 Moderately Dissatisfied	2 Slightly Dissatisfied	3 Neutral	4 Slightly Satisfied	5 Moderately Satisfied	6 Very Satisfied
1. Communication and openness							
2. Resolving conflicts and arguments							
3. Degree of affection and caring							
4. Intimacy and closeness							
5. Satisfaction with your role in the relationship							
6. Satisfaction with the other person's role							
7. Overall satisfaction with your relationship							
Total score on items 1–7 →							

Note: Although this test assesses your marriage or most intimate relationship, you can also use it to evaluate your relationship with a friend, family member, or colleague. If you do not have any intimate relationships at this time, you can simply think of people in general when you take the test.

*Copyright © 1983 by David D. Burns, M.D., from *Ten Days to Self-esteem*, copyright © 1993.

HEALTHY VS. UNHEALTHY FEELINGS

In the last session we talked about the huge impact of your thoughts and attitudes on the way you feel. Your emotions result more from the way you view things than from what happens to you. That simple idea can help you change the way you think and feel. In today's step, you'll learn more about the nuts and bolts of doing this.

However, before we go too far with this, we need to backtrack just a bit. When *should* we change our negative feelings? Are all negative feelings bad? Are some negative feelings normal and healthy? Should we try to be happy all the time?

I believe that some negative feelings are healthy and some negative feelings are unhealthy. For every negative emotion, there's a healthy and an unhealthy version. Healthy sadness is not the same as clinical depression. Healthy fear is not the same as neurotic guilt. Healthy, constructive anger is not the same as unhealthy, destructive anger. And so forth.

For example, if a loved one dies, it's healthy to grieve and to share your feelings with friends and family members. Your sadness is the expression of the love that you felt for that person, and the feelings of loss will naturally disappear after a period of time. Clinical depression is very different.

What are some of the differences between healthy sadness and depression? I have listed them below. Think about this question a little bit before you look!

Characteristics of Healthy Sadness	Characteristics of Depression
1. You are sad but don't feel a loss of self-esteem.	1. You feel a loss of self-esteem.
2. Your negative feelings are an appropriate reaction to an upsetting event.	2. Your negative feelings are far out of proportion to the event that triggered your bad mood.
3. Your feelings go away after a period of time.	3. Your feelings may go on and on endlessly.
4. Although you feel sad, you do not feel discouraged about the future.	4. You feel demoralized and convinced that things will never get better.
5. You continue to be productively involved with life.	5. You give up on life and lose interest in your friends and your career.
6. Your negative thoughts are realistic.	6. Your negative thoughts are exaggerated and distorted, even though they seem valid.

What are some of the characteristics of healthy, constructive anger? How does it differ from destructive, unhealthy anger? I have listed characteristics of both in the table on page 69. Think about the differences before you look.

Characteristics of Healthy, Constructive Anger	Characteristics of Unhealthy, Destructive Anger
1. You express your feelings in a tactful way.	1. You deny your feelings and pout (passive aggression) or lash out and attack the other person (active aggression).
2. You try to see the world through the other person's eyes, even if you disagree.	2. You argue defensively and insist there's no validity in what the other person is saying.
3. You convey a spirit of respect for the other person, even though you may feel quite angry with him or her.	3. You believe the other person is despicable and deserving of punishment. You appear condescending or disrespectful.
4. You do something productive and try to solve the problem.	4. You give up and see yourself as a helpless victim.
5. You try to learn from the situation so you will be wiser in the future.	5. You don't learn anything new. You feel that your view of the situation is absolutely valid.
6. You eventually let go of the anger and feel happy again.	6. Your anger becomes addictive. You won't let go of it.
7. You examine your own behavior to see how you may have contributed to the problem.	7. You blame the other person and see yourself as an innocent victim.
8. You believe that you and the other person both have valid ideas and feelings that deserve to be understood.	8. You insist that you are entirely right and the other person is entirely wrong. You feel convinced that *truth* and *justice* are on your side.
9. Your commitment to the other person increases. Your goal is to feel closer to him or her.	9. You avoid or reject the other person. You write him or her off.
10. You look for a solution where you can both win and nobody has to lose.	10. You feel like you're in a battle or a competition. If one person wins, you feel that the other one will be a loser.

Now that you've examined sadness and anger, I'd like you to compare healthy fear with neurotic anxiety. What are some of the differences? Think about the kinds of events that might bring on these feelings, how long the feelings last, whether the thoughts are realistic or distorted, and so forth. See if you can think of five differences, and list them here. The answer to this exercise is on page 88. Try to come up with your own ideas before you look.

Characteristics of Healthy Fear	Characteristics of Neurotic Anxiety
1.	1.
2.	2.
3.	3.
4.	4.
5.	5.

Similarly, healthy remorse is not the same as neurotic guilt. What are some of the differences? List them here.

Characteristics of Healthy Remorse	Characteristics of Neurotic Guilt
1.	1.
2.	2.
3.	3.
4.	4.
5.	5.

The same can be said of any positive or negative feeling. There is a healthy version and an unhealthy version. Healthy self-esteem is not the same as arrogance; genuine humility is not the same as inferiority. What are some of the differences? List them here:

Characteristics of Healthy Self-esteem	Characteristics of Arrogance or Self-centeredness
1.	1.
2.	2.
3.	3.
4.	4.
5.	5.

Why are we bothering to make this distinction between healthy and unhealthy emotions? Is it important to distinguish a healthy feeling from an unhealthy feeling? Why or why not?

It can be quite important because you do different things with healthy feelings and unhealthy feelings. If a feeling is healthy you have several good options:

- You can simply accept the feeling.

- You can express the feeling in a respectful way.

- You can act on the feeling in a constructive way.

In contrast, if your feelings are unhealthy, you can CHANGE your feelings by changing your Negative Thoughts.

A depressed woman named Ruby once told me that she felt angry all day long every day. Ruby said she was angry when she got up in the morning and she was angry when she went to bed at night. She said she felt annoyed and snapped at the bus driver when she got on the bus each morning, and she snapped at him again when she got off the bus. She said she was consumed by anger every minute of every day.

I asked what she was so mad about. Ruby told me she was mad at a teacher who had unfairly given her a B rather than an A on a paper she had slaved over. I asked if she had thought of talking it over with her teacher to find out what the problem was.

Ruby insisted that this was out of the question. She said that she couldn't *possibly* do that!

I was curious and asked why she felt she couldn't talk to him. She explained that he had died seventeen years ago!

I was flabbergasted: "Do you mean you've been angry with this professor every day for the past seventeen years?"

"No!" she exclaimed. "I've been feeling mad at him for *thirty-five* years—*that* was when he gave me the B! I've been ticked off about it ever since."

This is an example of *unhealthy* anger. Ruby's anger has been consuming her life, it never comes to an end, and it has no apparent purpose. If she doesn't change the way she is thinking and feeling, she might spend the rest of her life feeling sour and angry with the world!

In contrast, a woman named Joan recently came to me for treatment because she'd become depressed after her oldest daughter went away to college. She explained that she'd been feeling terribly sad and down in the dumps for six weeks. She said she was low on energy and moping around the house. She said this was very unexpected because she was usually a very up person who was full of energy and enthusiasm.

I asked her to tell me more about how she'd been feeling since her daughter left for school. Joan explained that she had a wonderful relationship with both of her daughters. She said that they were both fine athletes and that she'd coached many of their school teams when they were growing up. She said that she'd never had any problems with either daughter and loved them both dearly.

Joan seemed eager to talk about her own mother, whom she said she adored. She said she'd also been an athlete when she was young and that her mother had always been very involved in her activities. When she was thirteen, she'd been in a swimming meet and wanted to win to make her mother proud. Her mother was the coach of her swimming team, and was standing by the edge of the pool observing the competition.

Joan told me how she'd dived into the pool and swum with all her might, hoping to win. Suddenly there was a commotion and the judges stopped the race. As she got out of the water, she saw a crowd gathering near the edge of the pool where her mother had been standing. In the middle of the crowd she saw her mother lying on the ground. She tried to run to her mother's side, but the other coaches pulled her back and wouldn't let her get near.

Joan seemed to have tears welling up in her eyes as she told me, "I heard my mother say, 'Somebody call for a priest.' That's the last thing I ever heard my mother say."

She explained that her mother had had a sudden, massive heart attack, and she collapsed and died at the edge of the pool before the ambulance arrived.

I said that she must have grieved terribly over such a tragic loss of someone she'd loved so intensely. Joan explained that she had never actually cried about her mother's death even once. She said that her father had been a loving but stern man who told her and her brother that their mother would not want them to cry. He told them to keep a stiff upper lip, and never allowed them to grieve, even at the funeral.

Joan was shaky and still holding back the tears. I encouraged her to let the tears flow, and she wept freely in my office.

When the session was nearing an end, I suggested that she let herself grieve every night before she went to bed, and whenever she felt like it. I suggested she might visit her mother's grave and cry, if she thought that would help her get in touch with her tears and sad memories.

Joan's story made it clear why the separation from her own daughter hit her so hard. She had some grief work that she had not yet completed. Because the traumatic loss of her mother had not been brought to a natural closure, any separation and loss was exquisitely painful for her.

I'd been so absorbed by her story that I'd completely lost track of time and forgotten to do my normal diagnostic intake evaluation. This comprehensive evaluation usually takes two or three sessions. I apologized and told her we'd get back to the initial evaluation at the next session, which was scheduled in two weeks.

When Joan returned, she told me that she had cried and cried all day long after our session. She'd also talked with her husband and daughters about her mother's death. When she went to bed that night, she cried herself to sleep.

Joan said that when she woke up the next morning, her depression had vanished and she was back to her normal joyous self. She said she'd felt completely happy and energetic ever since. She asked if she was ready to terminate her treatment, which she was. I never did get to complete my initial evaluation!

The story illustrates the important difference between healthy and unhealthy emotions. Joan didn't need to *do* anything about her sadness. She didn't need any medications or fancy psychotherapy to get better. Her grief was healthy and only needed to be accepted. Once she allowed herself to feel all the sadness stored up inside, nature did the rest.

EMOTION COST-BENEFIT EXERCISE 1

So far we've discussed the difference between healthy and unhealthy emotions. How can we make a practical decision about our feelings when we get upset? We live in a real world where we get stuck in traffic and confronted by all kinds of frustrating and irritating situations. How can we decide whether to accept or change our feelings? We need useful guidelines.

Let's take a specific example. Imagine that you discover that Julie, your fourteen-year-old daughter, has been cutting classes and lying to you about her grades and homework. You feel shocked, disappointed, and angry with her. What should you do with these feelings? Should you express your angry feelings and give Julie a piece of your mind, or should you hold your breath and count to ten?

The Emotion Cost-Benefit Analysis on page 76 can help you with this decision. First, list the advantages of getting angry in this situation. Ask yourself, "How will it help me if I get angry? How will it help Julie?" List the advantages of getting angry in the left-hand column of the form.

Now list the disadvantages of getting angry in the right-hand column. Finally, weigh the advantages against the disadvantages. Are the advantages or disadvantages of getting angry greater? Write two numbers that add up to 100 in the circles at the bottom to indicate the results of your evaluation. For example, if the disadvantages feel slightly greater, you might put a 40 in the left-hand circle and a 60 in the right-hand circle. If, in contrast, the advantages feel quite a bit greater, you might put a 65 in the left-hand circle and a 35 in the right-hand circle.

The essence of the Emotion Cost-Benefit Analysis is that you ask yourself, "How will it help me to feel like this? What are the benefits? And how will it hurt me? What are the negative consequences?" If you decide that your negative feelings are healthy and appropriate, you can accept your feelings and express them constructively. In contrast, if you decide that your feelings are not beneficial, you can change the way you feel with the techniques you are learning.

EMOTION COST-BENEFIT ANALYSIS*

Describe Your Negative Feelings: *I'm angry with Julie for cutting classes, lying, and not doing her work.*

Advantages of Feeling Angry	Disadvantages of Feeling Angry

EMOTION COST-BENEFIT EXERCISE 2

Imagine that you are in one of the situations below. Describe the situation you have chosen at the top of the Emotion Cost-Benefit Analysis on page 78. Then list the advantages and the disadvantages of getting upset in the left- and right-hand columns. When you are done, weigh the advantages against the disadvantages on a 100-point scale. Put two numbers that add up to 100 in the two circles at the bottom.

If you decide that the advantages are greater, then you can accept or express your negative feelings. In contrast, if the disadvantages are greater, you can use the Daily Mood Log to change the way you feel.

Choose one of these situations and do a Cost-Benefit Analysis now:

- A car cuts in front of you in traffic. What are the advantages and disadvantages of getting angry?

- A family member makes a rude remark. What are the advantages and disadvantages of getting angry?

- You're in a big hurry, and the train or bus is thirty minutes late. What are the advantages and disadvantages of getting angry and frustrated?

- You are studying for an important exam. What are the advantages and disadvantages of getting nervous?

- Some ten-year-old children crowd in front of you in line at a movie theater. What are the advantages and disadvantages of getting angry?

- For women: Some workmen whistle at you when you pass a construction site. What are the advantages and disadvantages of getting annoyed?

- You discover that your new answering machine does not work properly after you carefully assembled it. You exchange it for another one, which you carefully unpack and install. You discover that it does not work properly either. All of this took about three hours. What are the advantages and disadvantages of getting annoyed?

EMOTION COST-BENEFIT ANALYSIS*

Describe Your Negative Feelings: _____

_____

Advantages of Feeling This Way	Disadvantages of Feeling This Way

THE DAILY MOOD LOG

In Step 2 you learned about the three steps in filling out the Daily Mood Log:

Step One: Write down a brief description of the upsetting event. Be specific as to *what* happened, *when* and *where* it happened, and *whom* you were with.

Step Two: Record your negative feelings and rate how intense each one is from 0% to 100%.

Step Three: Use the Triple-Column Technique:

- Write down your Negative Thoughts in the left-hand column.
- Identify the distortions in your Negative Thoughts using the Distorted Thinking chart on page 50.
- Write down more positive and realistic thoughts in the right-hand column. Once you have put the lie to all your Negative Thoughts, record how much you have improved. You will usually feel quite a bit better.

Today you'll learn more about using the Daily Mood Log. It might sound a little complicated, so we'll go through it with an actual example. I'll ask you to do some writing as we go along, so you can learn by doing. Once you have practiced this technique, it will become much easier.

Throughout the rest of the program, you should use the Daily Mood Log for ten to fifteen minutes per day to record your negative thoughts and feelings. You can find extra copies of the Daily Mood Log beginning on page 290.

DAILY MOOD LOG EXERCISE 1

Were you ever rejected by someone you loved? You probably felt hurt and lonely. Doug is an attractive but overly nice architect who rather easily falls in love. Unfortunately, he's such an excessively sweet guy that women sometimes walk all over him and his girlfriends all tend to dump him after a month or two. Then he mopes around, depressed and lovelorn for several months, until he falls desperately in love again. Not surprisingly, his new love interest is soon taking advantage of him and this unfortunate pattern of rejection is repeated.

His most recent girlfriend, Laura, recently gave him a Dear John phone call, just when he thought they were getting along famously. She said she "needed more space."

Imagine that you are Doug. How would you work through this depressing problem?

First you describe what happened and then you record your negative feelings, as in the example on the next page:

Step One: Describe the Upsetting Event. *Laura told me she wanted more space so she could date other people. She said she only wanted to be friends.*

Step Two: Record Your Negative Feelings— and rate them from 0% (the least) to 100% (the most). Use words like *sad, anxious, angry, guilty, lonely, hopeless, frustrated,* etc.

Emotion	Rating (0%–100%)	Emotion	Rating (0%–100%)
1. *sad*	99%	3. *hopeless*	99%
2. *hurt*	99%	4. *inferior*	99%

You will notice that Doug had a number of negative feelings, all quite intense. If this happened to you, you might have a number of other emotions as well: anger, jealousy, anxiety, and so forth.

Step Three: The Triple-Column Technique. Next, write down the Negative Thoughts that are associated with your feelings in the left-hand column of the Daily Mood Log, as in the example on page 81.

Because this pattern of rejection seemed to be happening over and over, Doug told himself, "I'll be alone forever." Notice that he put "100%" after this first thought to indicate that it seemed absolutely valid to him. If he didn't believe it quite so intensely, he would have a lower estimate, such as 75% or 50%.

Note: It is very important to record the percent that you believe each NT, just as in this example.

After you write down your Negative Thoughts, you can identify the distortions in them, using the Distorted Thinking list on page 50. How many distortions can you find in Doug's first Negative Thought? List them in the middle column of the Daily Mood Log on page 81.

When you list the distortions in the middle column of the DML, it will save time and space if you use abbreviations instead of writing them out. For example, instead of writing "all-or-nothing thinking," you can just put "A-O-N"; instead of writing "overgeneralization," you can put "OG"; and so forth.

(You can see the answers to this exercise on page 89 once you have written down the distortions you found. Please do the exercise *before* you read the answers. The practice in identifying distortions will be helpful and it is not difficult.)

DAILY MOOD LOG

Negative Thoughts	Distortions	Positive Thoughts
Write down the thoughts that make you upset and estimate your belief in each one (0%–100%).	Use the Distorted Thinking chart on page 50.	Substitute more positive and realistic thoughts and estimate your belief in each one (0%–100%).
1. I'll be alone forever. 100%	1.	1.
2.	2.	2.
3.	3.	3.

After you identify the distortions in the Negative Thought, write a Positive Thought in the right-hand column and indicate how strongly you believe it, on a scale from 0% to 100%. The Positive Thought should be a more positive and realistic idea that puts the lie to the Negative Thought. Try to come up with a Positive Thought to replace Doug's first Negative Thought, "I'll be alone forever." How would you talk back to this thought? Please write your Positive Thought in the right-hand column and estimate how strongly you believe it before you read on. Putting your thoughts in writing is very important to the success of this exercise.

This method works only when you do it on paper. Trying to do it in your head is a big mistake. Your Negative Thoughts will simply chase each other in endless circles. Once you write them down on the Daily Mood Log, it becomes far easier to see how illogical and unreasonable they are.

Your Positive Thought might be: "I haven't always been alone in the past, so I probably won't always be alone in the future, even though I'm having a bad time right now." You can write this down in the right-hand column of the Daily Mood Log, as in the example on page 83. Estimate how strongly you believe the PT, from 0% (not at all) to 100% (completely). Put your estimate at the end of the PT. In this example, the "75%" after the Positive Thought in the right-hand column indicates you do believe it fairly strongly but not entirely. You may still *feel* like you will be alone forever, even though you can rationally see that this probably isn't true.

To be helpful to you, a Positive Thought must have two characteristics:

- It must be 100% true, or nearly 100% true.
- It must reduce your belief in the NT.

Note: It is very important to record the percent that you believe each PT, just as in this example.

Finally, ask yourself how much you now believe your Negative Thought, "I'll be alone forever." You may now believe it only 25%. You would draw a line through your original estimate of 100%, and put the new estimate next to it, as in the example below. This shows that you now believe the Negative Thought much less.

Another Negative Thought you might have when you are rejected is "I'm unlovable." If you are feeling self-critical, you might believe it 100%. See if you can identify the distortions in this thought, using the Distorted Thinking chart on page 50. List the distortions in the middle column of the DML on page 83, just as in the previous example.

Now, put yourself into the shoes of someone like Doug who has been rejected and really feels unlovable. Perhaps you can think back on a time in your life when you felt that way. See how many Positive Thoughts you can generate for the thought "I'm unlovable." Put your best Positive Thought in the right-hand column on page 83 and estimate how strongly you believe it (from 0% to 100%). Then cross out the "100%" after "I'm unlovable" and put a new, lower estimate that indicates how strongly you now believe it.

DAILY MOOD LOG

Negative Thoughts Write down the thoughts that make you upset and estimate your belief in each one (0%–100%).	Distortions Use the Distorted Thinking chart on page 50.	Positive Thoughts Substitute more positive and realistic thoughts and estimate your belief in each one (0%–100%).
1. I'll be alone forever. ~~100%~~ 25%	1. A-O-N; OG; MF; DP; MR; FT; Mag; ER; Sh; BL	1. I haven't always been alone in the past, so I probably won't always be alone in the future, even though I'm having a bad time right now. 75%
2. I'm unlovable. 100%	2.	2.
3.	3.	3.

After you have successfully refuted all of your Negative Thoughts, estimate how much better you feel. Cross out your original ratings for each negative emotion (from 0% to 100%) and put a new estimate for each one that indicates how you now feel.

You will recall that Doug put "sad—99%" in the emotion section (Step Two) of the Daily Mood Log when he started the exercise. After the exercise, he felt a little less sad. He drew a line through his original estimate of 99% and made a new, lower estimate, like this:

Emotion	Rating (0%-100%)	Emotion	Rating (0%-100%)
1. sad	~~99%~~ 50%	3. hopeless	99%
2. hurt	99%	4. inferior	99%

If you were doing the DML, you would reestimate your other feelings as well.

If you have any difficulties when you work with the Daily Mood Log, it does not mean that you are stupid or hopeless. This is normal. It often takes many weeks to refute your own Negative Thoughts successfully. This is because you have probably believed these self-critical thoughts for many years, and it may require much persistent effort to put the lie to them.

At the beginning, you will probably find it easier to work with other people's negative thoughts. It is far easier to see how illogical other people are being, and how hard on themselves, when they feel depressed and self-critical. The exercises on the following pages will give you confidence and will make it a little easier when you begin to work with your own negative feelings and thoughts.

In the next several sessions you will learn a great number of techniques to turn your own Negative Thoughts around. When one method doesn't work you can try another, and another, and yet another. If you persist, you will nearly always find a Positive Thought that works for you. The effort is worth it, because the moment you see that your Negative Thoughts are not really true, you will feel an uplift in your self-esteem. Your attitudes and personal philosophy will often undergo a tremendous transformation as well.

DAILY MOOD LOG EXERCISE 2

Imagine that you are Bob, a thirty-six-year-old single construction foreman who felt nervous and insecure when a friend invited him to come over and play cards. Your Daily Mood Log is on page 86. Identify the distortions in your Negative Thoughts. Then substitute a Positive Thought for each of the four Negative Thoughts. Remember to put the percent to which you believe each Positive Thought (from 0% to 100%). Then reestimate how much you believe each Negative Thought (from 0% to 100%).

Finally, estimate how much you have improved. Draw a line through your old estimate for each negative emotion and put down a new, lower estimate.

HOW TO TROUBLESHOOT

The Troubleshooting Guide on page 87 can often be useful when you feel stuck and the Daily Mood Log does not seem to be working. Read it now.

The Troubleshooting Guide suggests that you may need to do a Cost-Benefit Analysis if you are having trouble changing the way you feel. This is especially important if anger is one of your negative feelings. Anger can sometimes be the most difficult emotion to change. Unlike some other negative feelings, anger is a choice you make. Even if your thoughts are grossly distorted and illogical, you may *intend* to feel angry. If so, the Daily Mood Log won't do you much good. The same can be said for any other negative emotion, such as depression, self-pity, worry, guilt, and so forth. If you *want* to feel that way, you won't have much luck trying to change your feelings!

When you feel like you *want* to be upset, you can do an Emotion Cost-Benefit Analysis, just like the ones you did earlier in this step. Suppose you're angry. List the advantages and disadvantages of feeling angry. Ask yourself, "Do I really *want* to feel this way?"

If you decide that the advantages of feeling angry are greater than the disadvantages, you can go ahead and be as angry as you want! You have that right! But ask yourself, "What am I going to do with these angry feelings?" You have several choices. First, you could express your angry feelings constructively, in a spirit of respect, to the person you're mad at. Second, you could tell the person off in an insulting way and do your best to put him or her down. Third, you could pout and keep your feelings hidden, feeling like a victim and telling yourself how unfair life is!

If you decide that the disadvantages of your anger (or any other negative emotion) are greater than the advantages, you will find it much easier to use the Daily Mood Log to CHANGE the way you FEEL.

DAILY MOOD LOG*

Step One: Describe the Upsetting Event *Jerry invited me to play cards.*

Step Two: Record Your Negative Feelings—and rate them from 0% (the least) to 100% (the most). Use words like *sad, anxious, angry, guilty, lonely, hopeless, frustrated,* etc.

Emotion	Rating (0%–100%)	Emotion	Rating (0%–100%)	Emotion	Rating (0%–100%)
1. nervous	90%	3. embarrassed	90%	5. sad	90%
2. inferior	90%	4. ashamed	90%	6.	

Step Three: The Triple-Column Technique

Negative Thoughts Write down the thoughts that make you upset and estimate your belief in each one (0%–100%).	Distortions Use the Distorted Thinking chart on page 50.	Positive Thoughts Substitute more realistic thoughts and estimate your belief in each one (0%–100%).
1. I won't understand the game. 100%		1.
2. Jerry will think I'm stupid. 100%		2.
3. Then he won't like me. 100%		3.
4. This means I'm no good. 100%		4.

TROUBLESHOOTING GUIDE*

If you still feel upset after you fill out a Daily Mood Log, ask yourself these questions:

1. **Have I correctly identified the problem or upsetting event?** Sometimes you can't put your finger on the problem that's bothering you. You will often discover what it is if you review your activities for the past day or two.

2. **Is my description of the negative event specific?** *What* happened? *Where* were you? *What* time was it? *With whom* were you involved? Avoid vague descriptions of problems such as "Life stinks."

3. **Do I want to change my negative feelings about this situation?** Use the Cost-Benefit Analysis to list the advantages and disadvantages of feeling upset.

4. **Have I identified my negative thoughts properly?** Remember not to put descriptions of feelings or upsetting events in the Negative Thoughts column. If you have trouble figuring out what your negative thoughts are, use the Stick Figure Technique.

5. **Are my Positive Thoughts convincing and true or are they just rationalizations?** Rationalizations won't make you feel any better. Your Positive Thoughts must be 100% or nearly 100% true to be helpful.

6. **Do my Positive Thoughts put the lie to my Negative Thoughts?** When you see that your Negative Thoughts are not really valid, you'll feel better. Often, many Positive Thoughts (and many weeks of work!) will be needed before you can put the lie to your Negative Thoughts.

ANSWER TO THE EXERCISE ON PAGE 70

Characteristics of Healthy Fear	Characteristics of Neurotic Anxiety
1. There is an actual danger, such as a rattlesnake that you see while hiking in the desert.	1. There is no real danger, or you greatly exaggerate the danger, such as avoiding planes because you fear they will crash.
2. Healthy fear usually doesn't last long and disappears when the danger is gone.	2. Neurotic anxiety can go on and on indefinitely and may become a way of life.
3. Healthy fear stimulates you to take action.	3. You typically avoid what you fear and may become paralyzed into inactivity. For example, people who are shy often avoid dating and making friends.
4. The thoughts that cause healthy fear are usually quite valid.	4. The thoughts that lead to neurotic anxiety are nearly always distorted and incorrect. For example, people who get panic attacks often tell themselves they are about to faint. However, people who are panicky cannot actually faint because their hearts are beating rapidly and pumping plenty of oxygen to their brains.
5. You are not ashamed of the fact that you are frightened.	5. You may see yourself as a weirdo or outcast and think your anxiety is something shameful you must hide from others.
6. What you see is what you get. There are no hidden motives in healthy fear.	6. People who are anxious are nearly always avoiding some problem they don't want to admit or deal with, such as a marital conflict or dissatisfaction at work.

ANSWER TO THE EXERCISE ON PAGE 81

Some of the distortions in the thought "I'll be alone forever" include:

- **All-or-nothing thinking:** You will feel lonely and dejected after a relationship breaks up. Are you completely alone? Do you have no friends or family?

- **Overgeneralization:** Is it really true that you will *always* be alone? Have you always been alone in the past? Do you honestly believe that no one will ever be interested in you again?

- **Mental filter:** Are you dwelling exclusively on this failed relationship that didn't work out the way you hoped it would?

- **Discounting the positives:** Have you had other relationships that were more successful in the past? Have there been people who were interested in you? Do you have some positive qualities that people value? Have you been able to learn from other mistakes in your life and grow and change?

- **Mind reading:** Are you assuming that you know how all human beings will think and feel about you? Do you have solid evidence that *no one* will *ever* find you interesting or attractive?

- **Fortune-telling:** Are you making a prediction without sufficient evidence? Can you predict tomorrow's stock market, next week's weather, or next year's politics?

- **Magnification:** Are you blowing the importance of this relationship out of proportion?

- **Emotional reasoning:** Are you telling yourself, "I *feel* like I'll always be alone, and so I really *will* always be alone. I *feel* unlovable, and so I must *be* unlovable"?

- **"Should" statements:** Do you have a hidden rule that says, "I must not be alone. If I am unloved, it means that I am worthless and life cannot be rewarding"?

- **Blame:** Are you blaming yourself entirely for the difficulties in the relationship and overlooking the other person's contribution?

Notice that this Negative Thought contained nearly every distortion. When you identify the distortions in your thoughts, it is not important to be precise. There is considerable overlap in the distortions. Once you find one or two distortions in a Negative Thought, you will often find several more.

EVALUATION OF STEP 3

What did you learn in Step 3? Put a brief summary of several of the most important ideas we discussed here:

1. _____

_____

2. _____

_____

3. _____

_____

Was there anything in today's step that bothered you or rubbed you the wrong way? If you are in a group, was there anything the leader or other members said that turned you off? Describe any negative feelings you had:

_____

_____

_____

_____

Was there anything in today's step that was particularly helpful, interesting, or useful? Did the leader or other participants say anything during today's session that you liked? Describe any positive reactions you had:

_____

_____

_____

_____

SELF-HELP ASSIGNMENTS FOR STEP 4

If you are participating in a Ten Days to Self-esteem group, your leader may give you self-help assignments to complete before the next session.

Assignments	Check (√) If Assigned	Check (√) When Finished
1. Complete the evaluation form for Step 3. Be prepared to discuss your positive and negative reactions at the next session.		
2. Take the three mood tests again. They are located at the beginning of the next step.		
3. Read the next step in this book and do as many of the written exercises as possible.		
4. Bring your copy of this book to the next session.		
5. Work with the Daily Mood Log for ten minutes per day. (Extra copies begin on page 290.)		
6. Do a Cost-Benefit Analysis of the advantages and disadvantages of a negative feeling.		
7. Bring any written homework to the next session.		
8. Bibliotherapy (was any reading assigned?)		
9.*		
10.		

*Use these spaces for any additional assignments.

SUPPLEMENTARY READING FOR STEP 3

1.	Read Chapter 4 of *The Feeling Good Handbook*.

HOW TO BREAK OUT OF A BAD MOOD

GOALS FOR STEP 4

In this step you will learn several techniques that can help you change the way you feel. These include:

1.   The Attitude Cost-Benefit Analysis
2.   The Experimental Method
3.   Examine the Evidence
4.   The Survey Method

MOOD TESTING

You have already taken three mood tests at the beginning of the previous steps. I would like you to take the three tests again at the beginning of this step to chart your progress. If you need help, you can review the instructions for these tests in Step 1 beginning on page 18.

THE BURNS DEPRESSION CHECKLIST*

Place a check (√) in the box to the right of each category to indicate how much this type of feeling has bothered you in the past several days.

	0 Not at All	1 Somewhat	2 Moderately	3 A Lot
1. **Sadness:** Do you feel sad or down in the dumps?				
2. **Discouragement:** Does the future look hopeless?				
3. **Low self-esteem:** Do you feel worthless?				
4. **Inferiority:** Do you feel inadequate or inferior to others?				
5. **Guilt:** Do you get self-critical and blame yourself?				
6. **Indecisiveness:** Is it hard to make decisions?				
7. **Irritability:** Do you frequently feel angry or resentful?				
8. **Loss of interest in life:** Have you lost interest in your career, hobbies, family, or friends?				
9. **Loss of motivation:** Do you have to push yourself hard to do things?				
10. **Poor self-image:** Do you feel old or unattractive?				
11. **Appetite changes:** Have you lost your appetite? Do you overeat or binge compulsively?				
12. **Sleep changes:** Is it hard to get a good night's sleep? Are you excessively tired and sleeping too much?				
13. **Loss of sex drive:** Have you lost your interest in sex?				
14. **Concerns about health:** Do you worry excessively about your health?				
15. **Suicidal impulses:** Do you have thoughts that life is not worth living or think you'd be better off dead?†				
Total score on items 1–15 →				

THE BURNS ANXIETY INVENTORY*

Place a check (√) in the box to the right of each category to indicate how much this type of feeling has bothered you in the past several days.

Category I: Anxious Feelings	0 Not at All	1 Somewhat	2 Moderately	3 A Lot
1. Anxiety, nervousness, worry, or fear				
2. Feeling that things around you are strange or unreal				
3. Feeling detached from all or part of your body				
4. Sudden unexpected panic spells				
5. Apprehension or a sense of impending doom				
6. Feeling tense, stressed, "uptight," or on edge				
Category II: Anxious Thoughts	0 Not at All	1 Somewhat	2 Moderately	3 A Lot
7. Difficulty concentrating				
8. Racing thoughts				
9. Frightening fantasies or daydreams				
10. Feeling that you're on the verge of losing control				
11. Fears of cracking up or going crazy				
12. Fears of fainting or passing out				
13. Fears of physical illnesses or heart attacks or dying				
14. Concerns about looking foolish or inadequate				
15. Fears of being alone, isolated, or abandoned				
16. Fears of criticism or disapproval				
17. Fears that something terrible is about to happen				

THE BURNS ANXIETY INVENTORY (Continued)

Category III: Physical Symptoms	0 Not at All	1 Somewhat	2 Moderately	3 A Lot
18. Skipping, racing, or pounding of the heart (palpitations)				
19. Pain, pressure, or tightness in the chest				
20. Tingling or numbness in the toes or fingers				
21. Butterflies or discomfort in the stomach				
22. Constipation or diarrhea				
23. Restlessness or jumpiness				
24. Tight, tense muscles				
25. Sweating not brought on by heat				
26. A lump in the throat				
27. Trembling or shaking				
28. Rubbery or ''jelly'' legs				
29. Feeling dizzy, lightheaded, or off balance				
30. Choking or smothering sensations or difficulty breathing				
31. Headaches or pains in the neck or back				
32. Hot flashes or cold chills				
33. Feeling tired, weak, or easily exhausted				
Total Score on items 1–33 →				

RELATIONSHIP SATISFACTION SCALE*

Place a check (√) in the box to the right of each category that best describes the amount of satisfaction you feel in your closest relationship.

	0 Very Dissatisfied	1 Moderately Dissatisfied	2 Slightly Dissatisfied	3 Neutral	4 Slightly Satisfied	5 Moderately Satisfied	6 Very Satisfied
1. Communication and openness							
2. Resolving conflicts and arguments							
3. Degree of affection and caring							
4. Intimacy and closeness							
5. Satisfaction with your role in the relationship							
6. Satisfaction with the other person's role							
7. Overall satisfaction with your relationship							
Total score on items 1–7 →							

Note: Although this test assesses your marriage or most intimate relationship, you can also use it to evaluate your relationship with a friend, family member, or colleague. If you do not have any intimate relationships at this time, you can simply think of people in general when you take the test.

HOW TO UNTWIST YOUR THINKING

Although it is usually easy to identify your Negative Thoughts when you feel upset, it is often difficult to put the lie to these thoughts because they seem so valid. My colleagues and I have developed a large number of techniques to help you develop more positive thinking patterns. These techniques are listed in the table entitled Fifteen Ways to Untwist Your Thinking on page 109.

You have already learned two techniques that can help you talk back to your Negative Thoughts:

1. **Identify the Distortions:** You use the Distorted Thinking chart on page 50 to identify the distortions in your Negative Thoughts. Although this usually won't be sufficient to change the way you feel, it's a helpful first step. Once you see that your Negative Thoughts are not realistic, it becomes a whole lot easier to replace them with thoughts that are more positive and realistic.

2. **The Straightforward Approach:** You simply ask yourself if you can think of a more positive and realistic thought.

Today you will learn about several additional techniques for talking back to Negative Thoughts.

3. **Do a Cost-Benefit Analysis:** You have already learned how to do an Emotion Cost-Benefit Analysis in Step 3 when you listed the advantages and disadvantages of getting angry or upset in various situations. You can do an Attitude Cost-Benefit Analysis for a Negative Thought (such as "I'm an inferior person") or an attitude (such as "I must always try to be perfect"). You ask yourself, "How will it help me, and how will it hurt me, to think like this?" We will do an Attitude Cost-Benefit Analysis in today's step.

4. **Examine the Evidence:** Ask yourself, "What is the evidence that this thought is true? What is the evidence that it's not true?"

5. **The Survey Method:** Do a survey to find out if your thoughts and attitudes are realistic. For example, if you believe that public speaking anxiety is abnormal, ask several friends if they ever felt that way.

6. **Use the Experimental Method:** You can often perform an experiment to test the accuracy of your Negative Thought. Ask yourself, "What experiment could I do to find out if this thought is really true?"

In future sessions you will learn about even more techniques for talking back to Negative Thoughts. You can review them here just to get a preliminary idea of how they work:

7. **Apply the Double-Standard Technique:** We are often much harder on ourselves than others. After you write down your Negative Thoughts, you can ask yourself, "Would I say this to a friend with a similar problem? Why not? What would I say to him or her?" You will often discover that you operate on a double standard—you have a realistic, fair, compassionate set of standards that you apply to other people whom you care about. You encourage them when they fail or when they are suffering. In contrast, you may have a stern, harsh, unrealistic set of standards that you apply to yourself. You beat yourself up relentlessly, as if this would somehow help you achieve perfection or become a better person. One secret of self-esteem is simply to make the decision to talk to yourself in the same way you would talk to a beloved friend who was upset.

8. **The Pleasure-Predicting Method:** You predict how satisfying various activities will be, on a scale from 0% (the least) to 100% (the most). After you complete each activity, record how satisfying it turned out to be. This technique can help you get moving when you feel lethargic. It can also be used to test Self-defeating Beliefs such as "If I'm alone, I'm bound to feel miserable."

9. **The Vertical Arrow Technique:** Instead of disputing your Negative Thought, draw a vertical arrow under it and ask yourself, "If this thought were true, why would it be upsetting to me? What would it mean to me?" You will generate a series of Negative Thoughts that will lead to your underlying beliefs.

10. **Thinking in Shades of Gray:** This is particularly helpful in combating all-or-nothing thinking. Instead of looking at things in black-and-white categories, evaluate them in shades of gray. For example, instead of thinking of yourself as a total failure when you're having trouble in your marriage or career, you could ask yourself, "What are my specific strengths and weaknesses? What are my positive qualities? What deficiencies could I work on?"

11. **Define Terms:** Ask yourself, "What do I really mean by this?" For example, if you call yourself a "total loser," what is the definition of a total loser? Does this definition really make sense? Is there any such thing as a total loser? You will discover that foolish behaviors exist, but fools do not. We all lose at times, but there's really no such thing as a "loser." Would you think of yourself as a "breather" simply because you breathe?

12. **Be Specific:** Stick with reality and avoid global judgments about reality. Instead of thinking of yourself as totally defective, focus on your specific strengths and weaknesses.

13. **Use the Semantic Method:** Use words that are more objective and less emotionally charged. This is especially effective for "should" statements and for labeling. For example, when you are upset you may beat yourself up by thinking, "I'm *such a jerk.*

I *shouldn't* have made that mistake. How could I possibly be so stupid?" Instead, you could tell yourself, "*It would be preferable* if I hadn't made that mistake. However, the world won't come to an end, so let's see what I can learn from this."

14. **Reattribution:** Instead of blaming yourself entirely for a problem, think about the many factors that may have contributed to it. Focus on solving the problem instead of using all your energy in blaming yourself and feeling guilty. Ask yourself, "What caused this problem? What did I contribute and what did other people (or fate) contribute? What can I learn from the situation?"

15. **The Acceptance Paradox:** Many of the techniques are based on the idea of Self-defense—you assume that the Negative Thought is illogical and you talk back to it. You refute it and defend yourself and build up your self-esteem. This approach is based on Western philosophy and on the scientific method. The idea is that "the truth shall make you free." The Acceptance Paradox is quite different. It is based on Eastern philosophy and on Buddhism. Instead of defending against your own self-criticism, you find some truth in it and accept it. You ask yourself, "Is there some truth in the criticism? Can I learn from it? Can I accept the fact that my performance was not up to par? I have many deficiencies. I am a human being and I am quite flawed." It's important to note that the Acceptance Paradox should never be used as a cop-out or a way to avoid your shortcomings. Often personal change through hard work is needed. Paradoxically, self-acceptance is frequently the crucial first step to personal change.

Why are there so many techniques? Actually, there are far more than fifteen, and you could think of this list as a beginner's toolkit. Many tools are needed because it can be very hard to change your own Negative Thoughts. If you've had feelings of self-doubt for many years, you're used to thinking about yourself and the world in a negative way. If it were easy to change these negative thinking patterns, you would have done it already!

Since it can be tough, we need different types of tools to get the job done properly. There's an old saying, different strokes for different folks. In my line of work, nothing could be more true. I never know ahead of time just what method will work for any particular person. So when one of my patients has a Negative Thought, we attack that thought over and over and over until we find a way to put the lie to it. Each technique represents a different way to attack the thought.

In the next several pages I will ask you to do some written exercises to get a better feel for some of these methods. You won't learn all of them in today's step, but you can make a good start.

ATTITUDE COST-BENEFIT ANALYSIS EXERCISE 1

So far you have learned about doing a Cost-Benefit Analysis for a negative emotion, such as guilt, anger, or anxiety. You can also use the Cost-Benefit Analysis to evaluate the advantages and disadvantages of a self-defeating attitude or Negative Thought. This procedure can sometimes make you aware of hidden motivations that keep you stuck in a bad mood.

Let's assume that someone criticized you or you had a setback in your career. You feel inadequate and frustrated and tell yourself that you're "a total failure." This mind-set is not especially useful, because you will get depressed and defensive instead of pinpointing the cause of the problem and making a plan for dealing with it. Nevertheless, you feel like your life is going nowhere and it's hard to shake the feeling.

List the advantages of telling yourself "I'm a total failure" in the left-hand column of the Cost-Benefit Analysis on page 101. How will it help you to think like this? There are actually quite a few payoffs. For example, you might feel that this kind of self-criticism will motivate you to try harder next time or give you an excuse for giving up. You might feel sorry for yourself and get other people to try to cheer you up. Can you think of any other advantages?

Then list the disadvantages in the right-hand column. How will this thought hurt you? One disadvantage is that you may use up all your energy in feeling inadequate and depressed instead of trying to learn from the experience. Can you think of any other disadvantages? Finally, weigh the advantages against the disadvantages on a 100-point basis. Put two numbers adding up to 100 in the circles at the bottom to indicated the results of your analysis. Which are greater?

In later sessions, you will learn about how the Cost-Benefit Analysis can be used to change a self-defeating belief (like perfectionism) or a self-defeating habit (like alcohol abuse or procrastination).

ATTITUDE COST-BENEFIT ANALYSIS EXERCISE 2

A doctor named Fred was chronically angry and resentful. When things didn't go his way, he would fume about all the injustice in the world and feel sorry for himself. Although he would try hard to act polite and sweep his angry feelings under the carpet, every month or so he would have a temper tantrum at home and act like a grouse at the hospital.

One day he learned that an obnoxious colleague of his had been promoted to associate professor in the Department of Medicine. He felt a surge of annoyance and told himself, "How can a phony like that get ahead? He's just a brownnoser. Promotions should be based on merit and original research, and not on politics. What's the world coming to? It's unfair!"

What are the distortions in his thoughts? After reviewing the Distorted Thinking chart on page 50, list them on page 102.

ATTITUDE COST-BENEFIT ANALYSIS*

The Attitude You Want to Change: _I'm a total failure._

Advantages of Believing This	Disadvantages of Believing This

1. _____   4. _____

2. _____   5. _____

3. _____   6. _____

Now imagine that you are Fred. You're fuming and ticked off and ruminating about the injustice of it all. You feel like a victim of unfair circumstances, and you wonder why the doctors in your department play games and don't have higher ethical standards. How would you use the Cost-Benefit Analysis to help you challenge your belief that "it's infair"? Put your ideas here:

_____

_____

_____

_____

_____

(The answer to this exercise is on page 117. Don't look until you've written your own answer first!)

ATTITUDE COST-BENEFIT ANALYSIS EXERCISE 3

Harry is an extremely shy thirty-two-year-old attorney who's had very little dating experience because he gets nervous around attractive women. Although Harry is tall and quite attractive, he wears rather shabby clothing and has a dumpy appearance. I gave Harry the homework assignment of buying some fashionable, attractive clothing so he could generate a little more charisma and sex appeal. I told him to wear his new clothes and begin flirting with a minimum of ten women every day.

After Harry left my office, he stubbornly resisted the assignment. He felt anxious and annoyed. His Negative Thoughts were: "Dr. Burns just doesn't understand that I *can't* do this. Women are looking for men who are confident and glib. I'm not like that. If any woman found out how nervous and insecure I am, she'd dump me like a ton of bricks. Besides, I'm a *nice* and *sincere* person and I *shouldn't have to* play social games just to get dates. I'm not like that. *I shouldn't have to* wear any stupid flashy clothing. That's not *the real me.* Women should like me just the way I am. If they don't like me the way I am, that's tough!"

What are the distortions in Harry's thoughts? After you review the Distorted Thinking chart on page 50, list them here:

1. _____   4. _____

2. _____   5. _____

3. _____   6. _____

Now imagine that you are Harry. How can you use the Cost-Benefit Analysis to change the way you are thinking, feeling, and behaving? Put your ideas here:

_____

_____

_____

_____

_____

(The answer to this exercise is on page 117. Don't look until you've written your own answer first!)

ATTITUDE COST-BENEFIT ANALYSIS EXERCISE 4

I recently treated a lovely but severely depressed woman who had suffered from horrendous sexual abuse by an alcoholic neighbor who baby-sat for her five days a week when she was between five and ten years old. He had forced her to have oral sex every day. If she didn't perform "good enough," she had to be punished. Her punishment was vaginal or anal intercourse. The neighbor told her she must keep it a secret, and that if she told on him, he would murder her baby brother. She was terrified and never did tell her parents. It became painful for her to eat food because of the ulcers in her mouth, and she hoped that her parents would notice and protect her, but they never did catch on.

She was loaded with extremely cruel, self-hating thoughts, such as "It was my fault. I should have been able to prevent it. If anybody knew about what happened to me, they'd think I was a horny little girl." Although she could see how unreasonable these thoughts were, she had an irrational compulsion to think them.

How could she use the Cost-Benefit Analysis to deal with her resistance to change? Are there any hidden advantages in these Negative Thoughts?

_____

_____

_____

_____

_____

(The answer to this problem is on page 118. Don't look until you've written your own answer first!)

EXPERIMENTAL METHOD EXERCISE 1

A twenty-eight-year-old chemist from India named Ronny suffered from painful shyness and nervousness in social situations. While standing in line at the grocery store, he would stare at the floor anxiously and tell himself, "These people are all poised and charming and chatting with each other. When I get to the cash register, they'll expect me to say something clever or witty to the checker." When he got up to the cash register, he imagined that every eye was staring at him, waiting for his Academy Award performance. He'd fumble nervously, saying nothing, and pay the bill, all the while staring at the floor and wishing he were invisible. Then he'd rush out of the grocery store to the parking lot like a dog with its tail between its legs, feeling humiliated and resentful.

What are the distortions in Ronny's thoughts? After you review the Distorted Thinking chart on page 50, list them here:

1. _____   4. _____

2. _____   5. _____

3. _____   6. _____

How could Ronny use the Experimental Method to evaluate the accuracy of his Negative Thoughts? Remember the definition of this method: You do an experiment to test the validity of your thought, in much the same way that a scientist gathers data to test a theory. Put your ideas here:

_____

_____

_____

_____

_____

(The answer to this problem is on page 118. Don't look until you've written your own answer first!)

EXPERIMENTAL METHOD EXERCISE 2

A successful but chronically anxious attorney named Bill could never relax because he was obsessed with the fear that he might make a mistake and lose a case in court. Although he had a superb record and a great career, he worried incessantly and believed that at any moment this might happen and screw up his career. He imagined that once his colleagues saw that he had lost a case, they'd lose all respect for him and stop sending him cases. Then, he imagined, he'd lose his job and end up in bankruptcy. Then, according to this scenario, his wife and children would leave him and he'd end up living as a bag man on the streets of New York. He had fantasies of his former colleagues walking by and laughing at him derisively as he begged, destitute and humiliated, for loose change to buy food.

Although Bill could see the absurdity of this chain of events from a rational perspective, he simply could not shake these concerns out of his mind, and they plagued him all day long. Of course, he was so nervous that he worked like a dog on every case, and this contributed to his incredible success. But by the same token, his life was miserable because he never had a chance to relax and smell the roses.

Bill's worrying always began with this Negative Thought: "If I lose a case, then my colleagues will look down on me and see how weak and inadequate I really am." How could he use the Experimental Method to challenge this belief? Put your ideas here:

_____

_____

_____

_____

_____

(The answer to this problem is on page 119. Don't look until you've written your own answer first!)

EXAMINE THE EVIDENCE EXERCISE

When you use the technique called Examine the Evidence, you evaluate all the facts that might tend to support or refute your Negative Thought. In a moment, I will ask you to use this method to challenge one of these four Negative Thoughts.

1. *I'm a total procrastinator. I can't seem to get <u>anything</u> done on time! What's wrong with me?*

2. *I just can't control my appetite. I have no willpower.*

3. *I'm so indecisive. I just can't make up my mind about anything!*

4. *I'm such a klutz. I can't do <u>anything</u> right.*

Choose one of those thoughts. Which thought have you chosen?

What are the distortions in the thought? Use the Distorted Thinking chart on page 50 and list them here:

1. _____ 4. _____

2. _____ 5. _____

3. _____ 6. _____

How could you use the method called Examine the Evidence to put the lie to the thought you have chosen? Put your ideas here:

_____

_____

_____

_____

_____

(The answer to this problem is on page 119. Don't look until you've written your own answer first!)

SURVEY METHOD EXERCISE

When you use the Survey Method, you conduct an informal survey to see if your thought or attitude is realistic. A depressed man was angry because he thought his wife was too lenient in disciplining their son. However, he was reluctant to tell her how he felt because he believed that loving couples shouldn't fight or argue. He thought that it would be dangerous to express his feelings. He feared that discussing the problem might alienate his wife and create even greater problems for their son.

What survey could he conduct to test the validity of his belief that loving couples never fight or argue? Put your answer here:

_____

_____

_____

_____

_____

(The answer to this problem is on page 120. Don't look until you've written your own answer first!)

DAILY MOOD LOG EXERCISE 1
PROBLEM—CRITICISM AT WORK

Choose a Negative Thought from the example on page 108. First, identify the distortions in the thought, using the Distorted Thinking chart on page 50. List the distortions in the middle column. Then write a Positive Thought that puts the lie to the Negative Thought in the right-hand column. Try to use several techniques from the table entitled Fifteen Ways to Untwist Your Thinking on page 109.

After you write down the Positive Thought, estimate how strongly you believe it, on a scale from 0% to 100%. Then reestimate your belief in the Negative Thought in the left-hand column.

DAILY MOOD LOG*

Step One: Describe the Upsetting Event *I got a bad evaluation from my boss.*

Step Two: Record Your Negative Feelings—and rate them from 0% (the least) to 100% (the most). Use words like *sad, anxious, angry, guilty, lonely, hopeless, frustrated,* etc.

Emotion	Rating (0%–100%)	Emotion	Rating (0%–100%)	Emotion	Rating (0%–100%)
1. discouraged	80%	3. sad	80%	5. angry	80%
2. inferior	80%	4. ashamed	80%		

Step Three: The Triple-Column Technique

Negative Thoughts Write down the thoughts that make you upset and estimate your belief in each one (0%–100%).	**Distortions** Use the Distorted Thinking chart on page 50.	**Positive Thoughts** Substitute more realistic thoughts and estimate your belief in each one (0%–100%).
1. I'm a total loser. 100%		
2. There must be something wrong with me. 100%		
3. This shouldn't have happened. It's unfair. 75%		

FIFTEEN WAYS TO UNTWIST YOUR THINKING*

Method	Description of This Method
1. Identify the Distortions	Use the Distorted Thinking chart on page 50 and write down the distortions in each Negative Thought.
2. The Straightforward Approach	Substitute a more positive and realistic thought.
3. The Cost-Benefit Analysis	List the advantages and disadvantages of a negative feeling, thought, belief, or behavior.
4. Examine the Evidence	Instead of assuming that a Negative Thought is true, examine the actual evidence for it.
5. The Survey Method	Do a survey to find out if your thoughts and attitudes are realistic.
6. The Experimental Method	Do an experiment to test the accuracy of your Negative Thought.
7. The Double-Standard Technique	Talk to yourself in the same compassionate way you might talk to a dear friend who was upset.
8. The Pleasure-Predicting Method	Predict how satisfying activities will be, from 0% to 100%. Record how satisfying they turn out to be.
9. The Vertical Arrow Technique	Draw a vertical arrow under your Negative Thought and ask why it would be upsetting if it were true.
10. Thinking in Shades of Gray	Instead of thinking about your problems in black-and-white categories, evaluate things in shades of gray.
11. Define Terms	When you label yourself as "inferior" or "a loser," ask yourself what you mean by these labels.
12. Be Specific	Stick with reality and avoid judgments about reality.
13. The Semantic Method	Substitute language that is less emotionally loaded for "should" statements and labeling.
14. Reattribution	Instead of blaming yourself for a problem, think about all the factors that may have contributed to it.
15. The Acceptance Paradox	Instead of defending yourself against your own self-criticisms, find truth in them and accept them.

DAILY MOOD LOG EXERCISE 2
PROBLEM—SOCIAL ANXIETY

Imagine that you are at a social gathering, such as a party or a meeting where you are expected to talk or introduce yourself. You feel nervous, panicky, and inferior. Put a brief description of the upsetting event where it says Step One at the top of the Daily Mood Log on page 111.

Now list your negative emotions where it says Step Two and estimate how strongly you would be feeling each of them, from 0% (not at all) to 100% (the worst).

These are the Negative Thoughts that make you feel upset:

1. I'm the only one who feels this way.

2. I *shouldn't* feel so nervous.

3. I don't have anything interesting to say.

4. All these people are so much smarter and more interesting. I'm such a boring person.

5. If anyone knew how nervous I felt, they'd really think I was a weirdo.

Copy these thoughts in the Negative Thoughts column of the DML on the next page. Estimate how strongly you would believe each of them, from 0% to 100%, if you were feeling upset in a social situation.

List the distortions in each NT in the middle column using the Distorted Thinking chart on page 50. Then substitute Positive Thoughts for one or more of the Negative Thoughts, using the table entitled Fifteen Ways to Untwist Your Thinking listed on page 109.

DAILY MOOD LOG*

Step One: Describe the Upsetting Event _____

_____

Step Two: Record Your Negative Feelings—and rate them from 0% (the least) to 100% (the most). Use words like *sad, anxious, angry, guilty, lonely, hopeless, frustrated,* etc.

Emotion	Rating (0%–100%)	Emotion	Rating (0%–100%)	Emotion	Rating (0%–100%)

Step Three: The Triple-Column Technique

Negative Thoughts Write down the thoughts that make you upset and estimate your belief in each one (0%–100%).	Distortions Use the Distorted Thinking chart on page 50.	Positive Thoughts Substitute more realistic thoughts and estimate your belief in each one (0%–100%).

DAILY MOOD LOG EXERCISE 3
PROBLEM—DEATH OF A FAMILY MEMBER

Imagine that your brother is a drug addict who has committed suicide. You feel devastated, guilty, despairing, hopeless. Your Negative Thoughts are:

1. It was my fault.

2. I should have known he was suicidal and done something to save him.

3. I shouldn't have been so angry and cold when I last spoke to him. I should have been more loving.

4. He felt rejected and that's why he killed himself.

Describe the event where it says Step One on the Daily Mood Log on page 113. Then record your negative feelings and rate how intensely you would be feeling each of them, from 0% (the least) to 100% (the most). Then record the four Negative Thoughts (or any others you might have) in the Negative Thoughts column of the DML. Remember to put the percent that you would believe each Negative Thought.

Next, list the distortions in each Negative Thought in the middle column using the checklist on page 50. Then substitute more positive and realistic thoughts in the Positive Thoughts column, using the table entitled Fifteen Ways to Untwist Your Thinking listed on page 109.

DAILY MOOD LOG*

Step One: Describe the Upsetting Event _____

_____

Step Two: Record Your Negative Feelings—and rate them from 0% (the least) to 100% (the most). Use words like _sad, anxious, angry, guilty, lonely, hopeless, frustrated,_ etc.

Emotion	Rating (0%–100%)	Emotion	Rating (0%–100%)	Emotion	Rating (0%–100%)

Step Three: The Triple-Column Technique

Negative Thoughts Write down the thoughts that make you upset and estimate your belief in each one (0%–100%).	Distortions Use the Distorted Thinking chart on page 50.	Positive Thoughts Substitute more realistic thoughts and estimate your belief in each one (0%–100%).

DAILY MOOD LOG EXERCISE 4

Fill out the Daily Mood Log on page 115 using a situation from your own life. Follow this format:

Step One: Identify the upsetting event or problem. Write a brief description of it at the top of the Daily Mood Log. Make sure it is specific and real, and not vague and general. Include precisely *what* happened, *where* it happened, and *when* it happened.

Step Two: Write down your negative emotions, using words like *angry, sad, frustrated, guilty,* or *anxious.* Rate how strongly you felt each one, from 0% (not at all) to 100% (the worst).

Step Three: Record your Negative Thoughts in the left-hand column of the Daily Mood Log. These are the thoughts that are associated with the negative emotions. Number each Negative Thought and record how strongly you believe it, from 0% (not at all) to 100% (completely).

Use the Distorted Thinking chart on page 50 to identify the distortions in your Negative Thoughts.

Try to generate a Positive Thought for each Negative Thought using techniques from the table on page 109. Write each Positive Thought in the right-hand column. Indicate how strongly you believe each Positive Thought, from 0% to 100%.

Estimate how strongly you now believe each Negative Thought. Has your belief in it been reduced? If so, put a line through the original estimate and write your new estimate.

After you have put the lie to all of your NTs, reestimate your belief in each of your negative emotions to see how much you have improved. Do you feel less upset? If so, put a line through the original rating for each negative emotion and write your new estimate.

If you run out of space, you can use the supplement to the Daily Mood Log on page 116.

DAILY MOOD LOG*

Step One: Describe the Upsetting Event _____

_____

Step Two: Record Your Negative Feelings—and rate them from 0% (the least) to 100% (the most). Use words like *sad, anxious, angry, guilty, lonely, hopeless, frustrated,* etc.

Emotion	Rating (0%–100%)	Emotion	Rating (0%–100%)	Emotion	Rating (0%–100%)

Step Three: The Triple-Column Technique

Negative Thoughts Write down the thoughts that make you upset and estimate your belief in each one (0%–100%).	Distortions Use the Distorted Thinking chart on page 50.	Positive Thoughts Substitute more realistic thoughts and estimate your belief in each one (0%–100%).

(Continued on next page)

DAILY MOOD LOG (Continued)

Negative Thoughts	Distortions	Positive Thoughts

ANSWER TO ATTITUDE CBA EXERCISE 2 ON PAGE 102

Fred can list all the advantages of telling himself "it's unfair" and getting angry about his phony colleague who was promoted. The advantages include:

1. He can feel morally superior and convinced that he's *right* about something very important.

2. He will have an excuse for the fact that he hasn't been promoted recently.

3. He can feel sorry for himself.

4. He won't have to be assertive with the department chairman and negotiate for his own promotion. He can avoid the issue, telling himself that the system is basically political and unfair.

5. He can feel angry and powerful.

There may be many additional advantages. Can you think of any?

The disadvantages of this mind-set may include:

1. He will feel sour and resentful.

2. He will get hostile and irritable and turn people off.

3. He will feel powerless and helpless.

4. He won't be creative or effective when he does negotiate with the department chairman for a promotion.

5. He won't feel happy and positive about his life, his career, or his colleagues. Instead, he'll be constantly at war with everyone, including himself.

Can you think of any other disadvantages of telling himself "it's unfair"? Once Fred lists the advantages and disadvantages, he can weigh them against each other. He will need to be aware that his cynical mind-set and chronic anger are quite addictive because he gets many rewards from being like this. If he wants to change, he will have to recognize these benefits and make a conscious decision to let go of them.

ANSWER TO ATTITUDE CBA EXERCISE 3 ON PAGE 103

Harry can list the advantages of his Negative Thoughts:

1. He won't have to change.

2. He won't have to flirt with women and risk getting turned down.

3. He can complain and feel self-righteous.

4. He can avoid doing something new and different that might make him feel anxious.

5. He will have an excuse for being alone.

Can you think of any other advantages? Actually, there are quite a few more.

Harry could also list the disadvantages of this mind-set. There are many. Can you think of some of them?

Once Harry lists the advantages and disadvantages, then he can make a decision about whether he wants to change.

ANSWER TO ATTITUDE CBA EXERCISE 4 ON PAGE 103

When she did the Cost-Benefit Analysis, she saw that there were actually a number of hidden advantages in her Negative Thoughts. She felt that by being severely depressed, irritable, and grossly overweight, she could make herself unattractive to men. Then she wouldn't have to have sex with her husband. Although she loved him dearly, she was quite turned off by sex. She also felt that the men at the office where she worked wouldn't make passes at her.

Once she became aware of these benefits, she decided that it really wasn't worth it. She agreed to talk back to her Negative Thoughts for a month to see what it would be like to be free of depression. Over the next several weeks, she experienced a rapid improvement in her outlook and self-esteem.

ANSWER TO EXPERIMENTAL METHOD EXERCISE 1 ON PAGE 104

Because Ronny was a scientist, his therapist suggested that he could do an experiment to test his belief that all the people in line at the grocery store were charming and witty and talking to each other in a lighthearted way. She told Ronny to raise his eyes from the floor and observe what the people were doing. How many were actually talking to each other and telling jokes in a lighthearted way, as he imagined they were doing? What did the people actually say to the checker when they paid for their groceries? Were any of them simply staring off into space, as he did? She suggested that he could bring his pocket calculator with him, and put the data about these people in different categories. Then he could analyze the data and test his hypothesis, just as he did in the laboratory.

Ronny was quite surprised to discover that very few people were talking to each other. Most were simply gazing off into space or looking at the *National Enquirer* and its cover story about how a Martian had impregnated Priscilla Presley. When people got to the checker, they mostly just paid for their groceries and left, exactly as he did.

ANSWER TO EXPERIMENTAL METHOD EXERCISE 2
ON PAGE 105

I suggested that Bill tell ten of his colleagues about a case he had lost when he went to the next bar association meeting. In this way, he could test his belief that people would look down on him if he wasn't always a winner.

Although he was very reluctant to do this, he finally agreed. He was quite surprised that none of his colleagues seemed to care that he had lost a case. Several were so preoccupied with what they were saying that they didn't even seem to notice what Bill had said. Others appeared relieved to hear that Bill had finally lost a case and poured out their hearts about all the cases they had recently lost. Several also opened up about marital and family problems.

Bill said that this was actually the first time he'd felt close to his colleagues. He was surprised to learn that what he had been trying so hard to hide—his imperfections—actually became his greatest assets in terms of getting close to others. His real problem was not his failures and shortcomings, but his tendency to hide them in shame.

ANSWER TO EXAMINE THE EVIDENCE EXERCISE ON
PAGE 105

Here's how you could Examine the Evidence for the first Negative Thought. Ask yourself if it's really true that you procrastinate about *everything* and never get *anything* done on time. What is the evidence for this? To find out, make a list of everything you did today from the moment you woke up. Did you wake up on time? Did you procrastinate about getting dressed? Did you go to the bathroom on time? Did you procrastinate about brushing your teeth? Drinking a cup of coffee?

You will learn that you do almost everything on time. Therefore, it can hardly be true that you procrastinate about *everything*. You are probably procrastinating about a number of things, but you won't help yourself by exaggerating the extent of your procrastination. You'll feel totally inadequate and think this is your basic nature.

You might now claim that you procrastinate about everything *important*. If so, you could Examine the Evidence for this Negative Thought. You could list twenty of the most important events in your life. Was it important to be born? Did you do that on time? Was it important to take your first breath? Did you do that on time? Was it important to learn to walk and talk? Did you do that on time? When you Examine the Evidence, you will realize that this new claim is not very valid either.

You would use a similar approach on the other Negative Thoughts. For example, if you claim you are a klutz who cannot do anything right, you could list a number of things that you are good at. If you claim you are so indecisive that you can't make up your mind about anything, you could remind yourself that every day you make hundreds of decisions automatically. Right now you are deciding to read this. After a period of time you may decide to stop and take a break. Then you may decide to eat a snack, jog, or do something else.

ANSWER TO SURVEY METHOD EXERCISE ON PAGE 106

His therapist suggested that he ask several happily married friends whether they ever fought or argued. He was surprised to learn that they fought frequently like cats and dogs and considered it entirely normal. This was not consistent with his belief that people with successful and normal marriages never get angry or have disagreements.

EVALUATION OF STEP 4

What did you learn in Step 4? Put a brief summary of several of the most important ideas we discussed here:

1. _____

_____

2. _____

_____

3. _____

_____

Was there anything in today's step that bothered you or rubbed you the wrong way? If you are in a group, was there anything the leader or other members said that turned you off? Describe any negative feelings you had:

_____

_____

_____

_____

Was there anything in today's step that was particularly helpful, interesting, or useful? Did the leader or other participants say anything during today's session that you liked? Describe any positive reactions you had:

_____

_____

_____

_____

SELF-HELP ASSIGNMENTS FOR STEP 5

If you are participating in a Ten Days to Self-esteem group, your leader may give you self-help assignments to complete before the next session.

Assignments	Check (√) If Assigned	Check (√) When Finished
1. Complete the evaluation form for Step 4. Be prepared to discuss your positive and negative reactions at the next session.		
2. Take the three mood tests again. They are located at the beginning of the next step.		
3. Read the next step in this book and do as many of the written exercises as possible.		
4. Bring your copy of this book to the next session.		
5. Work with the Daily Mood Log for ten minutes per day. (Extra copies begin on page 290.)		
6. Do a Cost-Benefit Analysis of the advantages and disadvantages of a Negative Thought.		
7. Bring any written homework to the next session.		
8. Bibliotherapy (was any reading assigned?)		
9.*		
10.		

*Use these spaces for any additional assignments.

SUPPLEMENTARY READING FOR STEP 4

1. Read Chapter 6 of *The Feeling Good Handbook*.
2. Read pages 137 to 143 from Chapter 8 of *The Feeling Good Handbook*.

STEP 5

THE ACCEPTANCE PARADOX

GOALS FOR STEP 5

1. You will learn about a powerful method for modifying Negative Thoughts called the Externalization of Voices. If you are in a Ten Days to Self-esteem group, you can work in a group of two or three to practice. If you are working on your own, you can practice with a friend or do it on your own with the help of a mirror.

2. You will learn about two completely different ways of talking back to Negative Thoughts. One of them is called Self-defense and the other is called the Acceptance Paradox. Self-defense is based on Western religion and scientific thinking. The Acceptance Paradox is based more on Eastern philosophies such as Buddhism. When used together, they can be exceedingly helpful.

MOOD TESTING

You have already taken three mood tests at the beginning of the previous steps. I would like you to take the three tests again now to chart your progress. If you need help, you can review the instructions for these tests beginning on page 18.

THE BURNS DEPRESSION CHECKLIST*

Place a check (√) in the box to the right of each category to indicate how much this type of feeling has bothered you in the past several days.

	0 Not at All	1 Somewhat	2 Moderately	3 A Lot
1. **Sadness:** Do you feel sad or down in the dumps?				
2. **Discouragement:** Does the future look hopeless?				
3. **Low self-esteem:** Do you feel worthless?				
4. **Inferiority:** Do you feel inadequate or inferior to others?				
5. **Guilt:** Do you get self-critical and blame yourself?				
6. **Indecisiveness:** Is it hard to make decisions?				
7. **Irritability:** Do you frequently feel angry or resentful?				
8. **Loss of interest in life:** Have you lost interest in your career, hobbies, family, or friends?				
9. **Loss of motivation:** Do you have to push yourself hard to do things?				
10. **Poor self-image:** Do you feel old or unattractive?				
11. **Appetite changes:** Have you lost your appetite? Do you overeat or binge compulsively?				
12. **Sleep changes:** Is it hard to get a good night's sleep? Are you excessively tired and sleeping too much?				
13. **Loss of sex drive:** Have you lost your interest in sex?				
14. **Concerns about health:** Do you worry excessively about your health?				
15. **Suicidal impulses:** Do you have thoughts that life is not worth living or think you'd be better off dead?†				
Total score on items 1–15 →				

†Anyone with suicidal urges should seek immediate help from a mental health professional.

THE BURNS ANXIETY INVENTORY*

Place a check (√) in the box to the right of each category to indicate how much this type of feeling has bothered you in the past several days.

Category I: Anxious Feelings	0 Not at All	1 Somewhat	2 Moderately	3 A Lot
1. Anxiety, nervousness, worry, or fear				
2. Feeling that things around you are strange or unreal				
3. Feeling detached from all or part of your body				
4. Sudden unexpected panic spells				
5. Apprehension or a sense of impending doom				
6. Feeling tense, stressed, "uptight," or on edge				
Category II: Anxious Thoughts	0 Not at All	1 Somewhat	2 Moderately	3 A Lot
7. Difficulty concentrating				
8. Racing thoughts				
9. Frightening fantasies or daydreams				
10. Feeling that you're on the verge of losing control				
11. Fears of cracking up or going crazy				
12. Fears of fainting or passing out				
13. Fears of physical illnesses or heart attacks or dying				
14. Concerns about looking foolish or inadequate				
15. Fears of being alone, isolated, or abandoned				
16. Fears of criticism or disapproval				
17. Fears that something terrible is about to happen				

*Copyright © 1984 by David D. Burns, M.D., from *Ten Days to Self-esteem,* copyright © 1993.

THE BURNS ANXIETY INVENTORY (Continued)

Category III: Physical Symptoms	0 Not at All	1 Somewhat	2 Moderately	3 A Lot
18. Skipping, racing, or pounding of the heart (palpitations)				
19. Pain, pressure, or tightness in the chest				
20. Tingling or numbness in the toes or fingers				
21. Butterflies or discomfort in the stomach				
22. Constipation or diarrhea				
23. Restlessness or jumpiness				
24. Tight, tense muscles				
25. Sweating not brought on by heat				
26. A lump in the throat				
27. Trembling or shaking				
28. Rubbery or "jelly" legs				
29. Feeling dizzy, lightheaded, or off balance				
30. Choking or smothering sensations or difficulty breathing				
31. Headaches or pains in the neck or back				
32. Hot flashes or cold chills				
33. Feeling tired, weak, or easily exhausted				
Total score on items 1–33 →				

RELATIONSHIP SATISFACTION SCALE*

Place a check (√) in the box to the right of each category that best describes the amount of satisfaction you feel in your closest relationship.

	0 Very Dissatisfied	1 Moderately Dissatisfied	2 Slightly Dissatisfied	3 Neutral	4 Slightly Satisfied	5 Moderately Satisfied	6 Very Satisfied
1. Communication and openness							
2. Resolving conflicts and arguments							
3. Degree of affection and caring							
4. Intimacy and closeness							
5. Satisfaction with your role in the relationship							
6. Satisfaction with the other person's role							
7. Overall satisfaction with your relationship							
Total score on items 1–7 →							

Note: Although this test assesses your marriage or most intimate relationship, you can also use it to evaluate your relationship with a friend, family member, or colleague. If you do not have any intimate relationships at this time, you can simply think of people in general when you take the test.

*Copyright © 1983 by David D. Burns, M.D., from *Ten Days to Self-esteem,* copyright © 1993.

EXTERNALIZATION OF VOICES

Role playing is a particularly powerful way of modifying Negative Thoughts. If you are in a self-esteem training group, the leader will ask for two brave volunteers to demonstrate a new technique called the Externalization of Voices. If you are not in a group, I will show how you can do the Externalization of Voices with a mirror. You can also practice with a friend or family member.

This technique can transform intellectual understanding into real emotional change at the gut level. It is called the Externalization of Voices because you externalize—or verbalize— the negative, self-critical thoughts that make you feel so upset. You get them out of your head and talk back to them, as if they were actually another person.

Begin this exercise with a list of your own self-critical thoughts. Let's assume that you've been having a hard time and you're feeling discouraged and inferior to other people. You think you aren't smart enough, charming enough, or successful enough. You have written these Negative Thoughts on your Daily Mood Log:

1. If people knew what I was really like, they'd look down on me.

2. Other people are a lot smarter than I am.

3. I'm always screwing up.

4. I'm a loser and a failure.

5. I shouldn't be so depressed all the time. There must be something wrong with me.

6. I'll never get well.

7. I'm defective and inferior.

8. I'm not witty or clever enough. I don't have a good sense of humor.

Ask another person in your group (or a friend) to be your partner in this exercise. Your partner will play the role of your Negative Thoughts. He or she will be that self-critical, negative part of your mind that feels inferior. Your partner will say your Negative Thoughts out loud, using the first person (for example, "*I'm* a loser; *I'll* never get well; *I'm* defective and inferior," and so forth).

You will play the role of the Positive Thoughts. You will talk to your partner in the same way you would talk to a dear friend who was feeling down and out, using the second person. For example, you might say, "*You're* not a loser, *you're* a human being. *You* have weaknesses, just like other people, and *you* also have a number of strengths, which *you* can be proud of. Don't sell yourself short."

This method is intended to make you aware that you may be operating on a double standard. You probably have one set of standards for other people, which is realistic and compassionate. You give others a break, you don't expect them to be perfect, and you don't kick them when they're down. Am I right? But you have a completely different set of standards for yourself—you expect perfection. When things don't go well, you beat yourself up and punish yourself, as if this would somehow help.

If all that self-abuse were really so helpful, why not treat other people that way? Why not dump on others when they feel lousy? The answer is obvious—it's about as helpful as throwing gasoline on a fire you're trying to put out. The flames just get hotter! Are you willing to stop doing this? Are you willing to treat yourself as you would treat a dear friend who was upset?

This method can help you give up your double standard. You learn to treat all human beings, including yourself, with one single standard that's fair, realistic, and compassionate.

Let's assume that you've been rejected by someone you really cared about. You may get quite depressed and rip into yourself as if you were Public Enemy Number One. You may tell yourself, "It's all my fault. I'm no good. I'm unlovable. I'll be alone forever."

These Negative Thoughts probably come into your mind naturally—they're automatic. You didn't plan to do this to yourself—it's a habit. Ask yourself, "Would I say these things to a friend who had just been rejected?" Of course you wouldn't! You would probably *never* say something so illogical and mean to a friend in identical circumstances. Instead, you would comfort and encourage your friend. One secret of self-esteem is to treat yourself in the same compassionate way you would treat a dear friend who was hurting.

When you practice the Externalization of Voices with another person, keep in mind that these are really the parts of your mind battling it out. This exercise is not intended to illustrate an actual dialogue between two people. This is *not* an exercise in how to counsel a troubled friend. In the Externalization of Voices, the other person is simply the projection of your own self-criticisms. Essentially, you are talking to yourself.

When you practice the Externalization of Voices with a partner, one of you plays the role of the Negative Thoughts and the other plays the Positive Thoughts. If there are three of you, the third one can be the observer. The observer can provide feedback about how the other two are doing. You can use frequent role reversals when the person who is playing the Positive Thoughts gets stuck.

Let's summarize how to do the Externalization of Voices:

EXTERNALIZATION OF VOICES

1. Make a list of your own Negative Thoughts. You can use the thoughts you have written in the Negative Thoughts column of a Daily Mood Log.
2. Select a partner and face him or her.
3. Tell your partner to read your Negative Thoughts, one by one, using the first person ("I" statements).
4. Talk to your partner in the same way you would talk to a friend who was upset, using the second person ("you" statements). Use a gentle, supportive style of counseling.
5. If you get stuck, do a role reversal.

Remember that even though you are talking to another person, you are really talking to your own self-criticisms.

THE MIRROR METHOD

I recently participated in a two-day workshop in Ohio with a number of well-known psychotherapists, including Dr. Mike Mahoney. Dr. Mahoney told me how he had accidentally discovered a helpful new technique when he was working with a rebellious teenager named Juan. Like many teenagers, Juan thought he looked ugly. He was so convinced of this that he had developed a mirror phobia. He was terrified of seeing his reflection in a mirror and refused to look into one.

Dr. Mahoney coincidentally had a small decorative mirror on his desk in his office, and he noticed that Juan carefully avoided looking into it. One day Dr. Mahoney encouraged Juan to face his fears and look into the mirror and describe the young man he saw reflected there. Juan resisted for a time but finally consented. Although he became intensely anxious at first, he began to feel more relaxed as he described his appearance. He started to think about himself in a more positive manner and began to make friends with himself. After several sessions, he was able to let go of his self-hatred as well as his mistrust of Dr. Mahoney.

You may find that this Mirror Method will also be helpful to you when you practice the Externalization of Voices. Look at your reflection as you repeat your Negative Thoughts out loud:

I'm always screwing up. I'm just a loser and a failure.

Now continue looking into the mirror and talk to yourself in the second person, just as if you were talking to a friend who was very much like you. Encourage yourself just as you would encourage a good friend who was feeling discouraged. You might say:

Listen, you do sometimes screw up, but so does everybody else. You have strengths and weaknesses, victories and losses. This makes you very human, and you don't need to be ashamed of that. If you have some deficiencies, you can work on them.

You will probably discover that after you defend yourself, you will come up with another negative, self-critical thought, such as:

But I *shouldn't* be so depressed all the time. There must be something wrong with me. I'm defective.

Continue to look into the mirror and talk to yourself the way you would talk to a dear friend. You could say:

It would be great if you weren't so depressed all the time. Over a period of time, you will improve. If you are depressed, it shows that there's something wrong with the way you feel, but it doesn't make you a defective person.

Notice that this response illustrates one of the techniques from the chart on page 109. Look at the chart now and see if you can find out what method it is.

Although you might come up with several techniques, I am thinking of the Semantic Method. When you use the Semantic Method to talk back to a Negative Thought, you simply use less loaded, less colorful, more objective language. The Semantic Method is especially good for the distortions called "should" statements. For example, instead of telling yourself, "I *shouldn't* be so depressed," you can say, "*It would be preferable if* I weren't so depressed." This simple change in language takes a lot of the sting out of a "should" statement.

The Semantic Method works for labeling as well as for "should" statements. Instead of labeling yourself as "defective," you could think of yourself "a human being who feels depressed."

Let's practice the Mirror Method now. You begin with a list of your own self-critical thoughts from the Daily Mood Log. Suppose, like a patient of mine, you forgot your appointment with the dentist. She got busy and the appointment slipped her mind. When she discovered that she'd forgotten it, she started berating herself mercilessly. One of her Negative Thoughts was:

Gee, I forgot my dentist appointment! Anybody with half a brain would have remembered it. What a jerk I am!

Pretend that this is your Negative Thought. Stand in front of a mirror and play the role of the Negative Thought. Repeat it out loud, just as it's written. Use the first person ("I" statements). Allow yourself to feel self-critical, embarrassed, and put down.

Now play the role of the Positive Thoughts. Your job is to defend yourself with positive, self-loving statements. This time, you can use the second person ("*you*" statements) and say things like this:

You did forget the appointment and it is a little embarrassing. You've got a lot on your mind right now and it's not so unusual to forget something. Being a little absent-minded is not the end of the world. The world will probably just keep spinning right along in spite of your mistake! Just call the dentist and explain honestly what happened and reschedule the appointment. You can also think about what might have been going on subconsciously. Were you angry with the dentist? Were you anxious about the appointment?

Keep in mind that these are really the negative and positive parts of your mind talking to each other. This exercise is not intended to illustrate an actual dialogue between two people. In the Externalization of Voices, the critic you are grappling with is simply the projection of your own self-criticisms.

Let's summarize how to do the Mirror Method:

THE MIRROR METHOD

1. Make a list of your Negative Thoughts in the left-hand column of the Daily Mood Log. Make sure you complete Step One (identify the upsetting event) and Step Two (record your negative feelings) first.
2. Stand in front of a mirror and face yourself.
3. Read your Negative Thoughts out loud, one by one, using the *first* person ("I" statements).
4. Defend yourself against your negative, self-critical thoughts, using the *second* person ("you" statements). Talk to yourself in the same compassionate way you would counsel a dear friend with a similar problem.

THE ACCEPTANCE PARADOX

There are two opposite sources of healing in cognitive therapy: Self-defense and the Acceptance Paradox. In Self-defense, you use logic or evidence to disprove the Negative Thoughts that make you feel so bad. Once you see that your Negative Thoughts are distorted and untrue, you will usually feel better.

However, many NTs can be handled far more effectively with the Acceptance Paradox. Instead of arguing with the NT, you find some truth in it and agree with it. If you can do this with inner peace, self-esteem, and a little humor, the results can be quite spectacular.

For example, let's say that you are in a self-esteem training group. A member of your group has Negative Thoughts such as these:

1. I'm a rotten mother.

2. I'm an addict and I've wasted my life.

3. I'm not nearly as smart and successful as other people. I've never accomplished anything really outstanding.

4. I'm a phony and I'm dishonest with people.

5. I'm a loser and I have no friends.

6. I'm fat and I have no willpower.

The leader will demonstrate the Acceptance Paradox by asking for a volunteer who will play the role of the NTs. The volunteer will attack the leader, using the second person. The leader will play the PTs, using the first person. Remember that although this looks like a dialogue between two different people, it is actually the two voices in someone's mind that are battling. It might go like this:

VOLUNTEER (as NT): You're a rotten mother.

LEADER (as PT): I have so many shortcomings as a mother. There is much I need to improve on. I accept this.

VOLUNTEER: Yes, but you're an addict and you've wasted your life.

LEADER: That's correct. I have screwed up and wasted an awful lot of my life. I make no bones about this.

VOLUNTEER: Well, you should feel terrible and guilty then. You're admitting what a loser and what scum you are.

LEADER: Oh, absolutely, I do admit it! And believe me, I have often felt guilty and terrible about my life.

VOLUNTEER: So you admit you're a stupid loser!

LEADER: Without hesitation! Many people are smarter and more successful than I am. Millions, in fact.

VOLUNTEER: Half the time you hate everybody, and no one gives a damn about you either.

LEADER: You've hit the nail on the head again! My relationships with people have not been good either. I often get angry and irritable and that turns people off. I have a lot of growing up to do. That's the gospel truth!

You can see from this dialogue that the Acceptance Paradox is quite different from the usual strategy of defending yourself against your own self-criticisms. You don't try to build yourself up or fight back. Instead, you do just the opposite: You simply accept the fact that you are broken, imperfect, and defective. You accept your shortcomings with honesty and inner peace. The surprising result is that you can often gain invulnerability when you make yourself completely vulnerable and defenseless.

I often illustrate the Acceptance Paradox at workshops for mental health professionals. Therapists come to these programs to learn more about the latest psychotherapeutic methods. However, many of them have a hidden agenda. They attend because of personal difficulties. Many of them suffer from depression, anxiety, panic attacks, or broken marriages. They feel inadequate and burned out in their careers. These problems are sometimes intensified by feelings of shame. They frequently tell themselves that because they are mental health professionals, they *should* have it all together. Many fear that they would be seen as frauds if people discovered how little they really knew.

I ask the workshop participants to write down some of their Negative Thoughts about themselves and hand them in anonymously so that I can illustrate how to turn them around. I urge them to share the private, self-critical feelings that they usually keep hidden and would not ordinarily reveal to their colleagues.

Generally more than half of a typical audience of 250 mental health professionals will turn in slips of paper with Negative Thoughts written on them. The audience members describe inadequacies in their careers and personal lives. You may discover that their concerns are not so different from your own.

I have grouped their thoughts into four categories, although there is considerable overlap among them. The first category includes concerns about therapeutic skills. The following are typical of hundreds of comments that I have received.

- I have more of a personality disorder than most of my clients!!!! My therapeutic effectiveness is a delusion!

- Why am I doing this? I'm not any good at this. I should just go sell used cars. I'm no counselor.

- I am inadequate, insensitive, poorly trained, and totally hopeless at what I do—a fraud. I have no business messing around in other people's lives.

The second theme includes negative feelings these therapists have about their clients. They are frequently troubled by feelings of indifference, anxiety, frustration, or anger. Many of them feel burned out, drained, and unappreciated. The following are typical examples:

- I get sick and tired of people's neediness—and trying to help them.

- I want to take out all of my hidden anger at my husband on my male clients—in essence, "nailing their asses to the wall" because I can't do it with my husband.

- I am insensitive and shallow. I turn serious things into a laugh—I'm not serious or committed. A real hummingbird.

The third theme involves feelings of failure in marriage and family life. Here are some typical examples:

- I'm damaged. I'm not fit to be a mother, wife, or therapist. I'm not good enough and I'm not whole. I'll never be cured. Because I was sexually molested as a child, I wear a large *M* on my forehead.

- I should be able to take care of my child and never get angry with him and also keep the house clean and go to work and do my job, all at the same time, and *never* feel overwhelmed!

- I don't have enough guts to express myself to my own family or stand up for myself, but I tell *all* my clients to do that!

The final theme involves feelings of personal inadequacy, as in the following examples:

- I don't say enough during therapy sessions or social situations. I am too quiet. But it really irritates the shit out of me when people tell me I'm quiet.

- I feel more adequate intellectually than physically. People don't enjoy me personally, but are attracted to my wife. I am *willing* but not *effective*.

- I am inept and inadequate in handling chores of living, such as finances, getting tires fixed, and so forth. I'm an impostor—and soon others will discover how little I know and how incompetent I am.

- I'm a fat, ugly fraud. My body is old and should be hidden from sight! I'm spiritually bankrupt.

- I'm as screwed up as my clients and I shouldn't be trying to help them because I can do them no good.

- I'm irresponsible, incompetent, disorganized, unfeeling, uncaring, selfish, and self-centered.

Once I have gathered the Negative Thoughts from the therapists, I ask for a volunteer to help me illustrate how to deal with them. I use a technique called the Feared Fantasy, which is described in my *Feeling Good Handbook*. The Feared Fantasy is an Alice in Wonderland nightmare in which you meet an imaginary person, the Hostile Stranger, who knows all about your most shameful shortcomings. The Hostile Stranger confronts you with your weaknesses in the most cruel, humiliating manner possible. The Stranger does not represent another human being, but is the projection of your own self-critical tendencies. In Freudian terms, the Hostile Stranger would be your "superego," or harsh conscience.

Recently, in Milwaukee, I illustrated the Feared Fantasy just before the lunch break of a workshop. Sheryl Strong, then a counselor at the University of Wisconsin, volunteered to illustrate this method. I played the role of the Hostile Stranger and instructed Sheryl to play the self-loving, self-accepting role.

I gave her these two suggestions about how to respond to the accusations of the Hostile Stranger:

1. Do not defend yourself or argue. Instead, immediately agree with every brutal accusation. Find some truth in the criticisms.

2. Do this with a sense of inner peace and self-esteem.

My first criticism of her was:

You're basically a stupid and incompetent therapist and you don't even know what you're doing half the time. Lots of the people in this group are a whole lot smarter and better than you are.

Keep in mind that this is not my criticism of Sheryl Strong, who is actually a talented and compassionate counselor. As the Hostile Stranger, I am simply expressing the kinds of self-critical thoughts that many of the therapists in the group wrote down.

Sheryl replied:

Well, I may not always know how to help every client, but I've been able to help many of them. All of my therapeutic skills may not be outstanding, but I'm probably as good as lots of other therapists.

This was a *Self-defense* response. Although her reply was rational, it sounds defensive. I could easily attack her again by pointing out that there were many patients she couldn't help, that many therapists have superior skills, and that she has had many personal failures in her life. Sooner or later, she would probably feel put down and befuddled. But why should she have to defend herself against all of these self-criticisms in the first place?

I did a role reversal to illustrate the Acceptance Paradox. I told Sheryl to be the Hostile Stranger. When she accused me of being stupid and incompetent, I simply responded:

> As a matter of fact, I wouldn't ever claim to be the smartest or most talented therapist. I often make mistakes and I have a great deal to learn from my colleagues. And furthermore, if you knew me well, you'd see that I have even more inadequacies—huge numbers of them, in fact!

She said that a light bulb went on then and she suddenly grasped the Acceptance Paradox. She said my response disarmed her and she couldn't continue to attack me. Essentially, you defeat the criticism by surrendering to it. You win by losing. The effect of the Acceptance Paradox can be startling and powerful.

We went back to our original roles so that she could try again. As the Hostile Stranger, I said:

> You know, you really have more of a personality disorder than most of your patients. Your therapeutic effectiveness is a delusion! You're pathetic!

Unperturbed, Sheryl smiled and calmly responded:

> As a matter of fact, when I look through the diagnostic manual, I can see myself in *all sorts* of categories! In addition, I would like to increase my therapeutic effectiveness, which frequently is a delusion. The truth is that I have many patients who seem to improve slowly or not at all!

The audience laughed and broke into spontaneous applause—and then it was time to break for lunch.

Why is this method so powerful? First, it is based on reality. The fact is, we all *are* human, and most of us are broken in many ways. No matter what your station in life—whether you are a mental health professional, a parent, a talented athlete, or a teacher—it simply does not take away the fact that you have flaws and shortcomings. When you accept your inadequacies with a sense of inner peace, instead of keeping them shamefully hidden in the dark, it removes the burden that you feel. The judgments and mental put-downs suddenly lose their power. You will often experience a sudden freedom and exhilaration.

The Acceptance Paradox is based on the idea that you can achieve success by accepting your failure. You can transcend your limits when you accept them. You can gain renewed strength when you accept your weakness. You can suddenly feel whole when you accept the fact that you are broken.

Many people will strenuously resist this, because we are terrified by the prospect of being "average," "ordinary," or "less than." The possibility that the greatest gain is often achieved through loss is unfamiliar territory to the Western mind, but I have found this idea to be tremendously healing in my clinical practice.

If you are in a Ten Days to Self-esteem group, you can discuss these two approaches: Self-defense and the Acceptance Paradox. Which approach seems more useful for you? What are the philosophical and practical implications of the Acceptance Paradox? If it seems helpful, why is it helpful? How does it tie in with the philosophy of twelve-step groups such as Alcoholics Anonymous, or with your own religious beliefs? When does self-acceptance lead to self-esteem and personal change, and when does self-acceptance lead to hopelessness and depression? When is it best to *accept* your negative, self-critical thoughts, and when is it best to *challenge* them?

If you have had any experience with AA or other self-help groups, you will know the importance of Reinhold Niebuhr's Serenity Prayer:

THE SERENITY PRAYER

God grant me the *serenity* to accept what I can't change, the *courage* to change what I can, and the *wisdom* to know the difference.

—Adapted from REINHOLD NIEBUHR (1943)

The Acceptance Paradox is one way of turning this principle into an emotional reality. It provides an important philosophical bridge between what you are learning here and what you may be learning in twelve-step programs such as Alcoholics Anonymous.

After the discussion of the Acceptance Paradox, the leader may divide your group into clusters of three to practice. You can use your own Negative Thoughts. Person A will play the role of the Negative Thoughts, Person B will play the role of the Positive Thoughts, and Person C can be the observer. Use frequent role reversals so A and B can both practice defending. Rotate chairs every two or three minutes so that the observer can participate in the role playing.

If you are not in a group and are doing it on your own, you can practice with a friend or use a mirror, as described previously.

Afterward, the group as a whole will reconvene so you can talk about your experiences. How did the exercise feel? Was it frightening? Did you feel upset? What worked and what did not work? Was the Self-defense approach or the Acceptance Paradox more helpful to you? Is there a place for both of them? Which one seemed more powerful?

Here are the specific steps:

THE ACCEPTANCE PARADOX / 137

CONFRONTING YOUR NEGATIVE THOUGHTS

1. Make a list of your Negative Thoughts. You can use the thoughts you have written in the Negative Thoughts column of a Daily Mood Log.
2. Select a partner and face him or her. You are Person A and your partner is Person B.
3. Attack Person B by reading your own Negative Thoughts out loud, one by one, using the *second* person ("you" statements). Pretend that Person B is actually you; it will be your goal to upset him or her.
4. Your partner, Person B, will try to defend against your criticisms, using the *first* person ("I" statements). He or she should use both the Self-defense approach and the Acceptance Paradox.
5. Do frequent role reversals. Remember that the person who plays the Negative Thoughts always uses the second person ("you" statements) and the person who plays the Positive Thoughts uses the first person ("I" statements).

Notice that this is a more confrontational way of doing the Externalization of Voices, since the person who is playing the Negative Thoughts is using the *second* person ("you" statements) and is on the attack. The person who plays the role of the Positive Thoughts defends against these criticisms, using the *first* person ("I" statements). He or she can use Self-defense as well as the Acceptance Paradox.

If you do the exercise, you may become upset when you are attacked with your own Negative Thoughts. If you can't think of effective responses—which is common—you can switch roles. You become your own Negative Thoughts and attack using the second person ("you" statements). Your partner in the exercise will play the role of your Positive Thoughts and can show how you can talk back more effectively, using "I" statements. Once you see how to defend against the Negative Thoughts, reverse roles again.

Keep in mind that this is not an encounter group or psychodrama or assertiveness training! The person you are battling it out with is simply the projection of the negative, critical part of your own mind. This method is designed to show you how to cope with your own Negative Thoughts, *not* the criticisms of another person such as your spouse or your boss.

I frequently use this method with the patients I treat in my office. It is dramatic and can be emotionally charged, especially for a person who is quite depressed or anxious. You should attempt it *only* if you are under the supervision of a mental health professional, because it is more powerful than the Double-Standard Technique described previously. Like any form of power, it has the potential to heal—if used properly—or to hurt—if used irresponsibly. I use it only with patients who trust me and who feel reasonably stable. If someone is feeling exceedingly fragile, tearful, or confused, I do not use this method.

When someone is feeling more fragile, I stick with the Double-Standard Technique. This technique is nonthreatening. Remember that, in the Double-Standard Technique, your partner plays the role of your Negative Thoughts and uses the first person ("I" statements). You play the role of the Positive Thoughts and use the second person ("you" statements). Remember to counsel your partner—who is really the depressed side of yourself—in the same supportive way you would counsel a dear friend who was upset. Use Self-defense as well as the Acceptance Paradox, so you can see the relative merits of both styles of responding.

HEALTHY VS. UNHEALTHY SELF-ACCEPTANCE

When you are thinking about the Acceptance Paradox, it is important to distinguish between healthy and unhealthy self-acceptance. This is a subtle but tremendously important distinction.

Many people who feel depressed believe that they are inferior, worthless losers. Some people have trouble comprehending how the Acceptance Paradox could help anyone who is already convinced that he or she is no good. The Acceptance Paradox may simply appear to confirm the feelings of hopelessness and inadequacy.

There are three important differences between healthy and unhealthy self-acceptance. First, in healthy self-acceptance, you accept the fact that you have *specific* deficiencies, but you reject the idea that you are globally and totally worthless. Suppose you have the thought "I'm a defective human being." This Negative Thought is condemning and lacking in compassion. It leaves no room for growth.

If you are using the Acceptance Paradox, your Positive Thought might be "I'm a human being with many defects and shortcomings. I accept this." This Positive Thought is thoroughly honest and it puts things in a more realistic and compassionate perspective. You are accepting many specific deficiencies (in fact, huge numbers of them!) but not one big, *global* defect.

The second difference is that in unhealthy self-acceptance you view your defects as unacceptable and worthy of condemnation. There is no hope or forgiveness or room for growth. In contrast, in healthy acceptance you acknowledge that you have many shortcomings, but you refuse to write yourself off and you maintain a spirit of self-respect. You declare that it's okay to have deficiencies. This is part of the human condition. You can either fight and protest and make yourself miserable, or you can accept your humanness and rejoice.

The third difference between healthy and unhealthy self-acceptance has to do with change. Healthy self-acceptance often leads to personal growth. People who feel hopeless and worthless often write themselves off. They use all their energy feeling inadequate and criticizing themselves, but *nothing ever changes*. It's like the perennially fat person who always diets, but never loses any weight! In contrast, when you accept your shortcomings without any loss of self-esteem, you will often have more energy and motivation to change.

EVALUATION OF STEP 5

What did you learn in Step 5? Put a brief summary of several of the most important ideas we discussed here:

1. _____

_____

2. _____

_____

3. _____

_____

Was there anything in today's step that bothered you or rubbed you the wrong way? If you are in a group, was there anything the leader or other members said that turned you off? Describe any negative feelings you had:

_____

_____

_____

_____

Was there anything in today's step that was particularly helpful, interesting, or useful? Did the leader or other participants say anything during today's session that you liked? Describe any positive reactions you had:

_____

_____

_____

_____

SELF-HELP ASSIGNMENTS FOR STEP 6

If you are participating in a Ten Days to Self-esteem group, your leader may give you Self-help Assignments to complete before the next session.

Assignments	Check (√) If Assigned	Check (√) When Finished
1. Complete the evaluation form for Step 5.		
2. Take the three mood tests again. They are located at the beginning of the next step.		
3. Read the next step in this book and do as many of the written exercises as possible.		
4. Bring your copy of this book to the next session.		
5. Work with the Daily Mood Log for ten minutes per day. (Extra copies begin on page 290.)		
6. Bring any written homework to the next session.		
7. Bibliotherapy (was any reading assigned?)		
8.*		
9.		
10.		

*Use these spaces for any additional assignments.

SUPPLEMENTARY READING FOR STEP 5

1. Complete Chapter 8 of *The Feeling Good Handbook.*
2. Study pages 133–135, 141, and 173–174 in *The Feeling Good Handbook,* which describe the Externalization of Voices presented in Step 5.

STEP 6

GETTING DOWN TO ROOT CAUSES

GOALS FOR STEP 6

1. In today's step you will learn how self-defeating attitudes and beliefs can make you vulnerable to painful mood swings and to conflicts in personal relationships.
2. You will identify your own self-defeating attitudes with the Vertical Arrow Technique and with the Self-defeating Belief Scale.
3. You will learn how to develop a personal value system that will lead to greater happiness, productivity, and intimacy, now *and* in the future.

MOOD TESTING

You have already taken three mood tests at the beginning of the previous steps. I would like you to take the three tests again at the beginning of this step to chart your progress. If you need help, you can review the instructions for these tests in Step 1 beginning on page 18.

THE BURNS DEPRESSION CHECKLIST*

Place a check (√) in the box to the right of each category to indicate how much this type of feeling has bothered you in the past several days.

	0 Not at All	1 Somewhat	2 Moderately	3 A Lot
1. **Sadness:** Do you feel sad or down in the dumps?				
2. **Discouragement:** Does the future look hopeless?				
3. **Low self-esteem:** Do you feel worthless?				
4. **Inferiority:** Do you feel inadequate or inferior to others?				
5. **Guilt:** Do you get self-critical and blame yourself?				
6. **Indecisiveness:** Is it hard to make decisions?				
7. **Irritability:** Do you frequently feel angry or resentful?				
8. **Loss of interest in life:** Have you lost interest in your career, hobbies, family, or friends?				
9. **Loss of motivation:** Do you have to push yourself hard to do things?				
10. **Poor self-image:** Do you feel old or unattractive?				
11. **Appetite changes:** Have you lost your appetite? Do you overeat or binge compulsively?				
12. **Sleep changes:** Is it hard to get a good night's sleep? Are you excessively tired and sleeping too much?				
13. **Loss of sex drive:** Have you lost your interest in sex?				
14. **Concerns about health:** Do you worry excessively about your health?				
15. **Suicidal impulses:** Do you have thoughts that life is not worth living or think you'd be better off dead?†				
Total score on items 1–15 →				

*Copyright © 1984 by David D. Burns, M.D., from *Ten Days to Self-esteem*, copyright © 1993.

THE BURNS ANXIETY INVENTORY*

Place a check (√) in the box to the right of each category to indicate how much this type of feeling has bothered you in the past several days.

Category I: Anxious Feelings	0 Not at All	1 Somewhat	2 Moderately	3 A Lot
1. Anxiety, nervousness, worry, or fear				
2. Feeling that things around you are strange or unreal				
3. Feeling detached from all or part of your body				
4. Sudden unexpected panic spells				
5. Apprehension or a sense of impending doom				
6. Feeling tense, stressed, "uptight," or on edge				
Category II: Anxious Thoughts	0 Not at All	1 Somewhat	2 Moderately	3 A Lot
7. Difficulty concentrating				
8. Racing thoughts				
9. Frightening fantasies or daydreams				
10. Feeling that you're on the verge of losing control				
11. Fears of cracking up or going crazy				
12. Fears of fainting or passing out				
13. Fears of physical illnesses or heart attacks or dying				
14. Concerns about looking foolish or inadequate				
15. Fears of being alone, isolated, or abandoned				
16. Fears of criticism or disapproval				
17. Fears that something terrible is about to happen				

THE BURNS ANXIETY INVENTORY (Continued)

Category III: Physical Symptoms	0 Not at All	1 Somewhat	2 Moderately	3 A Lot
18. Skipping, racing, or pounding of the heart (palpitations)				
19. Pain, pressure, or tightness in the chest				
20. Tingling or numbness in the toes or fingers				
21. Butterflies or discomfort in the stomach				
22. Constipation or diarrhea				
23. Restlessness or jumpiness				
24. Tight, tense muscles				
25. Sweating not brought on by heat				
26. A lump in the throat				
27. Trembling or shaking				
28. Rubbery or "jelly" legs				
29. Feeling dizzy, lightheaded, or off balance				
30. Choking or smothering sensations or difficulty breathing				
31. Headaches or pains in the neck or back				
32. Hot flashes or cold chills				
33. Feeling tired, weak, or easily exhausted				
Total score on items 1–33　→				

RELATIONSHIP SATISFACTION SCALE*

Place a check (√) in the box to the right of each category that best describes the amount of satisfaction you feel in your closest relationship.

	0 Very Dissatisfied	1 Moderately Dissatisfied	2 Slightly Dissatisfied	3 Neutral	4 Slightly Satisfied	5 Moderately Satisfied	6 Very Satisfied
1. Communication and openness							
2. Resolving conflicts and arguments							
3. Degree of affection and caring							
4. Intimacy and closeness							
5. Satisfaction with your role in the relationship							
6. Satisfaction with the other person's role							
7. Overall satisfaction with your relationship							
Total score on items 1–7 →							

Note: Although this test assesses your marriage or most intimate relationship, you can also use it to evaluate your relationship with a friend, family member, or colleague. If you do not have any intimate relationships at this time, you can simply think of people in general when you take the test.

*Copyright © 1983 by David D. Burns, M.D., from *Ten Days to Self-esteem,* copyright © 1993.

WHAT ARE SELF-DEFEATING BELIEFS?

A Self-defeating Belief is an attitude that may make you vulnerable to painful mood swings as well as conflicts in your personal relationships. Ten common Self-defeating Beliefs are listed on page 147.

A Self-defeating Belief is different from a Negative Thought (NT). NTs occur only when you are feeling unhappy, but a Self-defeating Belief is an attitude that is always with you. It is part of your personal philosophy, your value system. While some attitudes can be very healthy, others can get you into trouble.

For example, let's suppose you have this belief: "I must be a success in life to be a worthwhile person." Lots of people in our society think like this. It goes back to Calvinism—the so-called work ethic. The idea is that if you're lazy and unproductive, you're no good and people will look down on you. In contrast, if you are hardworking and productive, you are a good and worthwhile person. Do you have this attitude? Do you base your self-esteem on your work, your intelligence, or your accomplishments?

There can be certain benefits in this mind-set. If you work hard and do your best, you will enjoy the benefits of your efforts. The more successful and productive you are, the more worthwhile you may feel. By the same token, there can be certain hazards. If you fail, you may feel depressed and worthless. If you aren't as successful as you think you *should* be, you may feel inferior and jealous of others who have achieved more. Most of these attitudes are actually two-edged swords, with a healthy, productive side and an unhealthy, destructive side.

Some people base their self-esteem more on personal relationships than on work. Suppose you have the belief "I must be loved to be worthwhile." This belief is also very common in our society. Barbra Streisand sings that people who need people are lucky—in fact, they're the luckiest people in the world. Lots of readers—including you—may believe that if they are criticized or rejected or unloved and alone, it means they are less worthwhile and destined to feel unhappy. In contrast, if you have many friends and good relationships with people who care about you, you may feel happy and worthwhile. Do you ever think like this? Do you base your self-esteem on your relationships with others?

This belief has many benefits. If you think this way, you will work hard on your personal relationships and value others. If you have a conflict with a friend or family member, you will feel hurt and try darn hard to work the problem out. As long as you feel loved and accepted, you will feel happy and secure. That's good.

But there's a down side to this belief. If you are rejected by someone you care about, you may feel worthless and inadequate. If someone is mad at you, you may feel threatened and avoid the conflict instead of trying to listen and learn what the other person is upset about. If a friend or colleague criticizes you, you may get defensive because your self-esteem is on the line.

Review the list of Common Self-defeating Beliefs on page 147 and see if any of them are typical of how you think.

COMMON SELF-DEFEATING BELIEFS

1. **Emotional perfectionism:** "I should always feel happy, confident, and in control of my emotions."
2. **Performance perfectionism:** "I must never fail or make a mistake."
3. **Perceived perfectionism:** "People will not love and accept me as a flawed and vulnerable human being."
4. **Fear of disapproval or criticism:** "I need everybody's approval to be worthwhile."
5. **Fear of rejection:** "If I'm not loved, then life is not worth living."
6. **Fear of being alone:** "If I'm alone, then I'm bound to feel miserable and unfulfilled."
7. **Fear of failure:** "My worthwhileness depends on my achievements (or my intelligence or status or attractiveness)."
8. **Conflict phobia:** "People who love each other shouldn't fight."
9. **Emotophobia:** "I should not feel angry, anxious, inadequate, jealous, or vulnerable."
10. **Entitlement:** "People should always be the way I expect them to be."

THE VERTICAL ARROW TECHNIQUE

You can identify your Self-defeating Beliefs in two ways. The first method is called the Vertical Arrow Technique, and this exercise will illustrate it.

A first-year law student was troubled by feelings of panic when she was in class because this Negative Thought raced through her mind: "If the professor calls on me in class, I might not know the answer to the question." She wrote this Negative Thought on the Daily Mood Log and drew a vertical arrow directly underneath it. The vertical arrow is like shorthand that means "If that thought was true, why would it be upsetting to me? What would it mean to me?"

The next thought that crossed her mind was "I might make a fool of myself in front of the other students." She recorded this Negative Thought and put a new vertical arrow directly under it, just as she had done before. You can see how she did this on page 48.

The vertical arrow always means "If that was true, why would it be upsetting to me? What would it mean to me?" After you ask yourself this question, write down the next thought that comes to mind. Then draw another vertical arrow underneath and repeat the process over and over.

Imagine that you are this student. Complete the Vertical Arrow Technique on the next page. Write down several additional Negative Thoughts. Then review the list of Negative

NEGATIVE THOUGHTS

1. *If the professor calls on me, I might not know the answer.*

   ↓   If that was true, why would it be upsetting to me? What would it mean to me?

2. *I might make a fool of myself in front of the other students.*

   ↓   If that was true, why would it be upsetting to me? What would it mean to me?

3. _____

   _____

   ↓   If that was true, why would it be upsetting to me? What would it mean to me?

4. _____

   _____

   ↓   If that was true, why would it be upsetting to me? What would it mean to me?

5. _____

   _____

   ↓   If that was true, why would it be upsetting to me? What would it mean to me?

6. _____

   _____

   ↓   If that was true, why would it be upsetting to me? What would it mean to me?

7. _____

   _____

Thoughts and see if you can identify her Self-defeating Beliefs. List them here when you are done. You can refer to the list of Self-defeating Beliefs on page 147 when you do this.

1. _____

   _____

2. _____

   _____

3. _____

   _____

4. _____

   _____

Do this exercise now. Do it on paper, not in your head! When you are done, you can see a completed example of the exercise on page 159. Don't look there until you're done. Also keep in mind that your answers may be very different. That's perfectly okay. Everyone is different. The purpose of the exercise is to bring out the way you think.

THE SELF-DEFEATING BELIEF SCALE

There is a second, easier method for identifying Self-defeating Beliefs. All you have to do is fill out the Self-defeating Belief Scale on the page 150.

Answering the test is quite simple. After each of the thirty-five attitudes, put a check in the column that represents how you think and feel *most* of the time. Be sure to choose only one answer for each attitude. We are all different, and there are no "right" or "wrong" answers. Decide whether a given attitude is typical of how you look at things and react *most of the time*.

Here's an example:

THE SELF-DEFEATING BELIEF SCALE

	0 Disagree Strongly	1 Disagree Slightly	2 Neutral	3 Agree Slightly	4 Agree Strongly
1. Criticism is usually very upsetting to me.				√	

You can see that the woman who answered this question put a check in the "Agree slightly" column. This indicated her tendency to get upset whenever she was criticized.

After you complete the test, I will show how you can generate a profile of your personal values. This will show your areas of psychological strength and vulnerability.

THE SELF-DEFEATING BELIEF SCALE*

	0 Disagree Strongly	1 Disagree Slightly	2 Neutral	3 Agree Slightly	4 Agree Strongly
1. Criticism is usually very upsetting to me.					
2. If someone disapproves of me, I feel like I am not very worthwhile.					
3. I need other people's approval to feel happy and worthwhile.					
4. I often get defensive when someone criticizes me.					
5. My self-esteem depends greatly on what others think of me.					
6. I cannot feel happy and fulfilled without being loved by another person.					
7. If I am not loved, I am bound to be unhappy.					
8. If someone rejected me, I would feel like there was something wrong with me.					
9. I must be loved to feel happy and worthwhile.					
10. Being alone and unloved is bound to lead to unhappiness.					

*This test was adapted from the Dysfunctional Attitude Scale, which was originally developed by Dr. Arlene Weissman, a clinical psychologist. Many of the items have been changed to make the test more useful for the readers of this book. The scoring system has also been simplified.

THE SELF-DEFEATING BELIEF SCALE (Continued)

	0 Disagree Strongly	1 Disagree Slightly	2 Neutral	3 Agree Slightly	4 Agree Strongly
11. I sometimes feel upset because I have not been very successful in life.					
12. People with outstanding careers, social status, wealth, or fame are bound to be happier than people who are not especially successful.					
13. People who achieve a great deal are more worthwhile than those who do not.					
14. I sometimes feel inferior to people who are more intelligent and successful than I am.					
15. My self-esteem depends greatly on how productive and successful I am.					
16. People will think less of me if I fail or make a mistake.					
17. I feel less worthwhile when I fail.					
18. People would look down on me if they found out about all the mistakes I've made.					
19. I usually get very upset if I make a mistake.					
20. I feel like I should try to be perfect.					

THE SELF-DEFEATING BELIEF SCALE (Continued)

	0 Disagree Strongly	1 Disagree Slightly	2 Neutral	3 Agree Slightly	4 Agree Strongly
21. I often get upset when people do not meet my expectations.					
22. I often feel entitled to better treatment from others.					
23. Other people are usually to blame for the problems in my relationships with them.					
24. I often get frustrated or annoyed with people.					
25. I feel like I deserve better treatment from other people.					
26. I often feel guilty if someone is annoyed with me.					
27. I get very self-critical if I'm not getting along well with a friend or family member.					
28. I usually blame myself for the problems in my relationships with other people.					
29. If someone is upset with me, I usually feel like it's my fault.					
30. I get self-critical if I am not able to please everybody.					

THE SELF-DEFEATING BELIEF SCALE (Continued)

	0 Disagree Strongly	1 Disagree Slightly	2 Neutral	3 Agree Slightly	4 Agree Strongly
31. I feel pessimistic that things could ever change for the better.					
32. It would be extemely difficult or impossible to solve the problems in my life.					
33. I believe that my bad moods result from factors beyond my control.					
34. I don't believe I will ever feel truly happy or worthwhile.					
35. There's very little anyone could do to help me solve my problems.					

Now that you have completed the test, you can add up your score for each group of five items on the Self-defeating Belief Scale, beginning with the first item. Add up your scores on items 1–5, 6–10, 11–15, 16–20, 21–25, 26–30, and 31–35. Use this key when you score your answers:

SCORING KEY

Answer	Value
disagree strongly	0
disagree slightly	1
neutral	2
agree slightly	3
agree strongly	4

Your total score for each group of five questions will be between 0 (if you answered "disagree strongly" on all five items in that group) and 20 (if you answered "agree strongly" on all five items in that group).

For example, the first five items on the test measure your tendency to base your self-esteem on the amount of approval or criticism you receive. Suppose your scores on these five items were 2 + 1 + 3 + 4 + 2. Your total score for these five questions would be 12. Put your total score for each group of five items in the box below.

SCORING THE SELF-DEFEATING BELIEF SCALE

Belief	Items That Test This Belief	Total Score for This Belief
1. The Approval Addiction	1 – 5	
2. The Love Addiction	6 – 10	
3. The Achievement Addiction	11 – 15	
4. Perfectionism	16 – 20	
5. Entitlement	21 – 25	
6. Self-blame	26 – 30	
7. Hopelessness	31 – 35	

INTERPRETING YOUR SCORES

Low scores (between 0 and 10) represent areas of psychological strength. The lower the score, the better. High scores (between 11 and 20) represent areas of emotional vulnerability. The higher the score, the greater the vulnerability. These are areas where you may want to do some work.

For example, suppose you have the achievement belief: "I must be a success in life to be worthwhile." If you have this belief, you may work extremely hard to be successful, and when you are successful, you will feel happy and secure. On the other hand, when you experience a failure or setback in your career, you may have a tendency to feel worthless and depressed. Then you will have two problems for the price of one!

HOW TO MODIFY A SELF-DEFEATING BELIEF

The Cost-Benefit Analysis is the first step in modifying a Self-defeating Belief. You list the advantages and disadvantages of believing it. Choose a Self-defeating Belief from the following list so you can perform a Cost-Benefit Analysis:

- "I must be productive and successful to be worthwhile."
- "I must be loved to be a worthwhile and happy human being."
- "I should always try to be perfect."
- "I need everyone's approval to be a worthwhile human being."
- "If I'm depressed or unhappy, there's not much I can do about it. My moods result from forces beyond my control."
- "Other people are to blame for most of the problems in my relationships with them."
- "People should meet my expectations, because my expectations are reasonable."

Which Self-defeating Belief did you choose? Write it on the top of the form on page 156. Then list the advantages and disadvantages of this attitude. Ask yourself, "How will it help me to think this way, and how will it hurt me? What are the costs and benefits of this belief?"

Finally, weigh the advantages of this attitude against the disadvantages. Which are greater? If the disadvantages of the belief are greater, then you can replace it with a new belief that is more realistic and helpful to you. Write the new attitude or belief here:

_____

_____

_____

You will find an example of a completed Attitude Cost-Benefit analysis on page 160. You may want to look at it before you do this exercise to give you an idea of how to do it.

Let's suppose you have completed a CBA on this belief: "I need everybody's approval to be worthwhile." You decide that the disadvantages of this attitude outweigh the advantages. How would you revise it?

An example of a revised belief could be: "It is desirable to have people like me and approve of me, but I don't *need* people's approval to be worthwhile." You could also add: "If someone is upset with me, I can talk things over with them. There will often be some truth in their criticism, and I can try to learn from it. This won't ever make me any less worthwhile, but it might make me a little wiser." Of course, there are dozens of ways to revise any Self-defeating Belief.

When you revise a Self-defeating Belief, try to think of a new attitude that will maintain most of the advantages while getting rid of the disadvantages. After all, you don't want to throw out the baby with the bath water.

Try to make the attitude more objective and realistic than the Self-defeating Belief. You will notice that most Self-defeating Beliefs are contaminated by these distortions:

ATTITUDE COST-BENEFIT ANALYSIS*

The Attitude or Belief You Want to Change: _____

_____

Advantages of Believing This	Disadvantages of Believing This

- **Overgeneralization:** I should *always* be successful and *never* fail.
- **All-or-nothing thinking:** I need *everyone's* approval *all the time*.
- **"Should" statements:** People *should always be* fair and reasonable.

Several techniques from the list of Fifteen Ways to Untwist Your Thinking (see page 109) can help you make your revised beliefs less rigid and extreme. Here are some examples of how to revise Self-defeating Beliefs using Thinking in Shades of Gray, the Semantic Method, and the Acceptance Paradox:

SELF-DEFEATING BELIEF	REVISED BELIEF
1. I must be productive and successful to be worthwhile.	1. It's great to work hard and to be productive, but my value as a human being does not depend on how successful I am. Sometimes I will be quite successful and sometimes I won't. This is all part of being human.
2. The world should meet my expectations. People should always be fair and reasonable.	2. The world will sometimes meet my expectations, but not always. People will often be fair and reasonable, but sometimes they won't!

SELF-DEFEATING BELIEF EXERCISE

If you are working individually, you can do this exercise on your own. If you are in a Ten Days to Self-esteem group, the leader may divide the members into small teams of three to six members. Each team will work on a different Self-defeating Belief. One group can discuss the need for approval, another group can discuss the need for love, a third group can discuss entitlement, and so forth. You can choose the group working on the attitude or belief of greatest personal interest to you.

Each small group will write a paragraph on why that attitude or belief can be self-defeating. When your group is done, select a spokesperson to read the paragraph and report on the work that your group completed.

Which belief did you choose? Write it down here:

_____

_____

Now write a paragraph describing why the attitude or belief can be self-defeating. Please describe specific problems that may result from this mind-set:

_____

_____

_____

_____

_____

_____

_____

_____

_____

_____

_____

_____

ANSWER TO THE EXERCISE ON PAGE 148

NEGATIVE THOUGHTS

1. *If the professor calls on me, I might not know the answer.*

   ↓   If that was true, why would it be upsetting to me? What would it mean to me?

2. *I might make a fool of myself in front of the other students.*

   ↓   If that was true, why would it be upsetting to me? What would it mean to me?

3. *That would show I was stupid.*

   ↓   If that was true, why would it be upsetting to me? What would it mean to me?

4. *Then no one would like me.*

   ↓   If that was true, why would it be upsetting to me? What would it mean to me?

5. *Then I'd have no friends and I'd be alone.*

   ↓   If that was true, why would it be upsetting to me? What would it mean to me?

6. *That would mean I was a failure.*

   ↓   If that was true, why would it be upsetting to me? What would it mean to me?

7. *Then I'd be worthless and life would not be worth living.*

Based on these Negative Thoughts, her Self-defeating Beliefs would include perfectionism, perceived perfectionism, fear of failure, fear of disapproval, and the fear of being alone.

ANSWER TO THE EXERCISE ON PAGE 155

ATTITUDE COST-BENEFIT ANALYSIS*

The Attitude or Belief You Want to Change: *Other people are to blame for most of the problems in my relationships with them.*

Advantages of Believing This	Disadvantages of Believing This
1. I won't have to feel guilty.	1. If I blame other people, they'll blame me right back again.
2. I won't have to change.	2. The problem won't get corrected.
3. I can feel self-righteous.	3. I'll have more enemies than friends.
4. I can feel that I'm right and other people are wrong.	4. I'll feel helpless.
5. I can feel like a victim and resent other people.	5. I'll be sour, cynical, and unhappy.
6. I can feel sorry for myself.	6. I won't feel close to people.
7. I can feel powerful.	7. I won't grow and learn.
8. I can get back at people.	8. I won't examine my own behavior and discover what I'm doing to contribute to the problem.
9. I won't have to give in or appear weak.	9. I'll be rigid and judgmental.
10. I can be angry and harbor resentment.	10. I'll turn people off.

45   55

EVALUATION OF STEP 6

What did you learn in Step 6? Put a brief summary of several of the most important ideas we discussed here:

1. _____

_____

2. _____

_____

3. _____

_____

Was there anything in today's step that bothered you or rubbed you the wrong way? If you are in a group, was there anything the leader or other members said that turned you off? Describe any negative feelings you had:

_____

_____

_____

_____

Was there anything in today's step that was particularly helpful, interesting, or useful? Did the leader or other participants say anything during today's session that you liked? Describe any positive reactions you had:

_____

_____

_____

_____

SELF-HELP ASSIGNMENTS FOR STEP 7

If you are participating in a Ten Days to Self-esteem group, your leader may give you self-help assignments to complete before the next session.

Assignments	Check (√) If Assigned	Check (√) When Finished
1. Complete the evaluation form for Step 6.		
2. Take the three mood tests again. They are located at the beginning of the next step.		
3. Read the next step in this book and do as many of the written exercises as possible.		
4. Bring your copy of this book to the next session.		
5. Use the Vertical Arrow Technique to identify one of your Self-defeating Beliefs.		
6. Do a Cost-Benefit Analysis of the advantages and disadvantages of a Self-defeating Belief.		
7. Work with the Daily Mood Log for ten minutes per day. (Extra copies begin on page 290.)		
8. Bring any written homework to the next session.		
9. Bibliotherapy (was any reading assigned?)		
10.*		

*Use this space for any additional assignments.

SUPPLEMENTARY READING FOR STEP 6

1. Read Chapter 7 in *The Feeling Good Handbook*.
2. Read Chapter 10 in *Feeling Good: The New Mood Therapy* (see Recommended Reading on page 317).

STEP 7

SELF-ESTEEM—WHAT IS IT?
HOW DO I GET IT?

GOALS FOR STEP 7

In this step, we will focus on a buzzword that is frequently discussed but not often understood: *self-esteem*. You will discover the answers to these questions:

1. When people say they have low self-esteem, what do they really mean?
2. What are the consequences of low self-esteem?
3. Can a person have too much self-esteem?
4. What is the difference between self-esteem and self-confidence?
5. Should you base your self-esteem on your looks, your personality, or your accomplishments?
6. Should you base your self-esteem on love and approval?
7. What are the hidden benefits of an inferiority complex?
8. What is a worthwhile human being? What is a worthless human being?
9. How can I develop unconditional self-esteem?

MOOD TESTING

You have already taken three mood tests at the beginning of the previous steps. I would like you to take the three tests again at the beginning of this step to chart your progress. If you need help, you can review the instructions for these tests in Step 1 beginning on page 18.

THE BURNS DEPRESSION CHECKLIST*

Place a check (√) in the box to the right of each category to indicate how much this type of feeling has bothered you in the past several days.

	0 Not at All	1 Somewhat	2 Moderately	3 A Lot
1. **Sadness:** Do you feel sad or down in the dumps?				
2. **Discouragement:** Does the future look hopeless?				
3. **Low self-esteem:** Do you feel worthless?				
4. **Inferiority:** Do you feel inadequate or inferior to others?				
5. **Guilt:** Do you get self-critical and blame yourself?				
6. **Indecisiveness:** Is it hard to make decisions?				
7. **Irritability:** Do you frequently feel angry or resentful?				
8. **Loss of interest in life:** Have you lost interest in your career, hobbies, family, or friends?				
9. **Loss of motivation:** Do you have to push yourself hard to do things?				
10. **Poor self-image:** Do you feel old or unattractive?				
11. **Appetite changes:** Have you lost your appetite? Do you overeat or binge compulsively?				
12. **Sleep changes:** Is it hard to get a good night's sleep? Are you excessively tired and sleeping too much?				
13. **Loss of sex drive:** Have you lost your interest in sex?				
14. **Concerns about health:** Do you worry excessively about your health?				
15. **Suicidal impulses:** Do you have thoughts that life is not worth living or think you'd be better off dead?†				
Total score on items 1–15 →				

THE BURNS ANXIETY INVENTORY*

Place a check (√) in the box to the right of each category to indicate how much this type of feeling has bothered you in the past several days.

Category I: Anxious Feelings	0 Not at All	1 Somewhat	2 Moderately	3 A Lot
1. Anxiety, nervousness, worry, or fear				
2. Feeling that things around you are strange or unreal				
3. Feeling detached from all or part of your body				
4. Sudden unexpected panic spells				
5. Apprehension or a sense of impending doom				
6. Feeling tense, stressed, "uptight," or on edge				
Category II: Anxious Thoughts	0 Not at All	1 Somewhat	2 Moderately	3 A Lot
7. Difficulty concentrating				
8. Racing thoughts				
9. Frightening fantasies or daydreams				
10. Feeling that you're on the verge of losing control				
11. Fears of cracking up or going crazy				
12. Fears of fainting or passing out				
13. Fears of physical illnesses or heart attacks or dying				
14. Concerns about looking foolish or inadequate				
15. Fears of being alone, isolated, or abandoned				
16. Fears of criticism or disapproval				
17. Fears that something terrible is about to happen				

THE BURNS ANXIETY INVENTORY (Continued)

Category III: Physical Symptoms	0 Not at All	1 Somewhat	2 Moderately	3 A Lot
18. Skipping, racing, or pounding of the heart (palpitations)				
19. Pain, pressure, or tightness in the chest				
20. Tingling or numbness in the toes or fingers				
21. Butterflies or discomfort in the stomach				
22. Constipation or diarrhea				
23. Restlessness or jumpiness				
24. Tight, tense muscles				
25. Sweating not brought on by heat				
26. A lump in the throat				
27. Trembling or shaking				
28. Rubbery or "jelly" legs				
29. Feeling dizzy, lightheaded, or off balance				
30. Choking or smothering sensations or difficulty breathing				
31. Headaches or pains in the neck or back				
32. Hot flashes or cold chills				
33. Feeling tired, weak, or easily exhausted				
Total score on items 1–33 →				

RELATIONSHIP SATISFACTION SCALE*

Place a check ($\sqrt{}$) in the box to the right of each category that best describes the amount of satisfaction you feel in your closest relationship.

	0 Very Dissatisfied	1 Moderately Dissatisfied	2 Slightly Dissatisfied	3 Neutral	4 Slightly Satisfied	5 Moderately Satisfied	6 Very Satisfied
1. Communication and openness							
2. Resolving conflicts and arguments							
3. Degree of affection and caring							
4. Intimacy and closeness							
5. Satisfaction with your role in the relationship							
6. Satisfaction with the other person's role							
7. Overall satisfaction with your relationship							
Total score on items 1–7 $\longrightarrow$							

Note: Although this test assesses your marriage or most intimate relationship, you can also use it to evaluate your relationship with a friend, family member, or colleague. If you do not have any intimate relationships at this time, you can simply think of people in general when you take the test.

*Copyright © 1983 by David D. Burns, M.D., from *Ten Days to Self-esteem,* copyright © 1993.

SELF-ESTEEM EXERCISE 1

What are some of the situations that make you feel inferior or low on self-esteem? Is it when you feel criticized? Unloved? Rejected? Unsuccessful? Please describe several upsetting situations here:

1. _____

_____

2. _____

_____

3. _____

_____

What kinds of negative emotions do you have in these situations? Do you feel sad? Inferior? Jealous? Angry? Put down? Rejected? Describe your negative feelings here:

1. _____
2. _____
3. _____
4. _____
5. _____

What are you thinking in these situations? What do you tell yourself? Describe your Negative Thoughts here:

1. _____
2. _____
3. _____
4. _____
5. _____

What are the consequences of low self-esteem? How does it affect your productivity and your personal relationships?

_____

_____

_____

_____

_____

Can you think of someone you knew or admired who you felt was especially worthwhile? Who was that person? What was it that made him or her worthwhile? Describe that person here:

_____

_____

_____

_____

_____

SELF-ESTEEM VS. ARROGANCE

What are the consequences of high self-esteem? Can a person have too much self-esteem? What's the difference between self-esteem and arrogance? Write down your ideas here (for the answer see page 189):

_____

_____

_____

_____

_____

SELF-ESTEEM VS. SELF-CONFIDENCE

What are the differences between self-esteem and self-confidence? Are they the same or different? Can you have self-esteem without having self-confidence? Write down your ideas here (for the answer see page 189):

_____

_____

_____

_____

_____

SELF-ESTEEM EXERCISE 2

On the following pages you will find two Self-esteem Cost-Benefit Analyses. Choose one of them and then list the advantages and disadvantages of thinking in the way indicated. Ask yourself, "How will it help me, and how will it hurt me, to believe this?"

Let's suppose you choose the second one, in which you base your self-esteem on popularity. Do not list the advantages and disadvantages of *being* popular. Instead, list the advantages and disadvantages of basing your self-esteem on how popular you are. You can see this CBA filled out on page 190 once you have completed your own.

When you have completed your lists, balance the advantages against the disadvantages on a 100-point scale and write the numbers in the circles at the bottom. For example, if the advantages slightly outweigh the disadvantages, you might put 60 in the left-hand circle and 40 in the right-hand circle. In contrast, if the disadvantages are significantly stronger, you might put 30 in the left-hand circle and 70 in the right-hand circle.

If you decide that it's not to your advantage to measure your self-esteem in this way, then what new attitude or belief could you substitute for this one? Put your revised attitude here:

_____

_____

_____

SELF-ESTEEM COST-BENEFIT ANALYSIS*

The Basis of Your Feelings of Self-esteem: <u>*I am a worthwhile person if I am successful*</u>
<u>*and achieve something worthwhile.*</u>

Advantages of Believing This	Disadvantages of Believing This

SELF-ESTEEM COST-BENEFIT ANALYSIS*

The Basis of Your Feelings of Self-esteem: *I am a worthwhile person if I am popular and people like and respect me.*

Advantages of Believing This	Disadvantages of Believing This

SELF-ESTEEM EXERCISE 3

There are many other ways that people measure their self-esteem. Some of these include:

- I am worthwhile if I have close, loving relationships with others.
- I am worthwhile if I am attractive and in good physical condition.
- I am worthwhile if I treat other people in a fair, generous, and ethical way.
- I am worthwhile if I'm happy and like myself.
- I am worthwhile if I work hard and do the best I can to fulfill my potential.
- I am worthwhile if I contribute to society.
- I am worthwhile if I am talented or outstanding in at least one area.

On the next page you will find a blank Self-esteem Cost-Benefit Analysis. Choose one of the attitudes above and enter it at the top of the page. Then list the advantages and disadvantages of thinking that way. Balance the advantages against the disadvantages on a 100-point scale, just as you did in the previous exercise.

If you decide that it's not to your advantage to measure your self-esteem in this way, then what new attitude or belief could you substitute for this one? Put your revised attitude here:

_____

_____

_____

FEARED FANTASY EXERCISE

After you have completed the Cost-Benefit Analyses, you will probably see that these formulations of self-esteem are not very helpful. However, you may still believe that they are realistic and true.

A woman named Sue in a Ten Days to Self-esteem group at the Presbyterian Medical Center had always believed that people who are socially successful and popular are more worthwhile than others. After she listed the advantages and disadvantages of believing this, Sue recognized that this attitude was the cause of much unhappiness throughout her life. She said she'd begun to feel inferior to the more popular kids when she was in junior high school, and she still felt inferior to socially successful people with lots of money and charm and expensive clothing. In spite of her rational awareness that this mind-set was not beneficial, she still believed it was true. At the gut level, she felt convinced that extremely successful and popular people *really are* superior human beings.

To make Sue more vividly aware of how cruel and unrealistic this notion is, the leader

SELF-ESTEEM COST-BENEFIT ANALYSIS*

The Basis of Your Feelings of Self-esteem: _____
_____

Advantages of Believing This	Disadvantages of Believing This

suggested she do an exercise called the Feared Fantasy with a group member named Joan. In this exercise, Sue entered an Alice-in-Wonderland nightmare world where she came face to face with her worst fears. You should be aware that this is not assertiveness training, because Sue and the other volunteer acted far differently than normal human beings would act. They said outrageous things that real people would never dare to say.

Sue and Joan sat facing each other on two chairs in the middle of the group. The leader asked Sue to imagine that she was extremely successful and popular. Joan played the role of someone who was not especially successful or popular. Sue's job was to explain that she was superior to Joan because of her popularity and success. Even though she was a shy and sensitive person in real life, Sue tried to be as snotty and mean as possible in this particular exercise.

Sue was quite reluctant at first. She protested that she was a *nice* person who couldn't possibly say such mean things to another person. The leader reminded her that this was just role playing, and reassured her that she and Joan would not be real but would be fantasy figures who represented Sue's worst fears. Sue decided to take a chance and try, after the leader reassured her that he would suggest what to say if she got stuck during the exercise. After a little coaching, Sue said things like this:

SUE (as fantasy figure): Joan, you probably saw my picture on the cover of *Time* magazine this week as "Woman of the Year." This was only one small tribute to my many incredible achievements. Of course, in addition to being enormously successful in my career, I'm also gorgeous and charming. In fact, at virtually every social occasion I'm the center of attention. *Everyone* wants to be seen with me because I'm so *special*.

JOAN (as "ordinary" person): Gee, that must be quite exciting.

SUE (as fantasy figure): Oh, it is. In fact, I go around in a constant state of euphoria when I think of how great I am. But the main thing I wanted to let you know, Joan, is that I'm quite superior to you. You're just ordinary and don't enjoy even a tiny fraction of my incredible success and popularity. So it just logically follows that you're inferior to me, I mean *really* inferior. Remember that I'll be looking down on you whenever we're together. I hate to hurt your feelings, but I was sure you wanted to know the truth so you wouldn't have any mistaken idea that I considered you my equal!

Once Sue began to talk, she *really* got into it! These bottled-up feelings had never really had the chance to come out. The rest of the group seemed spellbound by her performance!

Once Joan and Sue finished their brief dialogue, the members discussed what they had just heard. How did they feel about it? What did they learn?

The group members had powerful reactions to the Feared Fantasy role playing. Sue said that verbalizing this value system out loud made it suddenly appear quite unrealistic. The other members agreed that the imaginary Sue was so obviously self-centered and shallow that it became difficult to believe that social success and popularity really made anybody more "worthwhile." Although popularity may be enjoyable and desirable, it does not make a person superior to anyone else.

A college student named Hank said that although it is obviously absurd to believe that the so-called beautiful people are more worthwhile as human beings, he still believed that people who are spiritual or philanthropic, as well as those who contribute to society through their research and scientific discoveries, *really are* more worthwhile. He said he felt that people like Gandhi, the Rockefellers, and Edison really were superior human beings.

To help Hank evaluate the consequences of this value system, the leader suggested a second Feared Fantasy exercise. The result was similar to that of the previous exercise. If you say, "Some people are more worthwhile because of their great generosity and contributions to mankind," you are in the awkward position of claiming that a few people are superior and that most of the people you know, including your friends and family, are inferior. We will examine the logic of this type of thinking in the next exercise.

I am not arguing that popularity is undesirable or that scientific discoveries and philanthropic contributions are unimportant. Nothing could be further from the truth. Compassion, generosity, and rewarding personal relationships are tremendously important. Doing your best with your mind and with your career can be exceedingly worthwhile. But popularity, success, and generosity can never make you a more worthwhile human being or any better than someone else.

WHAT IS A WORTHLESS PERSON?
WHAT IS A WORTHWHILE PERSON?

So far, we have used the Cost-Benefit Analysis to ask this question: "Is there any value in measuring my worthwhileness? What are the benefits and what are the costs of basing my self-esteem on my characteristics or my performance?" In the Feared Fantasy, you saw that any system for measuring your self-esteem can be unrealistic and destructive.

In this exercise you will ask yourself, "Is there any such thing as a worthless or worthwhile human being? Is there any such thing as an superior or inferior human being? Are these concepts meaningful or meaningless?"

The purpose of this exercise is to help you stop trying to measure your inherent value as a human being. Good or bad behaviors exist, but good or bad human beings do not. We can rate our *traits,* but not our *selves.*

We can demonstrate this with the method called Define Terms. Write your definition of a "worthless person" (or an "inferior person" or a "bad person"):

_____

_____

_____

After you write down your definition, ask yourself, "Is there anything fishy or suspicious about this definition?" Once you examine your definition in a critical and thoughtful way, you will see that it is useless or meaningless. Nearly all these definitions of a worthless or inferior human being suffer from one of these three difficulties:

- The definition applies to all human beings.
- The definition does not apply to any human being.
- The definition is based on all-or-nothing thinking.

For example, let's assume that you came up with this definition:

A worthless or inferior person is one who can't do anything right.

The problem with this definition is that every one can do *some* things right. Therefore no one is worthless or inferior.

Next, you may come up with this definition:

A worthless or inferior person is one who isn't as smart or talented as other people.

The problem with this definition is that no matter how smart or talented you are, you can always find people who are smarter and more talented than you are. Even the world's top tennis players lose many matches. Are they worthless or inferior human beings on those occasions? According to this definition, we are *all* worthless and inferior human beings!

See if you can write a rebuttal to several of the other definitions of a worthless person on the chart on page 178. You can also make up some additional definitions of your own. See if you can refute them. After you have written your own rebuttals, you can compare your answers with the ones I have provided on page 191.

Definition of a Worthless or Inferior Person	Rebuttal
1. Someone who does bad things.	
2. Someone who fails or make mistakes.	
3. Someone who fails or make mistakes 51% of the time.	
4. Someone who does mean, hateful things on purpose to hurt other people.	

Definition of a Worthless or Inferior Person	Rebuttal
5. Someone who is lazy, self-centered, and unproductive, and has no value to society.	
6. Someone whom nobody likes.	
7. Someone who is stupid and untalented.	
8. Someone who does not have *any* talent. To be worthwhile, you have to be good at *one* thing at least.	

179

Definition of a Worthless or Inferior Person	Rebuttal
9. To be worthwhile, you have to be very good at one thing that is regarded as very important by society. You have to be in the top 5% at that one thing.	
10. Someone who does not like himself or herself. Someone who does not feel worthwhile.	
11. A murderer is a worthless person because he or she has killed another human being on purpose.	
12. Other (put your definition here):	

INFERIORITY EXERCISE

Although we often feel that it would be wonderful to have self-esteem, an inferiority complex can have many hidden payoffs. This exercise will make you more aware of the many rewards of an inferiority complex. This insight can often give people the courage to change their self-image.

On page 182, list the advantages of believing that you are a defective or inferior person. Ask yourself how it might help you to have this attitude. Then list the disadvantages of this mind-set. How will it hurt you to think this way?

If you decide that the disadvantages of thinking of yourself as an inferior or defective human being outweigh the advantages, then what new attitude or belief could you substitute for this one? Put your revised attitude here:

_____

_____

_____

If you decide that you do want to change your self-image, you may want to save the Inferiority Cost-Benefit Analysis and read it from time to time. You should also continue working on your Negative Thoughts for ten or fifteen minutes per day, using the Daily Mood Log. Finally, you will want to *treat* yourself in a positive, kindly, loving way, the same way you would treat a friend you respected greatly. Later, you will learn how the Pleasure-Predicting Sheet can help you do this.

INFERIORITY COST-BENEFIT ANALYSIS*

The Attitude or Belief You Want to Change: _I am a defective, inferior human being. I am not as good as other people._

Advantages of Believing This	Disadvantages of Believing This

HOW TO USE THE PLEASURE-PREDICTING SHEET

One purpose of the Pleasure-Predicting Sheet is to help you become more involved in rewarding activities. A second purpose is to help you develop greater self-reliance by testing beliefs such as "I'm bound to feel miserable when I'm alone," or "The only true happiness comes from a loving relationship with someone I really care about." As you begin to enjoy your own company, you will naturally experience an increase in self-esteem.

Here's how to use the Pleasure-Predicting Sheet. In the "Activity" column, schedule activities with the potential for satisfaction, learning, or personal growth. If you feel depressed and can't think of anything that seems rewarding or worthwhile, you can schedule activities that used to be enjoyable, even if you don't think they'll be very satisfying now. Include activities you can do by yourself (such as jogging or reading) as well as activities you can do with friends.

Indicate whom you plan to do each activity with in the "Companion" column. Do not put the word *alone* in this column. Instead, use the word *self* to describe your companion when you schedule an activity by yourself. This will remind you that you never really need to feel alone if you regard yourself as a companion and friend.

In the third column, labeled "Predicted Satisfaction," estimate how satisfying each activity will be on a scale from 0% (for the least possible satisfaction) to 100% (for the most). Make these written predictions *before* you do each activity. Finally, in the last column, which is labeled "Actual Satisfaction," record how satisfying the various activities turned out to be after you've completed them, using the same 0% to 100% rating system.

The "Actual Satisfaction" column will show you how pleasurable and rewarding the various activities were. This will help you discover what gives you the most satisfaction. You may find that many of the things you usually do, such as watching TV or overeating, turn out to be unrewarding. In contrast, certain things you might ordinarily avoid, such as cleaning your desk or exercising, may turn out to be more rewarding than you anticipated.

You can also compare the satisfaction of activities by yourself with the satisfaction of activities with others. Discovering that you can often be as happy when you're alone as when you're with friends or loved ones can be a tremendous source of self-confidence. This can help you disprove the belief that happiness always comes from loving relationships with other people. Paradoxically, the self-esteem you feel when you realize that you don't really "need" others will often lead to improved relationships with people, because you won't feel so desperate and afraid of rejection.

PLEASURE-PREDICTING SHEET*

Activity Schedule activities with the potential for pleasure, learning, or personal growth.	Companion If alone, specify *self.*	Predicted Satisfaction Record this *before* each activity on a scale from 0% to 100%.	Actual Satisfaction Record this *after* each activity on a scale from 0% to 100%.

CONDITIONAL VS. UNCONDITIONAL SELF-ESTEEM

The message in this step is similar in some ways to the message in Step 5 on the Acceptance Paradox. In that session you learned about two ways of refuting Negative Thoughts: Self-defense and the Acceptance Paradox. When you use Self-defense, you talk back to your Negative Thoughts. You defend against your self-criticisms and try to build yourself up. For example, instead of dwelling on all your shortcomings and writing yourself off as a total loser, you can emphasize your strengths.

The difficulty with this strategy is that you may get trapped in a battle when you defend yourself. Every self-defense—no matter how persuasive—will be followed by a new self-criticism. You will never know for sure if you are really good enough or if you have lived up to the image of who you think you *should* be.

In contrast, when you use the Acceptance Paradox, you refuse to do battle with the inner critic. You accept your shortcomings with ruthless honesty, inner peace, and objectivity. If you comprehend this strategy, it can be incredibly liberating.

By the same token, there are two dramatically different ways a person can achieve self-esteem. You can say, "I am a worthwhile person because . . ." After the "because," you can include the basis you have decided upon for self-esteem. This could be your success and hard work in life or your altruism or the fact that you are loved. For example, you can say, "I am a worthwhile person because I have done the best I can with my God-given talents and abilities." This kind of reasoning is based on the Calvinist work ethic, which is widespread in our culture.

This formulation makes self-esteem conditional, because your self-esteem has to be earned. Conditional self-esteem has its benefits: If you base your self-esteem on your hard work and accomplishments, it may motivate you to work hard and do your best. Conditional self-esteem also has its downside. What happens when, in spite of your best efforts, you are not particularly productive or successful? Does this mean you are now worthless and inferior? Few people can achieve extreme levels of fame and recognition, and even the most successful people experience many failures along the way.

No matter how you try to measure or earn your self-esteem, there will be times when you do not measure up to the criterion you have chosen. Then you will be vulnerable to anxiety and depression. Instead of thinking, "I have failed," and trying to learn from the situation, you may think, "I am *a failure*."

Suppose, in contrast, that you work hard and experience outstanding success for a period of time. Are you now more worthwhile than other people who are less successful? Do you really need this feeling of superiority? What would you say to a less successful person if you were being really honest? "Hi, Joe, I just wanted you to know that I've been quite successful lately and so I'm superior to you now. I'll be looking down on you because I'm so great!" Of course, it sounds pretty ridiculous when you put it like that, but that's precisely where this type of thinking leads.

Alternatively, you can make your self-esteem unconditional. You can love and respect yourself because you are a human being or simply because you have chosen to do so. You can love yourself because you need the compassion and support, and not because you have earned it. Although unconditional self-esteem may be more difficult to comprehend, it is far more liberating.

You can use the Cost-Benefit Analysis on page 187 to decide whether this concept is right for you. In the left-hand column you can list the advantages of unconditional self-esteem. Ask yourself, "How will unconditional self-esteem help me? What are the benefits?" Your list of the advantages of unconditional self-esteem might include:

- I will always know I am worthwhile, even if I'm having a tough time.

- I won't be so afraid of failure or rejection. I may be willing to take more risks with my career and with my personal life.

- Although I will feel disappointed when things don't go well, I won't have to feel inferior or ashamed.

- I will always feel equal to other people—never superior or inferior. This will make my personal relationships more rewarding.

- I won't have to get so defensive when I'm criticized because my self-esteem won't be on the line.

- I can enjoy life far more because I won't use up all my energy worrying about whether I'm good enough.

- I'll face my shortcomings more honestly.

- I will have a greater capacity to love others and accept myself.

Of course, you will also want to list any disadvantages of unconditional self-esteem in the right-hand column of your CBA. Ask yourself, "How will unconditional self-esteem hurt me? What are the costs?" Your list of disadvantages might include:

- I may be complacent and less motivated to do my best.

- I may become self-centered and insensitive to the needs of other people.

- I may say "screw you" instead of listening and trying to learn from people who are critical of me.

I'm sure you can think of some additional advantages and disadvantages of unconditional self-esteem. After you have listed them, put two numbers adding up to 100 in the two circles at the bottom of the CBA to indicate the results of your analysis.

I like to think about the process of gaining self-esteem as climbing up a ladder. If you feel worthless and inferior, you may start out on the ground because you have very little self-esteem. On the first rung of the ladder you develop conditional self-esteem. You decide to like yourself because of your strengths rather than hating yourself because of your weaknesses. You stick up for yourself and defend yourself against your critical inner voice. For many people who feel inadequate, this can be an extremely important first step.

ATTITUDE COST-BENEFIT ANALYSIS*

List the advantages and disadvantages of unconditional self-esteem _____

_____

Advantages	Disadvantages

Once you have conditional self-esteem, you can climb up to the next rung on the ladder. On this step you develop unconditional self-esteem. You realize that self-esteem is a gift that you and all human beings receive at birth. Your worthwhileness is already there and you don't have to earn it. It suddenly dawns on you that you will always be worthwhile simply because you are a human being. It ultimately makes no difference if you are fat or thin, young or old, loved or rejected, successful or unsuccessful.

Unconditional self-esteem is given freely. It is much like hugging a child who is upset and needs comforting. The child doesn't have to earn your love. In Step 10, you will see that the concept of unconditional self-esteem is quite consistent with both the Jewish and Christian religions.

After you achieve unconditional self-esteem, you can climb another step up the ladder if you want. On the next step, you can adopt the even more radical position that there is no such thing as self-esteem, just as there is no such thing as a worthwhile person or a worthless person. You began to work on this idea in the exercise on "What Is a Worthless Person? What Is a Worthwhile Person?" Since there's no such thing as a worthwhile person, there's no point in trying to become one!

On this level, you can discard the notion of self-esteem entirely and simply refuse to deal with it! This solution to the problem of self-esteem is in the Buddhist tradition because self-esteem is rejected as a useless illusion.

Giving up your self-esteem once you have discovered it may sound like a negative notion! It may feel like a loss and seem like something inside you dies. All of us naturally want to feel "special" and "worthwhile." However, there is a rebirth, because the death of your pride and your ego can lead to new life and to a more profound vision. When you discover that you are nothing, you have nothing to lose, and you inherit the world.

This last formulation might sound abstract, mystical, or confusing, but it is immensely practical. Instead of worrying about whether you are sufficiently worthwhile, each day you can have goals that involve learning, personal growth, helping others, being productive, having fun, spending time with people you care about, improving the quality of your relationships, and so on. You will discover unexpected opportunities for intimacy, for productivity, and for joy in daily living.

ANSWER TO THE QUESTION ON PAGE 169 ON ARROGANCE

A person *can* have too much self-esteem! A person with healthy self-esteem also respects and likes others. In contrast, a person with excessive self-esteem is arrogant and self-centered and disrespectful of others. In its most extreme form, excessive self-esteem is known as narcissistic personality disorder. People with this disorder have fantasies of grandeur and an inflated sense of self-esteem. They are insensitive to the needs and feelings of others and exploit other people for their own purposes. When they are criticized or confronted, they react with rage or with feelings of shame. They have difficulties forming close, trusting, equal relationships with others.

ANSWER TO THE QUESTION ON PAGE 170 ON SELF-CONFIDENCE

Genuine self-esteem is *not* the same as self-confidence. Self-confidence is based on the knowledge that you will probably be successful at an activity because you have been successful at similar activities in the past. In contrast, self-esteem is the capacity to like and respect yourself when you lose just as much as when you win. If I were to play a top tennis star like Jimmy Connors, I would not have much self-confidence because I would know I would lose. In fact, I probably wouldn't get a single point unless he made a mistake! However, I would still have self-esteem if I lost, because I would not look down on myself or rate myself as a less worthwhile human being.

ANSWER TO THE EXERCISE ON PAGE 172

SELF-ESTEEM COST-BENEFIT ANALYSIS*

The Basis of Your Feelings of Self-esteem: *I am worthwhile if I am popular and people like and respect me.*

Advantages of Believing This	Disadvantages of Believing This
1. I'll work hard to earn other people's respect.	1. If someone doesn't like me I may get depressed.
2. When people like me, I'll feel great!	2. You can't please all the people all the time.
3. I won't have to think for myself. I can go along with the crowd.	3. Other people will do my thinking for me.
	4. Other people will control my self-esteem.
	5. Other people will be able to manipulate me pretty easily.

(35) —————— (65)

ANSWER TO THE EXERCISE ON PAGE 177

Definition of a Worthless or Inferior Person	Rebuttal
1. Someone who does bad things.	Then we're all worthless because we all do some bad things.
2. Someone who fails or make mistakes.	Then we're all worthless because we all fail and make mistakes.
3. Someone who fails or make mistakes 51% of the time.	Does this mean that someone who fails 50% of the time is a worthwhile human being and someone who fails 51% of the time is a worthless human being?
4. Someone who does mean, hateful things on purpose to hurt other people.	We all do things that are somewhat mean or hateful at times when we feel hurt and angry. The urge to get back at someone who has wronged us is an unattractive but nearly universal human characteristic. Does it mean that we are all worthless? How many mean, nasty impulses does it take before we become worthless?
5. Someone who is lazy, self-centered, and unproductive, and has no value to society.	We are all lazy and unproductive at times. Does it mean that we are all worthless?
6. Someone whom nobody likes.	Even our greatest heroes, like Abraham Lincoln, had many enemies. By the same token, some of the most destructive people, like Saddam Hussein, Hitler, and Charles Manson, were idolized by many people.
7. Someone who is stupid and untalented.	We're all stupid about most things and untalented in many areas. For example, David Burns, your author, knows little about physics, Greek, or French (and in fact was a lousy French student). He has a drab singing voice, almost no ability to play any musical instrument, etc. According to this definition, all of us are worthless.
8. Someone who does not have *any* talent. To be worthwhile, you have to be good at *one thing* at least.	How good do you have to be, between 0% and 100%, at that one thing, to be worthwhile? After all, we all are somewhat talented at dozens of things: walking, talking, listening to music, cooking, drawing, arithmetic, etc.

Definition of a Worthless or Inferior Person	Rebuttal
9. To be worthwhile, you have to be *very* good at *one* thing that is regarded as very important by society. You have to be in the top 5% at that one thing.	According to this definition, a surgeon who is better than 94% of all surgeons would be considered a worthless human being.
10. Someone who does not like himself or herself. Someone who does not feel worthwhile.	Most depressed people do not feel worthwhile. They do not like themselves. Low self-esteem is a symptom of depression. Does it follow that all depressed people are worthless? In addition, many serial killers like themselves intensely. Does this make them worthwhile?
11. A murderer is a worthless person because he or she has killed another human being on purpose.	Killing another person is usually a bad, despicable action. But many murders are committed by lovers or spouses as a result of jealousy or marital conflicts. It would not be helpful to label a convicted murderer as a "bad" or "worthless" person. It would be accurate to say that a convicted murderer is dangerous and has severe difficulties with impulse control.
12. Other: A paranoid like Adolf Hitler who promoted grandiosity, hatred, and violence on a large scale is a bad or worthless person.	This definition is not likely to apply to anyone you know! Certainly, Hitler did many horrendous, evil things. But even he also had at least a few good qualities. For example, he helped start the Volkswagen company. Did his "good" traits make him a "good" person? Do we need to leap from the labeling of someone's actions to the labeling of that person's entire self? What is gained and lost in the process? What are the advantages and disadvantages of labeling some human beings "bad" or "worthless"? Once you begin this type of labeling, you open a can of worms. Hitler was very committed to this labeling process. He sold the German people on the notion that they were a "superior" race and insisted that the Jewish people (as well as many other minority groups) were "inferior." Once you start this labeling process, where does it end?

EVALUATION OF STEP 7

What did you learn in Step 7? Put a brief summary of several of the most important ideas we discussed here:

1. _____

_____

2. _____

_____

3. _____

_____

Was there anything in today's step that bothered you or rubbed you the wrong way? If you are in a group, was there anything the leader or other members said that turned you off? Describe any negative feelings you had:

_____

_____

_____

_____

Was there anything in today's step that was particularly helpful, interesting, or useful? Did the leader or other participants say anything during today's session that you liked? Describe any positive reactions you had:

_____

_____

_____

_____

SELF-HELP ASSIGNMENTS FOR STEP 8

If you are participating in a Ten Days to Self-esteem group, your leader may give you self-help assignments to complete before the next session.

Assignments	Check (√) If Assigned	Check (√) When Finished
1. Complete the evaluation form for Step 7.		
2. Take the three mood tests again. They are located at the beginning of the next step.		
3. Read the next step in this book and do as many of the written exercises as possible.		
4. Bring your copy of this book to the next session.		
5. List the advantages and disadvantages of believing that you must be loved by others (or successful) to be happy and worthwhile.		
6. Work with the Daily Mood Log for ten minutes per day. (Extra copies begin on page 290.)		
7. Fill out a Pleasure-Predicting Sheet.		
8. Bring any written homework to the next session.		
9. Bibliotherapy (was any reading assigned?)		
10.*		

*Use this space for any additional assignments.

SUPPLEMENTARY READING FOR STEP 7

1. Read Chapters 11–13 in *Feeling Good: The New Mood Therapy.*
2. Concentrate on the "Four Paths to Self-esteem" in Chapter 13, "Your Work Is Not Your Worth," in *Feeling Good: The New Mood Therapy.*
3. Read "How to Overcome an Inferiority Complex." (This is Appendix C in *Intimate Connections;* see Recommended Reading on page 317.)

THE PERFECTIONIST'S SCRIPT FOR SELF-DEFEAT

GOALS FOR STEP 8

1. You will learn about several types of perfectionism, including physical perfectionism, achievement perfectionism, perceived perfectionism, emotional perfectionism, romantic perfectionism, relationship perfectionism, and obsessive-compulsive illness.
2. You will learn about the price you pay for being a perfectionist—along with the hidden benefits of this mind-set.
3. You will learn about the differences between neurotic perfectionism and the healthy pursuit of excellence.
4. You will discover the illogical thinking patterns that cause perfectionism.
5. You will learn how to attack perfectionism with the Cost-Benefit Analysis and the Daily Mood Log.
6. You will explore a radical philosophical position based on accepting one's flaws and shortcomings without a sense of shame.

MOOD TESTING

You have already taken three mood tests at the beginning of the previous steps. I would like you to take the three tests again at the beginning of this step to chart your progress. If you need help, you can review the instructions for these tests in Step 1 beginning on page 18.

THE BURNS DEPRESSION CHECKLIST*

Place a check (√) in the box to the right of each category to indicate how much this type of feeling has bothered you in the past several days.

	0 Not at All	1 Somewhat	2 Moderately	3 A Lot
1. **Sadness:** Do you feel sad or down in the dumps?				
2. **Discouragement:** Does the future look hopeless?				
3. **Low self-esteem:** Do you feel worthless?				
4. **Inferiority:** Do you feel inadequate or inferior to others?				
5. **Guilt:** Do you get self-critical and blame yourself?				
6. **Indecisiveness:** Is it hard to make decisions?				
7. **Irritability:** Do you frequently feel angry or resentful?				
8. **Loss of interest in life:** Have you lost interest in your career, hobbies, family, or friends?				
9. **Loss of motivation:** Do you have to push yourself hard to do things?				
10. **Poor self-image:** Do you feel old or unattractive?				
11. **Appetite changes:** Have you lost your appetite? Do you overeat or binge compulsively?				
12. **Sleep changes:** Is it hard to get a good night's sleep? Are you excessively tired and sleeping too much?				
13. **Loss of sex drive:** Have you lost your interest in sex?				
14. **Concerns about health:** Do you worry excessively about your health?				
15. **Suicidal impulses:** Do you have thoughts that life is not worth living or think you'd be better off dead?†				
Total score on items 1–15 ⟶				

THE BURNS ANXIETY INVENTORY*

Place a check (√) in the box to the right of each category to indicate how much this type of feeling has bothered you in the past several days.

Category I: Anxious Feelings	0 Not at All	1 Somewhat	2 Moderately	3 A Lot
1. Anxiety, nervousness, worry, or fear				
2. Feeling that things around you are strange or unreal				
3. Feeling detached from all or part of your body				
4. Sudden unexpected panic spells				
5. Apprehension or a sense of impending doom				
6. Feeling tense, stressed, "uptight," or on edge				
Category II: Anxious Thoughts	0 Not at All	1 Somewhat	2 Moderately	3 A Lot
7. Difficulty concentrating				
8. Racing thoughts				
9. Frightening fantasies or daydreams				
10. Feeling that you're on the verge of losing control				
11. Fears of cracking up or going crazy				
12. Fears of fainting or passing out				
13. Fears of physical illnesses or heart attacks or dying				
14. Concerns about looking foolish or inadequate				
15. Fears of being alone, isolated, or abandoned				
16. Fears of criticism or disapproval				
17. Fears that something terrible is about to happen				

*Copyright © 1984 by David D. Burns, M.D., from *Ten Days to Self-esteem*, copyright © 1993.

THE BURNS ANXIETY INVENTORY (Continued)

Category III: Physical Symptoms	0 Not at All	1 Somewhat	2 Moderately	3 A Lot
18. Skipping, racing, or pounding of the heart (palpitations)				
19. Pain, pressure, or tightness in the chest				
20. Tingling or numbness in the toes or fingers				
21. Butterflies or discomfort in the stomach				
22. Constipation or diarrhea				
23. Restlessness or jumpiness				
24. Tight, tense muscles				
25. Sweating not brought on by heat				
26. A lump in the throat				
27. Trembling or shaking				
28. Rubbery or "jelly" legs				
29. Feeling dizzy, lightheaded, or off balance				
30. Choking or smothering sensations or difficulty breathing				
31. Headaches or pains in the neck or back				
32. Hot flashes or cold chills				
33. Feeling tired, weak, or easily exhausted				
Total score on items 1–33 →				

RELATIONSHIP SATISFACTION SCALE*

Place a check (√) in the box to the right of each category that best describes the amount of satisfaction you feel in your closest relationship.

	0 Very Dissatisfied	1 Moderately Dissatisfied	2 Slightly Dissatisfied	3 Neutral	4 Slightly Satisfied	5 Moderately Satisfied	6 Very Satisfied
1. Communication and openness							
2. Resolving conflicts and arguments							
3. Degree of affection and caring							
4. Intimacy and closeness							
5. Satisfaction with your role in the relationship							
6. Satisfaction with the other person's role							
7. Overall satisfaction with your relationship							
Total score on items 1–7 →							

Note: Although this test assesses your marriage or most intimate relationship, you can also use it to evaluate your relationship with a friend, family member, or colleague. If you do not have any intimate relationships at this time, you can simply think of people in general when you take the test.

*Copyright © 1983 by David D. Burns, M.D., from *Ten Days to Self-esteem*, copyright © 1993.

PERFECTIONISM VS. THE HEALTHY PURSUIT OF EXCELLENCE

Today's step will focus on one of the commonest Self-defeating Beliefs: perfectionism. This mind-set can make you vulnerable to all kinds of difficulties:

- stress at work or school;
- mood swings, like depression and anxiety;
- loneliness and difficulties forming close, intimate relationships;
- excessive frustration, anger, and conflicts in personal relationships;
- problems in learning from criticism, failure, or mistakes;
- procrastination as well as difficulties sticking with jobs that are tough.

Can you think of any other negative consequences of perfectionism? Describe them here:

_____

_____

_____

Let me emphasize that perfectionism is *not* the same as the healthy pursuit of excellence. Where would we be without the achievements of people like Einstein, Edison, or Mozart? The kind of perfectionism I am referring to is seen in people who feel driven, stressed, and constantly unhappy with themselves, their achievements, and their relationships with others.

Please review the table on page 201. Can you think of any more differences between perfectionism and the healthy pursuit of excellence? Put your ideas here:

_____

_____

_____

KINDS OF PERFECTIONISM

There are actually many types of perfectionism. As you review the table beginning on page 202, put checks in the two columns to the right to indicate if each type of perfectionism has ever been a problem for you or for anyone you interact with on a daily basis (such as a family member, friend, or colleague at work).

PERFECTIONISM VS. THE HEALTHY PURSUIT OF EXCELLENCE

Perfectionism	The Healthy Pursuit of Excellence
1. You feel stressed and driven and motivated by the fear of failure.	1. You feel creative and motivated by feelings of enthusiasm.
2. Your accomplishments never seem to satisfy you.	2. Your efforts give you feelings of joy and satisfaction.
3. You feel you must impress others with your intelligence or accomplishments to get them to like and respect you.	3. You do not feel that you have to earn love or friendship by impressing people. You know that people will accept you as you are.
4. If you make a mistake or fail to achieve an important goal, you become self-critical and feel like a failure as a human being.	4. You are not afraid to make mistakes. You see failure as an opportunity for growth and learning.
5. You think you must always be strong and in control of your emotions.	5. You are not afraid to be vulnerable or share your feelings with others.

PERFECTIONISM EXERCISE 1

Choose one of the following beliefs and write it at the top of the Attitude Cost-Benefit form on page 205:

- "I must always try to be perfect."
- "People will think less of me if I fail or make a mistake."
- "I must be outstanding to be worthwhile and loved by others."

Now list the advantages and disadvantages of that attitude. Ask yourself, "How will it help me if I believe this? What are the benefits of this mind-set? And how will it hurt me? What are the costs of thinking this way?"

When you complete your lists, balance the advantages against the disadvantages of perfectionism on a 100-point scale at the bottom of the Cost-Benefit Analysis. For example, if the advantages of perfectionism are higher, you might put a 60 in the circle on the left and a 40 in the circle on the right.

If you decide that the disadvantages of the attitude are greater, then what new attitude

ARE YOU A PERFECTIONIST?

Type of Perfectionism	Definition	Check (√) If This Describes You	Check (√) If This Describes Someone You Know
1. Physical perfectionism	You think you must have a perfect face or figure to be desirable and appealing.		
2. Achievement perfectionism	You feel it would be terrible to make a mistake, to fail, or to fall short of a personal goal in your career or studies.		
3. Perceived perfectionism	You believe that you have to impress people with your accomplishments, talent, or intelligence to get them to like and respect you. You are convinced that others will look down on you if you fail, look foolish, or make a mistake.		
4. Emotional perfectionism	You feel ashamed of negative and vulnerable feelings such as loneliness, depression, anger, anxiety, or panic. You believe that you should always feel happy and in control of your emotions.		
5. Self-esteem perfectionism	You feel inferior to others who are more intelligent, attractive, or successful.		

ARE YOU A PERFECTIONIST? (Continued)

Type of Perfectionism	Definition	Check (√) If This Describes You	Check (√) If This Describes Someone You Know
6. Relationship perfectionism	You believe that people who care for each other should never fight or argue.		
7. Romantic perfectionism	You find it difficult to form lasting intimate relationships because people are never quite good enough. You become preoccupied with people's shortcomings.		
8. Entitlement	You get upset when other people (or the world) do not measure up to your expectations. You may get excessively angry or frustrated when a train is late, when traffic is slow, or when people do not treat you with sufficient respect.		
9. Obsessive-compulsive tendencies	You feel your house or office must always be immaculate and you spend excessive amounts of time checking things, cleaning, or organizing.		
10. Other: Can you think of other kinds of perfectionism?			

would you substitute for it? Can you revise the belief so that you retain the advantages and get rid of the disadvantages? Put your revised belief here:

_____

_____

_____

You can see a completed CBA on page 212. Do not look at it until you have completed this exercise.

PERFECTIONISM EXERCISE 2

One of the funny things about perfectionism is that perfectionists always try to be right about everything, but often end up being very wrong, even when they don't know it. This is because the negative messages perfectionists give themselves are often very distorted and illogical, even though these thoughts may seem very valid when they feel upset.

The best way to illustrate this is to think of a specific time when perfectionism was a problem for you. Can you remember a time when you felt very self-critical because you screwed up or you failed to achieve an important personal goal? It could have been a failure in your role as a parent, or in your marriage, or in your career. Write a brief description of the situation at the top of the Daily Mood Log on page 207 where it says Step One.

Now record your negative emotions where it says Step Two on the Daily Mood Log. Were you feeling frustrated? Put down? Inferior? Discouraged? Rate each negative emotion on a scale from 0% (the least) to 100% (the most).

The third step is to record your Negative Thoughts in the left-hand column. What were you telling yourself? Write down each Negative Thought and number them sequentially. Put an estimate of how strongly you believed each Negative Thought, from 0% (not at all) to 100% (completely).

Now identify the distortions in your NTs using the list on page 208. This will make you aware of how unrealistic these thoughts can be.

Finally, substitute Positive Thoughts in the right-hand column using the strategies listed on page 109.

When I was a psychiatric resident, a supervisor criticized my approach to a patient. Like many psychiatrists in training, I was trying awfully hard to be perfect. I thought that if I tried hard enough, I should be able to cure every patient. Since my supervisor was obviously displeased with my imperfect performance, I felt anxious. Since I was clearly not *all* I thought I *should* be, I felt literally like a *nothing*.

That night when I was jogging, these Negative Thoughts came to mind: (1) "I'm a rotten person." (2) "I'm a lousy therapist." It seemed as if I had suddenly perceived the truth about myself, and there was no doubt in my mind about the validity of these two thoughts.

When I got home I decided to write these two thoughts on a piece of paper, just as I ask

ATTITUDE COST-BENEFIT ANALYSIS*

The Attitude or Belief You Want to Change: _____

_____

Advantages of Believing This	Disadvantages of Believing This

my patients to do. Once I looked at them, it dawned on me how unfair and hard I was being on myself. It was easy to identify the distortions in my thoughts: all-or-nothing thinking, overgeneralization, mental filter, discounting the positives, magnification, labeling, emotional reasoning, "should" statements, and blame.

It was obvious that I was not only imperfect as a psychiatrist, but I was also quite imperfect in my illogical way of thinking about my imperfections!

I decided to think about the problem like this instead: "It's natural to make errors in dealing with a difficult patient. In fact, the patient may have tried to provoke a negative response because of his belief that people will always let him down. Instead of hating myself for falling in this trap, I can learn from this incident to make my work with him more vital and more helpful. The fact is, I'm not a rotten human being or a terrible therapist. I'm a very human therapist, with strengths and weaknesses. I do not need to be ashamed of my errors. I only need to learn from them."

This new way of thinking about the problem gave me a tremendous sense of relief. Since those early days I have never even come close to achieving perfection in my work. In fact, every day I become aware of my errors and all I don't know. But I am no longer terrified by these errors because I realize that I don't have to be perfect. Now, when I make a mistake, and my patient is upset with me, I simply acknowledge my error and apologize. We talk it over and have a meeting of the minds. We usually end up feeling closer and more connected. I have discovered that these therapeutic "failures" are frequently the most successful part of the therapy because they provide the greatest opportunities for real therapeutic breakthroughs! I now look forward to these mistakes, because they nearly always turn out to be the most helpful and rewarding part of my work!

PERFECTIONISM EXERCISE 3

Many perfectionists believe that they must earn love and approval by being outstanding. An alternative philosophy would be that our vulnerabilities and flaws—and not our successes and strengths—ultimately make us lovable and human. People can be admired or resented—but never loved—for their successes and achievements.

To care for other people, you must be aware of who they are as human beings—this includes their pain and their shortcomings as well as their positive qualities. A person who was perfect and never made mistakes would be difficult to love. Our "brokenness" is essential to being human. Our failures and moments of despair can sometimes be our greatest opportunities for growth, for intimacy, for spiritual awareness, and for self-acceptance. What do you think about this idea? Does it make any sense? Or does it seem like nonsense?

One of the cardinal principles of cognitive therapy is that all human beings are inherently broken and flawed. We constantly battle against these flaws and try to become the person we think we *should* be. Nevertheless, our brokenness—our shortcomings and failings—can become a source of strength, once we confront and accept them. It is only when we hide our shortcomings in shame that they eat away at us and rob us of joy and cause us to feel

DAILY MOOD LOG*

Step One: Describe the Upsetting Event _____

_____

Step Two: Record Your Negative Feelings—and rate them from 0% (the least) to 100% (the most). Use words like *sad, anxious, angry, guilty, lonely, hopeless, frustrated,* etc.

Emotion	Rating (0%–100%)	Emotion	Rating (0%–100%)	Emotion	Rating (0%–100%)

Step Three: The Triple-Column Technique

Negative Thoughts Write down the thoughts that make you upset and estimate your belief in each one (0%–100%).	Distortions Use the Distorted Thinking chart on the next page.	Positive Thoughts Substitute more realistic thoughts and estimate your belief in each one (0%–100%).

(Continued on next page)

DAILY MOOD LOG (Continued)

Negative Thoughts	Distortions	Positive Thoughts

DISTORTED THINKING*

1. **All-or-nothing thinking:** You look at things in absolute, black-and-white categories.
2. **Overgeneralization:** You view a negative event as a never-ending pattern of defeat.
3. **Mental filter:** You dwell on the negatives and ignore the positives.
4. **Discounting the positives:** You insist that your accomplishments or positive qualities don't count.
5. **Jumping to conclusions:** You conclude things are bad without any definite evidence.
    (a) **Mind reading:** You assume people are reacting negatively to you.
    (b) **Fortune-telling:** You predict that things will turn out badly.
6. **Magnification or minimization:** You blow things way out of proportion or you shrink their importance.
7. **Emotional reasoning:** You reason from how you feel: "I feel like an idiot, so I must be one."
8. **"Should" statements:** You criticize yourself or other people with "shoulds," "shouldn'ts," "musts," "oughts," and "have-tos."
9. **Labeling:** Instead of saying, "I made a mistake," you tell yourself, "I'm a jerk" or "a loser."
10. **Blame:** You blame yourself for something you weren't entirely responsible for, or you blame other people and overlook ways that you contributed to a problem.

isolated from others. This vision is quite different from the value system of Western culture, which suggests that we must achieve as much as possible and aspire to perfection in life to be special, worthwhile, and lovable.

I once treated a man named Jerry who came to Philadelphia from Detroit for outpatient treatment at my clinic at the Presbyterian Medical Center. Jerry had always suffered from depression, from shyness and nervousness around people, and from marital unhappiness. Although he had substantial success in his career, he had never been successful in his search for happiness.

Jerry came from a blue-collar family. His parents were German immigrants, and his father was a tough disciplinarian. No matter what Jerry achieved in school, it never seemed quite good enough. For example, even if he got straight A's, his father would tell him to make sure he kept it up, instead of telling him how proud he felt.

Although Jerry was a model student and a good son, he always felt inadequate and lonely. As far back as he could remember, he had felt nervous and uncomfortable around other people—including his classmates and his family. He was ashamed to admit how he felt, so he kept it a secret. He didn't dare tell anyone that he felt vulnerable and afraid of people, because he thought he would be a failure in their eyes. He was convinced that people would look down on him if they knew how weak and defective he felt.

After graduation from college, Jerry took over a small business on the verge of bankruptcy and worked hard to turn it around. He worked tirelessly, seven days a week, and soon the company prospered. He expanded the business, and his plans were successful. After fifteen years, he had more than five thousand employees and his company was listed on the American Stock Exchange. Jerry married a beautiful woman, lived in a fancy house, and was financially secure.

In spite of his success, Jerry still felt anxious. He was constantly tense. At work, Jerry felt more in control because he was the boss. Outside of work, every social situation was awkward. Jerry even found it hard to be around his wife and family. He had little self-esteem and rarely experienced any real satisfaction from his accomplishments.

Jerry's difficulties stemmed from his belief that "I have to be a great success to be worthwhile and respected by others. If people knew what I was really like—self-doubting and insecure—they'd look down on me and reject me." If you are a perfectionist, you may have felt this way as well.

The therapists at my clinic came up with an innovative idea about how we might help Jerry. They proposed that Jerry could do an experiment to *test* his belief that people would not accept him if they knew what he was really like. We told Jerry that he could get on the subway that stops near our hospital and ride it for an hour or so. While he was riding, he could sit down next to ten people of various ages and races and start conversations with them. After introducing himself, he could tell them that although he was a successful businessman, he never really felt like much of a success in life because he was terribly anxious and felt inferior to other people. He could also tell them that he always tried to hide his feelings for fear that people would think less of him. Finally, he could tell them that as of today, he'd decided to stop keeping it a secret and simply tell people the truth about what he was really like.

Jerry was not at all enthusiastic about this assignment! In fact, he *stubbornly* refused to do it. He said it was *out of the question* and that he had no interest in making a fool of himself in front of a bunch of strangers. Although he *felt* insecure, he was actually quite a powerful and forceful businessman, and he could be quite intimidating when he wanted to be!

Despite his initial reluctance, Jerry finally agreed to give it a try. Accompanied by a psychology graduate student, Jerry bravely set out for the subway. I scheduled an appointment with Jerry immediately after the assignment so we could discuss what happened.

Jerry spent nearly two hours on the subway and talked to more than a dozen people. When he returned, he told me that although two young women seemed tense and may have been afraid he was a weirdo or a mugger, all the other people he'd spoken to had been incredibly kind and friendly. He said that they had offered him all kinds of encouragement and poured out their hearts to him. Instead of condemning him when he described his inadequacies, they told him about all of *their* feelings and problems. He said that most of them had treated him like a long-lost friend! An older African-American man said he was unemployed and worried he couldn't support his family. A young woman said that she was an alcoholic and attended AA meetings. She was grateful that he had opened up about his feelings. She said it made him seem very vulnerable and likable. Other people gave him advice on how to overcome his shyness.

Jerry said this was one of the first times in his life he had ever felt close to people, like a member of the human race. His nervousness disappeared, and he felt free to be himself and to connect with other people. He suddenly felt like he had something to offer, a way to form a bond.

When we discover new ideas that are very important, they often come in the form of paradoxes. The paradox for Jerry was that his weakness, which he had spent his entire life trying to hide, had suddenly become his greatest asset. The problem was not that he felt inadequate, but that he tried to hide his imperfections in the dark, where they ate away at him and robbed him of all vitality, like a cancer. The problem was the shame, not the imperfection. Once he exposed his weakness to the light of day, it became his greatest source of strength.

Jerry was a Christian, and he said this experience reminded him of Second Corinthians, chapter 12, where Saint Paul described his failure to rid himself of his "thorn in the flesh." The nature of Paul's affliction is unknown. Biblical scholars have speculated it might have been stuttering, a sexual problem, or an emotional difficulty such as manic-depressive illness or panic attacks.

Over and over, Saint Paul prayed that God would heal him and remove this affliction, but God would not answer his prayers. Finally, his prayer was answered, but in an unexpected way. Saint Paul wrote: "For this thing I besought the Lord thrice, that it might depart from me. And he said unto me, My grace is sufficient for thee: for my strength is made perfect in weakness. . . . for when I am weak, then I am strong."

Jerry said that he had heard this passage many times when going to services but had never really comprehended it. Now he said he understood. His weakness *was* his strength—he only needed to accept it.

Although I was also raised in the Christian religion, I do not mean to promote Christianity or any other religion. Similar passages can be found in other religious writings, including the Book of Mormon as well as the Old Testament. All of us have deep values that guide our lives. When you overcome your own emotional problems, you may develop a renewed appreciation of your spiritual heritage and discover fresh meaning in these beliefs. We will discuss a few of the connections between self-esteem and spirituality in Step 10.

If you are in a Ten Days to Self-esteem group, members may volunteer to share disappointments or failures in their careers or personal lives. The group leader can suggest common problems that would be suitable for this discussion, such as being criticized or rejected, failing to achieve a personal goal, a personal habit such as alcoholism or overeating or drug abuse, problems with marriage or children, and so forth. The group can discuss the positive and negative consequences of these negative experiences. Would we be better off having perfect lives? Or do these moments of despair and self-doubt actually enhance our lives? In what way?

ANSWER TO THE EXERCISE ON PAGE 205

ATTITUDE COST-BENEFIT ANALYSIS*

The Attitude or Belief You Want to Change: *I must always try to be perfect.*

Advantages of Believing This	Disadvantages of Believing This
1. I will do my best work.	1. When I fail or make a mistake I'll get very upset.
2. I will feel great when I do a good job.	2. I'll get defensive when people criticize me.
3. I won't settle for mediocrity.	3. It will be harder to learn from my mistakes.
4. This will mean I'm special, since only special people would have to be perfect.	4. I may never feel satisfied, since my work is never perfect enough.
5. People will admire me because I work so hard.	5. I'll be afraid to be creative and take chances doing something new.
	6. I may find it hard to get close to people, because I'll always think I have to impress them.
	7. I'll feel lonely.
	8. I'll always be on a treadmill, having to earn my self-esteem.

35 ———— 65

EVALUATION OF STEP 8

What did you learn in Step 8? Put a brief summary of several of the most important ideas we discussed here:

1. _____

_____

2. _____

_____

3. _____

_____

Was there anything in today's step that bothered you or rubbed you the wrong way? If you are in a group, was there anything the leader or other members said that turned you off? Describe any negative feelings you had:

_____

_____

_____

_____

Was there anything in today's step that was particularly helpful, interesting, or useful? Did the leader or other participant say anything during today's session that you liked? Describe any positive reactions you had:

_____

_____

_____

_____

SELF-HELP ASSIGNMENTS FOR STEP 9

If you are participating in a Ten Days to Self-esteem group, your leader may give you self-help assignments to complete before the next session.

Assignments	Check (√) If Assigned	Check (√) When Finished
1. Complete the evaluation form for Step 8.		
2. Take the three mood tests again. They are located at the beginning of the next step.		
3. Read the next step in this book and do as many of the written exercises as possible.		
4. Bring your copy of this book to the next session.		
5. Work with the Daily Mood Log for ten minutes per day. (Extra copies begin on page 290.)		
6. Bring any written homework to the next session.		
7. Bibliotherapy (was any reading assigned?)		
8.*		
9.		
10.		

*Use these spaces for any additional assignments.

SUPPLEMENTARY READING FOR STEP 8

1. Read Chapter 14 in *Feeling Good: The New Mood Therapy*.
2. Review Chapter 7 of *The Feeling Good Handbook*.

STEP 9

A PRESCRIPTION FOR PROCRASTINATORS

GOALS FOR STEP 9

1. You will learn about the ten characteristics of people who procrastinate.
2. You will discover the hidden benefits of procrastination.
3. You will learn how to attack procrastination with the Procrastination Cost-Benefit Analysis and with the Devil's Advocate Technique.
4. You will discover how to become a more productive and creative person.

MOOD TESTING

You have already taken three mood tests at the beginning of the previous steps. I would like you to take the three tests again at the beginning of this step to chart your progress. If you need help, you can review the instructions for these tests in Step 1 beginning on page 18.

THE BURNS DEPRESSION CHECKLIST*

Place a check (√) in the box to the right of each category to indicate how much this type of feeling has bothered you in the past several days.

	0 Not at All	1 Somewhat	2 Moderately	3 A Lot
1. **Sadness:** Do you feel sad or down in the dumps?				
2. **Discouragement:** Does the future look hopeless?				
3. **Low self-esteem:** Do you feel worthless?				
4. **Inferiority:** Do you feel inadequate or inferior to others?				
5. **Guilt:** Do you get self-critical and blame yourself?				
6. **Indecisiveness:** Is it hard to make decisions?				
7. **Irritability:** Do you frequently feel angry or resentful?				
8. **Loss of interest in life:** Have you lost interest in your career, hobbies, family, or friends?				
9. **Loss of motivation:** Do you have to push yourself hard to do things?				
10. **Poor self-image:** Do you feel old or unattractive?				
11. **Appetite changes:** Have you lost your appetite? Do you overeat or binge compulsively?				
12. **Sleep changes:** Is it hard to get a good night's sleep? Are you excessively tired and sleeping too much?				
13. **Loss of sex drive:** Have you lost your interest in sex?				
14. **Concerns about health:** Do you worry excessively about your health?				
15. **Suicidal impulses:** Do you have thoughts that life is not worth living or think you'd be better off dead?†				
Total score on items 1–15 →				

†Anyone with suicidal urges should seek immediate help from a mental health professional

THE BURNS ANXIETY INVENTORY*

Place a check (√) in the box to the right of each category to indicate how much this type of feeling has bothered you in the past several days.

Category I: Anxious Feelings	0 Not at All	1 Somewhat	2 Moderately	3 A Lot
1. Anxiety, nervousness, worry, or fear				
2. Feeling that things around you are strange or unreal				
3. Feeling detached from all or part of your body				
4. Sudden unexpected panic spells				
5. Apprehension or a sense of impending doom				
6. Feeling tense, stressed, "uptight," or on edge				

Category II: Anxious Thoughts	0 Not at All	1 Somewhat	2 Moderately	3 A Lot
7. Difficulty concentrating				
8. Racing thoughts				
9. Frightening fantasies or daydreams				
10. Feeling that you're on the verge of losing control				
11. Fears of cracking up or going crazy				
12. Fears of fainting or passing out				
13. Fears of physical illnesses or heart attacks or dying				
14. Concerns about looking foolish or inadequate				
15. Fears of being alone, isolated, or abandoned				
16. Fears of criticism or disapproval				
17. Fears that something terrible is about to happen				

*Copyright © 1984 by David D. Burns, M.D., from *Ten Days to Self-esteem*, copyright © 1993.

THE BURNS ANXIETY INVENTORY (Continued)

Category III: Physical Symptoms	0 Not at All	1 Somewhat	2 Moderately	3 A Lot
18. Skipping, racing, or pounding of the heart (palpitations)				
19. Pain, pressure, or tightness in the chest				
20. Tingling or numbness in the toes or fingers				
21. Butterflies or discomfort in the stomach				
22. Constipation or diarrhea				
23. Restlessness or jumpiness				
24. Tight, tense muscles				
25. Sweating not brought on by heat				
26. A lump in the throat				
27. Trembling or shaking				
28. Rubbery or "jelly" legs				
29. Feeling dizzy, lightheaded, or off balance				
30. Choking or smothering sensations or difficulty breathing				
31. Headaches or pains in the neck or back				
32. Hot flashes or cold chills				
33. Feeling tired, weak, or easily exhausted				
Total score on items 1–33 $\longrightarrow$				

RELATIONSHIP SATISFACTION SCALE*

Place a check (√) in the box to the right of each category that best describes the amount of satisfaction you feel in your relationship.

	0 Very Dissatisfied	1 Moderately Dissatisfied	2 Slightly Dissatisfied	3 Neutral	4 Slightly Satisfied	5 Moderately Satisfied	6 Very Satisfied
1. Communication and openness							
2. Resolving conflicts and arguments							
3. Degree of affection and caring							
4. Intimacy and closeness							
5. Satisfaction with your role in the relationship							
6. Satisfaction with the other person's role							
7. Overall satisfaction with your relationship							
Total score on items 1–7 →							

Note: Although this test assesses your marriage or most intimate relationship, you can also use it to evaluate your relationship with a friend, family member, or colleague. If you do not have any intimate relationships at this time, you can simply think of people in general when you take the test.

WHY PEOPLE PROCRASTINATE

Is procrastination ever a problem for you? Is there anything you have been procrastinating about lately? Do you procrastinate about doing the self-help assignments between sessions? Do you put off dieting? Balancing your checkbook? Studying? Applying for a new job?

Try to think of one or two specific things that you procrastinate about. List them here. If you aren't procrastinating about anything now, perhaps you can think of a time in the past when this was a problem for you. These examples can help to make today's step more interesting and helpful.

1. _____

_____

2. _____

_____

3. _____

_____

Do you know why you procrastinate? For a lot of people, it seems to be a puzzle. They tell themselves that they really *want* to clean the closet, but for some mysterious reason they just *can't seem to get around to it.*

The Procrastination Test on page 221 may help you answer this question. Please take it now.

THE PROCRASTINATION TEST

Put a check (√) in the box that best describes how you feel and behave.

	0 Not at All	1 Somewhat	2 Moderately	3 A Lot
1. I often put things off because I don't feel like doing them.				
2. I often tell myself, "I'll do it later when I'm in the mood."				
3. I often give up when things are harder than I expected.				
4. I get frustrated when things don't come easily.				
5. I avoid tasks because I'm afraid I might do a bad job.				
6. I'd rather not do something than try and fail.				
7. I don't like to do things if I can't do them perfectly.				
8. I often worry that I won't do a really outstanding job.				
9. I'm often critical of what I do, even if I do a good job.				
10. I don't usually feel very good about my accomplishments.				

THE PROCRASTINATION TEST

Put a check (√) in the box that best describes how you feel and behave.

	0 Not at All	1 Somewhat	2 Moderately	3 A Lot
11. I often feel guilty about all the things I *should* be doing.				
12. I put things off and then I feel guilty about not doing them.				
13. I usually feel reluctant to talk to someone I'm angry or upset with.				
14. I often avoid dealing with conflicts with other people.				
15. I often agree to do things I don't really want to do.				
16. It's hard for me to say no to people.				
17. I don't like it when people act bossy and try to tell me what to do.				
18. I dig in my heels when people make demands on me.				
19. I usually don't feel very enthusiastic about the things I have to do.				
20. I don't really want to do a lot of the things I have to do.				

SCORING THE PROCRASTINATION TEST

Add up your scores for items 1 and 2 and put the combined score at the top of the right-hand column of the Scoring Key. Then add up your scores on each of the following pairs of items on the Procrastination Test.

SCORING KEY

Item Numbers	Mind-set	Your Score
1 + 2	Putting the Cart Before the Horse	
3 + 4	The Mastery Model	
5 + 6	Fear of Failure	
7 + 8	Perfectionism	
9 + 10	Lack of Rewards	
11 + 12	"Should" Statements	
13 + 14	Passive Aggression	
15 + 16	Unassertiveness	
17 + 18	Coercion Sensitivity	
19 + 20	Lack of Desire	

Interpreting your scores: Your score on each mind-set will be between 0 and 6. Low scores (0 to 2) are good. Higher scores (3 to 6) indicate attitudes that may make you procrastinate.

PROCRASTINATION EXERCISE

Today you will learn about a new technique called the Procrastination Cost-Benefit Analysis. First, describe something that you are procrastinating about, such as housecleaning, doing the written self-help assignments in this book, writing letters, paying bills, dieting, asking someone for a date, applying for a new job, studying for a boring class, and so forth. Write a brief description of the actual task at the top of the Procrastination Cost-Benefit Analysis on page 226.

Next, list all the advantages of procrastinating about this task *today* in the left-hand column of that form. When you do this exercise, try to list the many *obvious* benefits:

- Procrastination is easy.

- You can avoid frustration and anxiety.

- You can do something else that's more fun.

- You can put it off and the world won't come to an end.

- In your heart of hearts, you don't really *want* to do it now and you don't *have* to do it now.

- It will get done sooner or later anyway.

List the *hidden* benefits of procrastination as well. These benefits might include:

- You can get back at the people who are pressuring you and making demands on you.

- If you don't do it, someone else may get fed up and do it for you.

- People won't make any more demands on you, since they'll know you're overwhelmed and doing more than you can handle already.

- You can feel "special," like a king or queen, since you won't have to work hard and do things that are unpleasant.

You will need to become aware of these benefits before you can break this habit.

Now list the *disadvantages* of procrastinating in the right-hand column of the Cost-Benefit Analysis on page 226. Are there any? What is the price you pay for procrastinating?

After you have listed several advantages and disadvantages of procrastinating, weigh the advantages against the disadvantages of procrastination on a 100-point scale. For example, if the advantages are somewhat greater, you might put a 60 in the left-hand circle at the bottom of the page and a 40 in the right-hand circle. This would show that you really do *not* intend to get started on the task at this time.

The list of the advantages and disadvantages may make it clear why you procrastinate. The problem is not really so mysterious. Most people procrastinate because that is precisely what they *want* to be doing. Procrastination is a *choice* you make, and you make this choice *knowingly* and *intentionally*. But you may want to keep your motives hidden, so you can act helpless, as if procrastination were some type of illness or disability, like the flu or a broken leg. It may feel more acceptable to say, "I *want to,* but I just can't seem to get around to it."

Remember that we're all free to choose if we will or won't do something. Sometimes making the conscious choice to procrastinate can be the first step in conquering this habit!

I once treated a young man from Israel who told me he procrastinated in just about everything—his room was a mess, he was way behind at work, he hadn't had a haircut for months, and he hadn't even opened six letters from his parents and friends.

He told me he had procrastinated for nine months in filling out his medical insurance forms so he could get reimbursement for his psychotherapy sessions. He procrastinated even though he was short on cash and desperately needed the money.

When we did the Procrastination Cost-Benefit Analysis, he was able to list fifteen advantages of putting off the insurance forms for another week. There were many tangible and hidden benefits for him. For one thing, he had recently taken dancing lessons and loved going out late every night to discos. In addition, he had the fantasy of being a prince who didn't have to do any hard work or boring jobs.

Once he saw all these advantages, he made a firm commitment not to do any work at all on the insurance forms for the next week. I made him promise not to do even five minutes' worth of work on the forms for seven days. He said this decision gave him a tremendous sense of relief.

When I saw him about ten days later, he said that as the week went by, he became more and more restless about the insurance forms. He found that he actually *wanted* to fill them out, but kept his promise and didn't touch them. At the end of the seventh day, he promptly sat down and finished all of them in about fifteen minutes. He said it had been *incredibly* easy, and he felt exhilarated.

If you also find that the advantages of procrastination outweigh the disadvantages, then you can also make a conscious decision *not* to do the task. If, after a period of time, you discover that there are unexpected negative consequences of procrastinating, then you may want to repeat the Cost-Benefit Analysis.

If you decide that the disadvantages of procrastination are greater than the advantages, I want you to pass one more acid test of your motivation before getting started. In order to be really sure, I want you to list the disadvantages of getting started *today* in the right-hand column of the Action Cost-Benefit Analysis on page 227. The disadvantages of getting started today may include these:

- The job may be difficult and boring.
- You can just as easily do it some other day.
- There are more rewarding things you can do instead.
- The task may seem overwhelming.
- Your efforts will just be a drop in the bucket.

Now list the *advantages* of getting started *today* in the left-hand column of the Action Cost-Benefit Analysis on page 227. Finally, weigh the advantages of getting started against the disadvantages on a 100-point scale. Put two numbers at the bottom to indicate the results of your analysis. For example, if the advantages are somewhat greater, you might put a 60 in the left-hand circle at the bottom of the page and a 40 in the right-hand circle.

What's the idea behind this final test? It's the same principle at work. Essentially you procrastinate because on some level you really want to do exactly that. Unless the advantages of getting started *now* outweigh the disadvantages, you'll just stay stuck in the same rut. The purpose of these lists is to bring the hidden benefits of procrastination to your conscious awareness. Once you understand your motivation, you'll have a greater chance to change. If you want to give up all those benefits, you'll be ready for action.

PROCRASTINATION COST-BENEFIT ANALYSIS*

What are you procrastinating about? _____

_____

Advantages of Procrastinating Today	Disadvantages of Procrastinating Today

ACTION COST-BENEFIT ANALYSIS*

What are you procrastinating about? _____

_____

Advantages of Getting Started Today	Disadvantages of Getting Started Today

THE DEVIL'S ADVOCATE TECHNIQUE

If you are in a Ten Days to Self-esteem group, the leader will demonstrate the Devil's Advocate Technique. After the demonstration, you will have a chance to practice it with another group member. If you are not in a group, you can practice with a friend or do it on your own in front of a mirror.

Here's how it works. A man named Michael procrastinates about cleaning up his garage and junk has been piling up for years. Michael's wife nags him to do it. He tells her he will clean it up, but he never seems to get around to it. This is a source of constant irritation in their marriage. He is puzzled about why he can't seem to get around to it, and sees this as a mysterious "problem."

According to his Cost-Benefit Analysis, he sees *lots* of advantages in cleaning the garage, and *lots* of disadvantages in procrastinating. And yet, in spite of his best intentions, Michael has put off cleaning it for eighteen months (or approximately five hundred days in a row!).

Whenever Michael thinks about cleaning the garage, he has lots of Negative Thoughts like these:

1. I really *should* do it, but I'm not in the mood.

2. I can do it a little later. I'll wait until I feel more like it.

3. Just think of all the junk in the garage! There must be a mountain of it.

4. It will take forever.

5. Even if I do get started it will just be a drop in the bucket. I better wait until I have a three-day weekend.

6. I have other, more important things to do right now. I can relax and have a beer and watch the football game on TV.

7. It will really be exhausting.

8. Once I'm done, it will just get messy again.

9. Why is my wife such a nag? What's so important about the garage anyway? It's fine the way it is.

10. Why don't we have sex more often? I shouldn't have to clean the garage if we don't have sex!

Imagine that you are Michael. We will attack these Negative Thoughts with the Devil's Advocate Technique. The Devil's Advocate Technique is similar to the Externalization of Voices you learned about in Step 5. You get a partner and talk back to him or her in a role-playing situation, just as if you were talking to another person. However, the other person is simply an extension of your own mind.

Select a partner who will volunteer to play the role of the thoughts that make you dread cleaning out the garage. Your partner will tempt you like the Devil and try to persuade you that you really *shouldn't* clean the garage today. Your partner advocates the status quo.

You, in turn, will argue and insist that you really do want to get started on the garage *today*. The dialogue could go like this:

PARTNER (as Devil's Advocate): It's really too late to get started on cleaning out the garage today. You're tired. Tomorrow will be a better day.

YOU (as Positive Thoughts): Well, I really *should* get started.

PARTNER: It's really late and you can't get much done today anyway.

YOU: Even if I only work in there for fifteen minutes, at least I will get started. That would be something.

PARTNER: That would only be a drop in the bucket. Besides, it will be cold and dark out there. You're all tired out and it will be more fun to have a beer and watch a little TV. There may be a good game on. You can wait until a long weekend to do the garage. Then you can get a whole lot done.

YOU: Yes, but my wife has been nagging me and I can get her off my back if I get started.

PARTNER: Yes, but your wife is a real nag and she doesn't seem to appreciate you very much. If you have a couple of beers you won't mind so much. Why should you break your butt for her?

YOU: But this is ruining our marriage. She's annoyed and we practically *never* have sex.

PARTNER: Yes, but you shouldn't have to clean the garage just to have sex with your wife. After all, you slave away sixty hours a week at the office and all she does is gripe at you when you get home. You deserve better. The garage can wait for a better day.

You can see in this dialogue that your partner—who plays the role of the tempting, lazy thoughts—should try his or her hardest to persuade you to do nothing. Your partner should use the *second* person ("you" statements). When you talk back, you should use the *first* person ("I" statements). If you can talk back to these tempting thoughts in a persuasive, convincing way, it will help you overcome your procrastination.

This is an emotional exercise, and it will help you change at the gut level. If you get stuck and can't think of a way to fight off the temptations of the Devil's Advocate, switch roles so your partner can model a more effective response.

Remember the steps in the box on the next page.

If you are doing the exercise on your own, you can do it in front of a mirror. Remember that you will be playing both roles. When you play the role of the Devil's Advocate, use the second person. When you argue with the Devil's Advocate, use the first person.

DEVIL'S ADVOCATE TECHNIQUE

1. Make a list of your Negative Thoughts when you procrastinate. Think of all the advantages of procrastinating. Write down what you tell yourself when you procrastinate, such as "I'm not really in the mood."
2. Select a partner. The two of you face each other.
3. Tell your partner to read your Negative Thoughts, one by one, using the second person ("you" statements). Tell your partner to try to tempt you or persuade you to procrastinate. Tell your partner to be as persuasive as he or she can possibly be.
4. Talk to back to your partner using the first person ("I" statements). Try to refute his or her arguments. Don't give in, fight back! Argue that it really would be to your advantage to get started today.
5. If you get stuck, do a role reversal.

THE TIC-TOC TECHNIQUE

By now you should be well aware of the fact that when you procrastinate, you give yourself negative messages that upset you. They are called TICs, or Task-Interfering Cognitions, because they prevent you from getting started on the task. (A TIC is just a Negative Thought with a cute name.)

Write some of your own TICs on the form on page 232. Then identify the distortions in these TICs using the checklist on page 50. Finally, write TOCs in the right-hand column of the TIC-TOC form. (A TOC, or Task-Oriented Cognition, is a positive challenge to your Negative Thought.)

Here's an example. Let's assume you are procrastinating about studying for a difficult exam. First write a TIC in the left-hand column:

TICs	Distortions	TOCs
1. There's so much to study. I'll never learn it all.		

Next, identify the distortions in the middle column:

TICs	Distortions	TOCs
1. There's so much to study. I'll never learn it all.	all-or-nothing thinking; mental filter; fortune-telling; magnification; emotional reasoning; "should" statement	

Finally, enter your TOC in the right-hand column:

TICs	Distortions	TOCs
1. There's so much to study. I'll never learn it all.	all-or-nothing thinking; mental filter; fortune-telling; magnification; emotional reasoning; "should" statement	1. I don't have to learn it all, but if I study for 15 minutes that would be a good start. In any 15-minute period, I only have to learn 15 minutes' worth of material.

Now you try it, using the form on page 232.

LITTLE STEPS FOR BIG FEATS

One of the secrets of people who are highly productive is that they rarely try to tackle a difficult job all at once. Instead, they break the task down into its smallest component parts and do one small step at a time.

There are two ways to break a task into small steps. One solution is simply to work for relatively brief periods of time, such as fifteen minutes. The rationale is that it's relatively easy to do something if you know you can quit after fifteen minutes. Of course, once you get started, you will often get in the mood and end up doing even more.

Many procrastinators stubbornly resist this simple plan, even though it is fabulously effective. List three excuses you could give yourself for refusing to do fifteen minutes of a task you've been putting off.

1. _____

THE TIC-TOC TECHNIQUE*

TICs	Distortions	TOCs

2. _____

_____

3. _____

_____

The answer to this exercise is on page 236. Write your own answers before you look there. There's no one correct answer, and your feelings are important.

If you examine these reasons, I think you'll see that they are actually TICs, as described in the previous section. Can you use the TIC-TOC Technique to deal with them?

The second solution is to organize the task in small steps that all follow one another in a logical sequence. I want you to break a task down into its smallest component parts using the Antiprocrastination Sheet on page 234 of this book. First, think of something you've been procrastinating about. Then think of the separate steps that go into completing this task. List the small steps and number each one in the left-hand column. Then predict how difficult and how satisfying (on a scale from 0% to 100%) each step will be. Record these predictions in the second and third columns of the sheet.

For example, suppose that Michael has decided to clean out the garage. He might list the following steps:

1. Go into the garage and look around.

2. Purchase or locate some trash bags.

3. Load several bags with trash.

4. Repeat Step 3 several times.

5. Organize the things we need to keep.

6. Sweep the floor.

After you have completed each step of the task, you can record how difficult and how satisfying (on a scale from 0% to 100%) it actually turned out to be. Record these values in the fourth and fifth columns of the sheet.

THE ANTIPROCRASTINATION SHEET

Activity Break the task into little steps and number each one.	Predicted Difficulty (0%–100%)	Predicted Satisfaction (0%–100%)	Actual Difficulty (0%–100%)	Actual Satisfaction (0%–100%)

MAKE A PLAN

If you would like to overcome procrastination, make a specific plan. First, what would you like to get started on? Describe it here:

_____

_____

_____

_____

What is the very first thing you would have to do to get started on the task? Make the first step a small one that can be completed in fifteen minutes or less. Describe the first small step here:

_____

_____

_____

_____

What time today would you like to get started on the task? Put the specific time here:

_____

_____

What problems do you anticipate that could cause you to procrastinate at that time (like not being in the mood, having someone call you on the phone at that time, and so forth)? List the two most likely problems here:

1. _____

_____

2. _____

_____

What are the best solutions to these two problems? (If someone calls, for example, you can say you will be busy for the next fifteen minutes.) List the solutions here:

1. _____

_____

2. _____

_____

The table on page 237 summarizes a five-step plan for overcoming procrastination, using the methods we've been discussing. Please study this chart so you can review the techniques that are the most helpful to you.

ANSWER TO THE EXERCISE ON PAGE 231

Here are three reasons you might not want to do fifteen minutes of a task you're procrastinating about:

1. You can tell yourself fifteen minutes would be only a drop in the bucket.

2. You can tell yourself you intend to do it all at once and get it over with.

3. You can tell yourself you're not really ready to get started.

HOW TO BEAT PROCRASTINATION*

Step 1. Don't put the cart before the horse.	Instead of waiting for motivation, get started. Remember: Action comes first, and motivation comes second.
Step 2. Make a specific plan.	Instead of telling yourself you'll get started one of these days, make a specific plan. Would you like to start today? At what time? What will you do first?
Step 3. Make the job easy (little steps for big feats).	Instead of telling yourself you have to do it all at once, decide to do just 10 or 15 minutes of the task. Break the task into small steps, and remind yourself that you only have to take the first small step today. After that, you can quit with a clear conscience, or do more.
Step 4. Think positively.	Write down the negative thoughts that make you feel guilty and anxious; substitute others that are more positive and realistic.
Step 5. Give yourself credit.	Instead of putting yourself down because your work wasn't good enough, give yourself credit for what you did accomplish.

*Copyright © 1989 by David D. Burns, M.D., from *Ten Days to Self-esteem,* copyright © 1993.

EVALUATION OF STEP 9

What did you learn in Step 9? Put a brief summary of several of the most important ideas we discussed here:

1. _____

_____

2. _____

_____

3. _____

_____

Was there anything in today's step that bothered you or rubbed you the wrong way? If you are in a group, was there anything the leader or other members said that turned you off? Describe any negative feelings you had:

_____

_____

_____

_____

Was there anything in today's step that was particularly helpful, interesting, or useful? Did the leader or other participants say anything during today's session that you liked? Describe any positive reactions you had:

_____

_____

_____

_____

SELF-HELP ASSIGNMENTS FOR STEP 10

If you are participating in a Ten Days to Self-esteem group, your leader may give you self-help assignments to complete before the next session.

Assignments	Check (√) If Assigned	Check (√) When Finished
1. Complete the evaluation form for Step 9.		
2. Take the three mood tests again. They are located at the beginning of the next step.		
3. Read the next step in this book and do as many of the written exercises as possible.		
4. Bring your copy of this book to the next session.		
5. Do one small part of any task you've been procrastinating about.		
6. Work with the Daily Mood Log for ten minutes per day. (Extra copies begin on page 290.)		
7. Bring any written homework to the next session.		
8. Bibliotherapy (was any reading assigned?)		
9.*		
10.		

*Use these spaces for any additional assignments.

SUPPLEMENTARY READING FOR STEP 9

1. Read Chapters 9 and 10 in *The Feeling Good Handbook*.

STEP 10

PRACTICE, PRACTICE, PRACTICE!

GOALS FOR STEP 10

1. In this step you will assess how much progress you have made so far. Have you achieved some of your goals? What work still remains to be done? I will emphasize the importance of continued practice so you can deal successfully with painful mood swings and enjoy greater self-esteem in the future.
2. You will learn how to deal with feelings of hopelessness and overcome the relapses into depression that may occur after you begin to feel better.
3. We will talk about the relationships between self-esteem and spirituality. You will examine the similarities and differences between what you have been learning and your own personal beliefs.
4. Since this is the last step of the series, you will review what you have learned. What are the basic principles of cognitive therapy? What has been the most helpful part of this experience for you?

MOOD TESTING

You have already taken three mood tests at the beginning of the previous steps. I would like you to take the three tests again at the beginning of this step to evaluate the progress you have made so far as a result of reading this book. If you need help, you can review the instructions for these tests in Step 1 beginning on page 18.

THE BURNS DEPRESSION CHECKLIST*

Place a check (√) in the box to the right of each category to indicate how much this type of feeling has bothered you in the past several days.

	0 Not at All	1 Somewhat	2 Moderately	3 A Lot
1. **Sadness:** Do you feel sad or down in the dumps?				
2. **Discouragement:** Does the future look hopeless?				
3. **Low self-esteem:** Do you feel worthless?				
4. **Inferiority:** Do you feel inadequate or inferior to others?				
5. **Guilt:** Do you get self-critical and blame yourself?				
6. **Indecisiveness:** Is it hard to make decisions?				
7. **Irritability:** Do you frequently feel angry or resentful?				
8. **Loss of interest in life:** Have you lost interest in your career, hobbies, family, or friends?				
9. **Loss of motivation:** Do you have to push yourself hard to do things?				
10. **Poor self-image:** Do you feel old or unattractive?				
11. **Appetite changes:** Have you lost your appetite? Do you overeat or binge compulsively?				
12. **Sleep changes:** Is it hard to get a good night's sleep? Are you excessively tired and sleeping too much?				
13. **Loss of sex drive:** Have you lost your interest in sex?				
14. **Concerns about health:** Do you worry excessively about your health?				
15. **Suicidal impulses:** Do you have thoughts that life is not worth living or think you'd be better off dead?†				
Total score on items 1–15 $\longrightarrow$				

*Copyright © 1984 by David D. Burns, M.D., from *Ten Days to Self-esteem*, copyright © 1993.

†Anyone with suicidal urges should seek immediate help from a mental health professional.

THE BURNS ANXIETY INVENTORY*

Place a check (√) in the box to the right of each category to indicate how much this type of feeling has bothered you in the past several days.

Category I: Anxious Feelings	0 Not at All	1 Somewhat	2 Moderately	3 A Lot
1. Anxiety, nervousness, worry, or fear				
2. Feeling that things around you are strange or unreal				
3. Feeling detached from all or part of your body				
4. Sudden unexpected panic spells				
5. Apprehension or a sense of impending doom				
6. Feeling tense, stressed, "uptight," or on edge				
Category II: Anxious Thoughts	0 Not at All	1 Somewhat	2 Moderately	3 A Lot
7. Difficulty concentrating				
8. Racing thoughts				
9. Frightening fantasies or daydreams				
10. Feeling that you're on the verge of losing control				
11. Fears of cracking up or going crazy				
12. Fears of fainting or passing out				
13. Fears of physical illnesses or heart attacks or dying				
14. Concerns about looking foolish or inadequate				
15. Fears of being alone, isolated, or abandoned				
16. Fears of criticism or disapproval				
17. Fears that something terrible is about to happen				

THE BURNS ANXIETY INVENTORY (Continued)

Category III: Physical Symptoms	0 Not at All	1 Somewhat	2 Moderately	3 A Lot
18. Skipping, racing, or pounding of the heart (palpitations)				
19. Pain, pressure, or tightness in the chest				
20. Tingling or numbness in the toes or fingers				
21. Butterflies or discomfort in the stomach				
22. Constipation or diarrhea				
23. Restlessness or jumpiness				
24. Tight, tense muscles				
25. Sweating not brought on by heat				
26. A lump in the throat				
27. Trembling or shaking				
28. Rubbery or "jelly" legs				
29. Feeling dizzy, lightheaded, or off balance				
30. Choking or smothering sensations or difficulty breathing				
31. Headaches or pains in the neck or back				
32. Hot flashes or cold chills				
33. Feeling tired, weak, or easily exhausted				
Total score on items 1–33 →				

RELATIONSHIP SATISFACTION SCALE*

Place a check (√) in the box to the right of each category that best describes the amount of satisfaction you feel in your closest relationship.

	0 Very Dissatisfied	1 Moderately Dissatisfied	2 Slightly Dissatisfied	3 Neutral	4 Slightly Satisfied	5 Moderately Satisfied	6 Very Satisfied
1. Communication and openness							
2. Resolving conflicts and arguments							
3. Degree of affection and caring							
4. Intimacy and closeness							
5. Satisfaction with your role in the relationship							
6. Satisfaction with the other person's role							
7. Overall satisfaction with your relationship							
Total score on items 1–7 ⟶							

Note: Although this test assesses your marriage or most intimate relationship, you can also use it to evaluate your relationship with a friend, family member, or colleague. If you do not have any intimate relationships at this time, you can simply think of people in general when you take the test.

*Copyright © 1983 by David D. Burns, M.D., from *Ten Days to Self-esteem*, copyright © 1993.

LET'S EVALUATE YOUR PROGRESS

Now that you have come to the last step, let's see what you have accomplished and what remains to be done. One way to evaluate your progress is to compare your scores on the three self-assessment tests you took just now with your scores the first time you took them in Step 1. Record both sets of scores in the boxes below. (See pages 21, 24, and 27.)

Test	Step 1 Score	Step 10 Score	Optimal Score
Burns Depression Checklist			less than 5
Burns Anxiety Inventory			less than 5
Relationship Satisfaction Scale			greater than 35

Have your scores on the depression, anxiety, and personal relationship tests improved? Are any of your scores now in the optimal range? Is there still some room for improvement? You may recall that a score between 5 and 10 on the BDC and BAI tests would be considered normal but lackluster, and a score below 5 would be normal and happy. Scores greater than 35 on the RSAT are very good. Ideally, your scores on these tests would be in the optimal range most (but not all!) of the time.

Another way to evaluate your progress is to review your goals for this experience, which you listed in Step 1 on page 28. Take a look at them now.

How much progress have you made so far? Have you accomplished some of your goals? Please describe what you have achieved, as well as the areas where there is still some room for improvement:

_____

_____

_____

_____

If you have not yet achieved all of your goals, or if your scores on the three self-assessment tests indicate that you are still depressed, anxious, or dissatisfied with your personal relationships, what should you conclude?

In the Introduction, I emphasized that people differ greatly in how rapidly they improve.

Some people recover rapidly, while others require a persistent effort over a longer period of time. If you are still unhappy, it is not unusual or shameful. This does *not* mean you are hopeless or different from other people; it only means that you still need to keep working with these ideas and techniques. You can consider these options:

- If you read this book on your own but did not do the written exercises, you can review the book and actually do the written assignments. The self-help assignments are often the key to improvement. You could also do some of the supplementary reading suggested at the end of each step. Sometimes when you hear an idea expressed a little differently, it suddenly begins to make sense. The longer you work with these ideas, the more deeply you will comprehend them.

- You could join a Ten Days to Self-esteem group, if there is one in your area, or another self-help group such as the local chapter of the National Depressive and Manic Depressive Association.

- If you are already a member of self-esteem training group, and this is your last step, you could repeat the group program. Many people find that repeated practice and exposure to these ideas can be extremely helpful.

- You could obtain a consultation with a mental health professional to see if individual psychotherapy or treatment with an antidepressant medication would be helpful to you.

AN OUNCE OF PREVENTION

Let's look at the other side of the coin. What should you do if you have improved and are now feeling a whole lot better?

After the first wave of solid improvement, I tell all my patients that they can expect a relapse *soon*—within days or weeks—and that *now* is the time to deal with it. When it comes to depression, an ounce of prevention can be worth a ton of cure!

Imagine that you have finally recovered completely from your depression. After a long period of misery that you thought would never end, you begin to feel the happiest you have felt in your entire life. You suddenly see clearly how irrational your Negative Thoughts and attitudes were. You feel joyous and optimistic again. Self-esteem feels so natural that it's hard for you to understand how you could have ever felt so gloomy and self-critical. It feels terrific—almost too good to be true.

One morning your bubble bursts. You wake up incredibly depressed again. You feel demoralized and angry. Just when you were beginning to feel great, you're back in the pits again! You feel an overwhelming desire to give up—but instead you reach for a Daily Mood Log. After all, one of the most important things you have learned is to *write down* your Negative Thoughts when you feel depressed. Even though you feel convinced it won't do any good, you decide to give it a try.

You can see the DML partially filled out on page 248. First, you write a brief description of the upsetting event: "I woke up feeling terribly depressed again." Remember that it's important to describe the actual situation that upsets you at the beginning of every DML. Remember, too, that you must do the exercise on paper. Doing it in your head simply won't work!

Next, you record your negative feelings, including hopelessness, inferiority, sadness, and frustration, and rate each of them on a scale from 0% (the least) to 100% (the most).

Then you record your Negative Thoughts in the left-hand column, and indicate the percent you believe each thought, from 0% (not at all) to 100% (completely).

I want you to complete the exercise. Identify the distortions in each Negative Thought using the Distorted Thinking checklist on page 249. I'll help you get started, and then I want you to continue.

Let's start with the second Negative Thought: "These techniques can't really help me after all." Using the Distorted Thinking checklist, see if you can identify several distortions in this thought. Write the distortions in the middle column of the DML on page 248, using abbreviations, before you read on.

The second thought is an example of **all-or-nothing thinking,** because you believe the techniques haven't helped you at all. But they must have helped you somewhat, because you did get better after you began to use them! You can put "A-O-N," as an abbreviation for all-or-nothing thinking, in the middle column of the Daily Mood Log. Do this now!

Feelings of hopelessness always result from all-or-nothing thinking. Many people reason, "I'm either a happy person or a depressed person." When they recover, they tell themselves that their problems are over for good and they'll be happy for the rest of their lives. This is actually a positive distortion, the "all" of all-or-nothing thinking.

Although this optimistic message feels wonderful, it may set you up for a big fall because you probably *will* feel crummy again. No one can be happy *all* the time. We all get upset from time to time. Then you may tell yourself, "I'm *not* a happy person after all. I'll be depressed forever." When you see it on paper, it looks awfully illogical—and it is! But that's exactly the way many depressed people think.

All-or-nothing thinking is not a very accurate or productive way to think about life, especially our moods. Our moods constantly change, much like a river that twists and winds its way to the ocean. Sometimes we feel happy and relaxed. Other times we feel discouraged and frustrated. The one thing we can say about our moods is that they *always* change.

Can you find some more distortions in the second Negative Thought, "These techniques can't really help me after all"? Look at the list of distortions on page 249. Write down several more distortions in the middle column on page 248 before you read on.

> # Stop! Have you written down several additional distortions that you found in the second negative thought yet? Do it before you read on!

DAILY MOOD LOG*

Step One: Describe the Upsetting Event _I woke up feeling terribly depressed again._

Step Two: Record Your Negative Feelings—and rate them from 0% (the least) to 100% (the most). Use words like _sad, anxious, angry, guilty, lonely, hopeless, frustrated,_ etc.

Emotion	Rating (0%–100%)	Emotion	Rating (0%–100%)	Emotion	Rating (0%–100%)
1. hopeless	100%	3. sad	100%	5. angry	75%
2. inferior	90%	4. frustrated	100%	6. defeated	100%

Step Three: The Triple-Column Technique

Negative Thoughts Write down the thoughts that make you upset and estimate your belief in each one (0%–100%).	Distortions Use the Distorted Thinking chart on the next page.	Positive Thoughts Substitute more realistic thoughts and estimate your belief in each one (0%–100%).
1. I feel worse now than I ever did. I'm back to the zero point. 100%		
2. These techniques can't really help me after all. 100%		
3. My improvement was just a fluke. I was just fooling myself. 100%		
4. This proves that I'm hopeless after all. 100%		
5. I'll never really improve. I'll be depressed forever. 100%		
6. I'm a worthless nothing. 100%		

(Continued on next page)

DAILY MOOD LOG (Continued)

Negative Thoughts	Distortions	Positive Thoughts

DISTORTED THINKING*

1. **All-or-nothing thinking:** You look at things in absolute, black-and-white categories.
2. **Overgeneralization:** You view a negative event as a never-ending pattern of defeat.
3. **Mental filter:** You dwell on the negatives and ignore the positives.
4. **Discounting the positives:** You insist that your accomplishments or positive qualities don't count.
5. **Jumping to conclusions:** You conclude things are bad without any definite evidence:
   (a) **Mind reading:** You assume people are reacting negatively to you.
   (b) **Fortune-telling:** You predict that things will turn out badly.
6. **Magnification or minimization:** You blow things way out of proportion or you shrink their importance.
7. **Emotional reasoning:** You reason from how you feel: "I feel like an idiot, so I must be one."
8. **"Should" statements:** You criticize yourself or other people with "shoulds," "shouldn'ts," "musts," "oughts," and "have-tos."
9. **Labeling:** Instead of saying "I made a mistake," you tell yourself "I'm a jerk" or "a loser."
10. **Blame:** You blame yourself for something you weren't entirely responsible for, or you blame other people and overlook ways that you contributed to a problem.

The second Negative Thought is also an example of **mental filter,** since you are thinking exclusively about how bad you feel just at this moment. You can put "MF" as an abbreviation in the middle column.

The second Negative Thought is also an example of **discounting the positives,** since you are ignoring your earlier improvement, as if it hadn't happened. You can put "DP" as an abbreviation in the middle column. It's also an example of **fortune-telling,** since you are predicting, without evidence, that the techniques won't be helpful to you anymore. You can put "FT" in the middle column. You are also involved in **emotional reasoning.** You may *feel* like the techniques can't help, so you conclude that they *really won't* help. You can put "ER" as an abbreviation in the middle column. You will find some other distortions in the second Negative Thought as well!

Please identify the distortions in all the Negative Thoughts on page 248 now. Do not continue reading until you are done.

After you have identified the distortions in the Negative Thoughts, use several of the techniques listed in the chart on page 251 to challenge these thoughts. Substitute Positive Thought (PT) in the right-hand column for each Negative Thought (NT). After you write down each PT, indicate how strongly you believe it, from 0% to 100%. Then reestimate how much you now believe the NT, from 0% to 100%.

Here's an example of how a woman named Rose used the method called Examine the Evidence to challenge the second Negative Thought:

Negative Thoughts	Distortions	Positive Thoughts
2. These techniques can't really help me after all. ~~100%~~ 25%	A-O-N; OG; MF; DP; FT; MAG; ER; SH	2. These techniques did help me before because I started to feel better. 100%

When you Examine the Evidence, you ask yourself, "What is the evidence that supports or disproves my Negative Thought?" Rose realized that the techniques must have been somewhat helpful, because she improved dramatically soon after she started using them. After she wrote this in the Positive Thoughts column, she put "100%" after it because it was convincing. Then she didn't believe the Negative Thought nearly so much. You can see that she crossed out her original estimate of "100%" for the Negative Thought, and put "25%" next to it in the left column. This indicated that her belief in the Negative Thought was now much lower.

If this method had not worked so well, Rose could have tried another of the techniques from the table on page 251. For example, she might try the Double-Standard Technique. She could ask herself, "Would I say this to a dear friend who had recovered from a depression and then woke up feeling bad one day? If not, why not? What would I say to my friend? Would I be more encouraging and supportive?"

How would you use the Experimental Method to deal with the fifth Negative Thought, "I'll never really improve. I'll be depressed forever"? When you use the Experimental

FIFTEEN WAYS TO UNTWIST YOUR THINKING*

Method	Description of This Method
1. Identify the Distortions	Use the Distorted Thinking chart on page 249 and write down the distortions in each Negative Thought.
2. The Straightforward Approach	Substitute a more positive and realistic thought.
3. The Cost-Benefit Analysis	List the advantages and disadvantages of a negative feeling, thought, belief, or behavior.
4. Examine the Evidence	Instead of assuming that a Negative Thought is true, examine the actual evidence for it.
5. The Survey Method	Do a survey to find out if your thoughts and attitudes are realistic.
6. The Experimental Method	Do an experiment to test the accuracy of your Negative Thought.
7. The Double-Standard Technique	Talk to yourself in the same compassionate way you might talk to a dear friend who was upset.
8. The Pleasure-Predicting Method	Predict how satisfying activities will be, from 0% to 100%. Record how satisfying they turn out to be.
9. The Vertical Arrow Technique	Draw a vertical arrow under your Negative Thought and ask why it would be upsetting if it was true.
10. Thinking in Shades of Gray	Instead of thinking about your problems in black-and-white categories, evaluate things in shades of gray.
11. Define Terms	When you label yourself as "inferior" or "a loser," ask yourself what you mean by these labels.
12. Be Specific	Stick with reality and avoid judgments about reality.
13. The Semantic Method	Substitute language that is less emotionally loaded for "should" statements and labeling.
14. Reattribution	Instead of blaming yourself for a problem, think about all the factors that may have contributed to it.
15. The Acceptance Paradox	Instead of defending yourself against your own self-criticisms, find truth in them and accept them.

Method, you do an actual experiment to see if the Negative Thought is true or false. How could you test your belief that you'll never improve? Put your ideas here. The answer is on page 266. Please jot down your ideas before you look there!

How would you use Thinking in Shades of Gray to deal with the same Negative Thought? This method can be especially helpful for all-or-nothing thinking, because all-or-nothing thinking is not a very accurate way to describe most things. For example, no one is totally smart or completely stupid. All of us are somewhere in between. But when you say "I'll be depressed forever," it sounds like you'll be stuck eternally in one lousy, horrible mood without any change whatsoever.

What could you tell yourself about your moods and your progress if you were Thinking in Shades of Gray? Put your ideas here. The answer is on page 266. Please record your ideas before you look there!

It is important to try many different techniques when you feel stuck and you can't put the lie to a Negative Thought. When one technique doesn't work, try another, and then another. It's worth a persistent effort, because sooner or later you will find the method that works. When you do, you'll feel much better.

Let's try one more technique, the Cost-Benefit Analysis. How would you use the Cost-Benefit Analysis to deal with the last Negative Thought, "I'm a worthless nothing"? Put your ideas here. The answer is on page 267. Please record your ideas before you look there!

You should be aware that the probability of relapse after you recover is extremely high. Nearly all human beings have bad moods from time to time. This need not be a problem if you prepare for these relapses ahead of time. It's a big mistake to do nothing and give up when the depression returns. This will make the relapse worse. If, instead, you apply the techniques you are beginning to learn, you can often turn these bad spells around quickly.

A relapse can actually be a positive experience—in spite of how awful it feels—because you will discover that you can overcome your bad moods. This will prove that the first improvement you experienced was not a fluke. The secret of self-esteem is not *feeling* better, but *getting* better. Getting better means that you are learning to cope with mood slumps more effectively.

Complete the Daily Mood Log on page 248 carefully. Give yourself at least fifteen minutes for this exercise. This is one of the best ways to prepare for a relapse.

The effort you put in now will be worth a great deal later on!

THE KEY TO RECOVERY

People seem to experience recovery in different ways. Some people may notice a difference in their attitudes when they begin to feel happy. For example, you may suddenly realize that you don't need everyone's approval to feel happy and worthwhile. If someone is angry with you, instead of getting defensive and feeling devastated, you may tell yourself, "Hey, there's probably some truth in their criticism. Let's see what I can learn from this." This new mind-set may improve your self-esteem and lead to much better relationships with others.

Some people notice more of a change in their behavior when they recover. They have to take action to break out of a bad mood. For example, a businessman named Burt had been depressed and anxious for more than ten years. Burt always complained that he wasn't earning enough money to be truly happy and worthwhile. He constantly compared himself to people with bigger cars and fancier houses. He told himself they were the beautiful people who enjoyed true happiness. He believed that he was inferior because he had never truly "made it" in life.

Although Burt is not rich, he has actually done quite well for himself. He lives in an affluent suburban Pittsburgh neighborhood, with an attractive, devoted wife and two small children. Nevertheless, he beats himself up endlessly because he thinks he *should* have done much better. He ruminates about business errors in years past and fantasizes about how wonderful life would be if only he had made better decisions and been more successful.

Burt and I spent months discussing whether it was reasonable to base his self-esteem and happiness on the amount of money he earned. Although we had wonderfully exciting philosophical discussions, these sessions never really seemed to help much. I also treated Burt with the antidepressant drug Prozac. Although it seemed to help somewhat, Burt was still dissatisfied with life. He was hooked on the idea that he could never feel truly happy and fulfilled until he was making enough money to buy a BMW and a fancy new house.

Burt talked a great deal about his father during these sessions. His described his father as a suspicious, bitter man. He said his parents had fought constantly. There had never been any harmony or love at home. He had many vivid memories of his parents' battles and his father's wrath. He lamented his past and wondered if the lack of love and affection at home was the real cause of his pessimism. But all our lengthy discussions of his childhood failed to bear fruit.

One day it dawned on me that Burt's actual problem might actually be quite simple: procrastination. I realized that whenever Burt started complaining about how inadequate he was, there was always something bugging him that he was not dealing with.

For example, Burt had generously agreed to a temporary 15% "salary" cut to help his firm make it through a business slowdown. He was proud of this sacrifice, because his boss was the owner of the firm and Burt considered him a close friend. His boss emphasized that all the senior staff members in the firm would be asked to take the same pay cut until the company recovered.

Several months later, Burt discovered a payroll memo revealing that he was the only staff member who had been asked to take a pay cut. Burt felt betrayed and taken advantage of.

The day that Burt discovered this memo, he began obsessing about how inadequate he was. However, he did not seem to notice the connection between this upsetting event and the sudden plunge in his self-esteem! All he wanted to do at our next therapy session was to talk about philosophy! I suggested it might be better to talk about how he was going to deal with his problem at work. For example, did he want to talk things over with his boss in a frank and respectful way? Burt insisted that it *wouldn't be appropriate* to discuss the situation with his boss. All he wanted to do was to talk on and on about how much happier he would be if only he had a happier childhood or a bigger house!

Fortunately, I was able to persuade Burt to stop procrastinating and take action. He agreed to discuss his feelings with his boss within twenty-four hours, even if it made him intensely uncomfortable. Burt and his boss were able to resolve the pay dispute in a friendly and fair manner, and Burt felt better.

Burt had to take *action* to recover from his depression. The moment he stopped procrastinating, his mood immediately brightened.

Will his new positive outlook last forever? You know the answer! Sooner or later, Burt will almost definitely fall again into the black hole of worry and self-criticism again. He will wake up one day and notice that he again feels inferior and dissatisfied with his life and envious of people with more money and bigger houses.

What should Burt do? He will need to ask himself, "What (or whom) am I upset with? What problem am I avoiding?" Once he stops procrastinating and takes action to solve the problem, he will again feel better.

Is there anything you have been putting off that might be contributing to your feelings of low self-esteem? It could be something as simple as going on a diet, doing the written exercises in this book, giving up alcohol or drugs, talking to a friend or family member you're upset with, or looking for a new job. Do you think your mood would improve if you stopped procrastinating and took action?

The key to recovery for each person is usually a little different. That's why recovery takes time and effort. Do you have any idea yet what the most important key is to your recovery?

Once you have discovered this key, it will very likely help you over and over again in the future. You probably won't have to go through a long process of figuring out what to do every time you're depressed.

What is the key to recovery for you? Can you identify one or two ideas or techniques that have been particularly helpful and important in your personal growth during the past nine steps? Please describe them here:

_____

_____

_____

_____

_____

SELF-ESTEEM AND SPIRITUALITY

Although psychotherapy and religion have been at odds with each other during much of the twentieth century, many of the ideas and techniques you have been learning about are actually quite compatible with a wide variety of religious and philosophical orientations. I would like you to become more aware of these connections. This can strengthen your own convictions and make your recovery more meaningful.

For example, you may be able to relate the following Old Testament passage to what you learned during the ten steps:

Proverbs 23:7: For as he thinketh in his heart, so is he.

The meaning of the passage is actually similar to one of the most basic ideas that was introduced in Step 2. Do you know what it is? Put your best guess below. (The answer to this problem is on page 267. Don't look until you have answered it!)

_____

_____

_____

_____

The lack of self-esteem is one of the most painful symptoms of depression. The central belief that causes low self-esteem is "I'm not a worthwhile human being. I am inferior to others." The evidence for this belief is generally "because my girlfriend (or boyfriend) rejected me," or "because I'm not as intelligent and successful as other people," or "because I'm socially awkward and nervous in crowds," and so forth.

The belief that you are not worthwhile rests on the assumption that human worth is a quality that people can have or not have. One way we dealt with this problem in Step 7 was called Define Terms. According to this method, if you believe that you are not worthwhile, I will ask you over and over, "What is the definition of a worthless human being?" Regardless of the definition you propose, I will show you that it does not apply to anybody, or that it applies to everybody in the world, and that it is a meaningless definition. The purpose of this discussion is to help you give up the idea that "worthless" and "worthwhile" people exist, so that you can focus on productive living instead.

Here's a brief example of the method. Suppose you say, "A worthless person is one who has never accomplished anything." I might ask you to list several things you have accomplished: learning to walk, to talk, to write, to relate to others, or to play piano, among many others. Since you have accomplished many things, you cannot be worthless, according to your definition. In fact, no one can be worthless according to this definition.

No matter how you try to define a worthless person, your definition will always fall apart. Why is this? It's because there is no such thing as a worthless or an inferior human being, nor is there any such thing as a worthwhile or superior human being. All human beings have strengths and weaknesses. Specific activities can be more or less worthwhile, but human beings cannot. People can have more or less talent, more or less intelligence, and so forth, but this does not make us superior or inferior as human beings.

Although this notion that we can be superior or inferior human beings is completely nonsensical, it is tremendously common, and it can cast a powerful spell on us. When you feel depressed, you will probably believe with all your heart that you *really are* inferior.

People can sometimes be just as easily seduced by the belief that they are superior to others, a vulnerability that Hitler exploited masterfully. He convinced the German people that they were a master race. Millions of ordinary people got caught up in this intoxicating idea.

This has been a difficult and challenging issue for psychologists and theologians. Just how do we determine human worth? On what should you base your self-esteem?

My philosophy of self-esteem can be stated in three ways. The first approach is to view all human beings as equally worthwhile. We have one unit of worth that we receive at the moment of birth, and we can do nothing to increase or decrease it. It is far more productive to focus on solving real problems (such as career dilemmas or difficulties in personal relationships) than to obsess about whether or not we are worthwhile.

This first formulation is quite consistent with the Jewish faith. In the book *Let Us Make Man: Self-esteem Through Jewishness* (Brooklyn, N.Y.: Traditional Press, 1987), Abraham J. Twerski argues that all people, regardless of sex or station in life, are equal in the eyes of God. He writes:

> The issue of role assignment is often compared to a team effort or to the interdependence of the members of an orchestra. All participants are important, the right fielder as well as the

pitcher, the percussionist as well as the violinist. . . . Equality in the eyes of God should be the only measure for the Torah Jew. . . . Any stratification which reflects upon a person's worth is an artifact, imposed by a non-Torah system. There are indeed varying assignments, but . . . in creation we are all equal. (P. 178)

In the second approach, you can view self-esteem as the decision to treat yourself in a respectful and loving way instead of putting yourself down with harsh, destructive messages, such as "I'm no good." This act of self-love is a gift, not a special status that has to be earned.

This second approach to self-esteem is quite consistent with Christian theology. Christianity emphasizes that all human beings are lovable in the eyes of God and that we cannot earn our way to heaven through good works. This idea is stated clearly in the New Testament.

Ephesians 2:8–9: For by grace are ye saved through faith; and that not of yourself: it is the gift of God: Not of works, lest any man should boast.

Romans 5:8: But God commendeth his love toward us, in that, while we were yet sinners, Christ died for us.

The concept of grace suggests that we cannot gain genuine self-esteem through our achievements, intelligence, or good works. We cannot gain genuine self-esteem by being loved or popular. We declare self-esteem, and love ourselves in spite of our shortcomings and not because of our accomplishments.

The notion of faith implies that you cannot demonstrate or prove that you are basically acceptable or lovable. In fact, you can never prove that any human being is worthwhile *or* worthless. You can only declare your own dignity as an act of faith. Genuine self-esteem cannot be earned or taken away.

The third approach to the problem of self-esteem is based on the notion that there is really no such thing as a worthwhile or worthless human being. There is also no such thing as a superior or inferior human being.

Instead of trying to figure out how to be worthwhile, you can focus on pursuing specific goals, such as learning, having fun, being helpful to others, being productive and creatively involved in your career or hobbies, or improving your personal relationships. Foolish and worthless behaviors exist, but fools and worthless human beings do not.

This third formulation, which denies the validity of self-esteem, is quite compatible with Buddhism. Buddhism not only denies the validity of self-esteem, but also denies the very existence of a personal identity of "self." In his article "The Buddhist-Christian Dialogue," M.S.J. Barnes states that Buddhism even denies the very sense of uniqueness or individuality that we all seem to have. He says that for the Buddhist, everything is a flux of becoming. The "self" does not really refer to anything that actually exists. The self is just a mythical concept. He writes:

For the Buddhist, linguistic forms are strictly functional. Like a boat they are to be used to enable the traveler to cross to the further shore; once on the other side they can be safely abandoned. (*The Way* 30, no. 1 [1990]: 58)

This Buddhist point of view is also quite consistent with what you have been learning. The concepts of identity and self are simply meaningless and useless abstractions, in the same sense that the concepts of self-esteem and worthwhileness are. In other words, now that you have learned how to develop self-esteem, I am suggesting that you may no longer need it! Although this may sound like double-talk, or like I am taking away something precious, please be assured that no real loss will occur!

While jogging the other day I realized that I had no identity or self. It was a pleasant relief, and it didn't slow me down at all!

Do you feel that you would lose something if you lost your identity or self? What is it that you think you would lose? What time of day do you think you would notice that you had lost something?

Of course, when you lose your "self," you have literally lost nothing, because there was nothing there to lose.

Like Buddhism, cognitive therapy is ruthlessly pragmatic. A young woman recently went to a colleague of mine because she felt extremely anxious and was convinced she was having an "identity crisis." She was a senior in high school, and wanted to know, "Who am I?"

He told her that he had unfortunately missed the lecture about identity in medical school and never did find out what an "identity" is. After apologizing for being unable to help her with that particular difficulty, he asked if she had any specific problems he might assist her with. She might well have been anxious about problems with family or friends or difficulties with her schoolwork. As it turned out, she was a top student and had been accepted by two colleges the same week her "identity crisis" developed. Although she wanted to go to the University of Pennsylvania, she felt pressured to go to Smith, since her mother had gone there. After she listed the advantages and disadvantages of these two schools, she decided to go to the University of Pennsylvania. This took only two sessions. She said she felt a whole lot better and was ready to terminate her therapy. Then my colleague reminded her that they had not yet dealt with her identity crisis. "Oh, I don't really have one of those anymore," she replied!

All three solutions to the problem of self-esteem are very similar. Each is simply expressed a little differently. The practical result is never to give in to the belief that you are worthless or inferior to anyone.

Can you describe how your own attitudes and values have changed as a result of the past nine steps? Have you begun to think about the meaning and purpose of life in a new and different way? Describe any changes in your personal philosophy here:

_____

_____

_____

_____

_____

Are some of the ideas you have learned about in this book compatible with your own personal philosophy or spiritual beliefs? Describe the areas of compatibility here:

_____

_____

_____

_____

Have any of your own personal or religious beliefs been strengthened as you progressed through the ten steps? Describe the changes here:

_____

_____

_____

_____

Can you think of anything you have learned in this book that seems in conflict with your personal philosophy or spiritual beliefs? Describe the conflict here:

_____

_____

_____

_____

Can you think of any way to reconcile the conflict? For example, some Christian Fundamentalists might feel a mistrust of secular psychotherapy and argue that only a belief in Christ as one's personal savior can help a person with emotional difficulties. However, the following biblical passages suggest that spiritual healing and psychological therapy need not be at odds:

John 1:14: And the Word was made flesh, and dwelt among us. . . .

John 3:16: For God so loved the world, that he gave his only begotten Son, that whosoever believeth in him should not perish, but have everlasting life.

Clergy and psychotherapists share the goal of understanding and relieving human suffering. In these New Testament passages, Saint John tells us that redemption is the result of God's spiritual work in the world. Jesus lived and worked among us as a flesh-and-blood human being. Christians believe that God loved the world and sent his son to work *in the world* to provide healing and salvation.

Similarly, psychological healing occurs through human interaction. This healing is a gift that occurs in the context of a compassionate and caring relationship between two people. Psychotherapy can be the expression of a spiritual commitment, even if the therapist does not believe in God or make any reference to prayer or to religious ideas in his or her daily practice.

PRACTICE, PRACTICE, PRACTICE!

In the Introduction and in Step 1, I reviewed a number of studies showing that self-help is an important key to recovery from depression and anxiety. This is true whether you are working on your own or receiving psychiatric treatment. You will make the greatest progress now and maintain those gains in the future if you continue to practice, practice, practice with the Daily Mood Log whenever you feel upset.

I would recommend that you use the DML for fifteen minutes per day whenever your score on the BDC is greater than 5. Write down your Negative Thoughts and identify the distortions in them. Then substitute more positive and realistic thoughts in the right-hand column. This can be invaluable anytime you are feeling unhappy.

I have included a blank Daily Mood Log on the following pages. Fill it out now! Think of a time in your life when you felt upset. Go through all the steps one by one, just as we did in the exercise on hopelessness and relapse prevention.

Suppose, for example, that right now you are feeling frustrated and telling yourself, "I'm not getting this. I should be doing better." In Step One of the Daily Mood Log, you might record the upsetting event as "Reading page 260 of the self-esteem book."

Next you can record your emotions on the DML. They might include frustration, inferiority, and discouragement.

Then you can record your Negative Thoughts in the left-hand column of the DML:

1. I'm not getting this. 100%

2. I *should* be doing better. 100%

Finally, you can identify the distortions, substitute Positive Thoughts, and estimate how much better you feel.

Remember that there are extra copies of the DML in the Appendix. Leave at least one copy blank so you can photocopy extras whenever you need them.

DAILY MOOD LOG*

Step One: Describe the Upsetting Event _____

_____

Step Two: Record Your Negative Feelings—and rate them from 0% (the least) to 100% (the most). Use words like *sad, anxious, angry, guilty, lonely, hopeless, frustrated,* etc.

Emotion	Rating (0%–100%)	Emotion	Rating (0%–100%)	Emotion	Rating (0%–100%)

Step Three: The Triple-Column Technique

Negative Thoughts Write down the thoughts that make you upset and estimate your belief in each one (0%–100%).	Distortions Use the Distorted Thinking chart on the next page.	Positive Thoughts Substitute more realistic thoughts and estimate your belief in each one (0%–100%).

(Continued on next page)

*Copyright © 1984 by David D. Burns, M.D., from *Ten Days to Self-esteem*, copyright © 1993.

DAILY MOOD LOG (Continued)

Negative Thoughts	Distortions	Positive Thoughts

DISTORTED THINKING*

1. **All-or-nothing thinking:** You look at things in absolute, black-and-white categories.
2. **Overgeneralization:** You view a negative event as a never-ending pattern of defeat.
3. **Mental filter:** You dwell on the negatives and ignore the positives.
4. **Discounting the positives:** You insist that your accomplishments or positive qualities don't count.
5. **Jumping to conclusions:** You conclude things are bad without any definite evidence.
   (a) **Mind reading:** You assume people are reacting negatively to you.
   (b) **Fortune-telling:** You predict that things will turn out badly.
6. **Magnification or minimization:** You blow things way out of proportion or you shrink their importance.
7. **Emotional reasoning:** You reason from how you feel: "I feel like an idiot, so I must be one."
8. **"Should" statements:** You criticize yourself or other people with "shoulds," "shouldn'ts," "musts," "oughts," and "have-tos."
9. **Labeling:** Instead of saying, "I made a mistake," you tell yourself, "I'm a jerk" or "a loser."
10. **Blame:** You blame yourself for something you weren't entirely responsible for, or you blame other people and overlook ways that you contributed to a problem.

REVIEW OF THE TEN STEPS TO SELF-ESTEEM

This review highlights a few of the most important ideas we have been discussing during the ten steps. What are the basic principles of cognitive therapy? I have listed one of them. See how many you can list. (The answer to this exercise is on page 267.)

1. *Your thoughts create your moods. When you are upset, it's not so much what's happening to you, but the way you think about it that causes you to feel the way you do.*

2. _____

3. _____

4. _____

5. _____

What are some of the differences between a healthy negative emotion and an unhealthy one? List as many as you can think of. (The answer to this exercise is on page 267.)

1. _____

2. _____

3. _____

4. _____

5. _____

What should you do if you have a healthy negative emotion, such as healthy sadness or anger? (The answer to this exercise is on page 268.)

_____

_____

_____

What are the steps in filling out a Daily Mood Log? (The answer to this exercise is on page 79.)

1. _____

_____

2. _____

_____

3. _____

_____

What is a Self-defeating Belief? How does it differ from a Negative Thought? (The answer to this exercise is on page 146.)

_____

_____

_____

_____

List several Self-defeating Beliefs here. (The answer to this exercise is on page 147.)

1. _____

_____

2. _____

_____

3. _____

_____

4. _____

_____

What's the difference between Self-defense and the Acceptance Paradox? (The answer to this exercise is on page 131.)

_____

_____

_____

_____

Write a Positive Thought to substitute for the Negative Thought "I'm a total loser." Use the Self-defense technique. (The answer to this exercise is on page 268.)

_____

_____

_____

_____

Now write a Positive Thought for the same Negative Thought, using the Acceptance Paradox. (The answer to this exercise is on page 268.)

_____

_____

_____

_____

Which approach was more useful to you?

Can you list five different kinds of perfectionism? (The answer to this exercise is on pages 202 and 203.)

1. _____

_____

2. _____

_____

3. _____

_____

4. _____

_____

5. _____

_____

If you are in a Ten Days to Self-esteem group, did the leader or the other members say or do anything that made a positive impact on your life or on the way you think and feel? What was it? What was the most positive part of the experience?

_____

_____

_____

_____

_____

ANSWER TO EXPERIMENTAL METHOD EXERCISE ON PAGE 252

You can do the following experiment. You could maintain your belief that you'll never really improve, but test it by working hard and doing the written exercises in this book every day for the next six weeks. You could take the BDC and BAI tests each week and see how much your scores improve. Suppose your BDC score now is 25, indicating a moderate depression. How much of a reduction in the score would show you were beginning to improve?

ANSWER TO SHADES OF GRAY EXERCISE ON PAGE 252

You can think about partial improvement, moving forward one step at a time, instead of trying to recover all at once. Would a 3-point improvement on the BDC be an improvement? Of course it would! And we know that you can improve by that small amount! Then you could improve another 3 points, and so on, until your score is in the normal range.

It's important to think about improvement in Shades of Gray, rather than using black-and-white categories. Some people reason, "If I improve and then relapse, my improvement doesn't count." But it *does* count! The first time you recover, you may feel happy and carefree for several days. The next time you recover, you may feel better for several weeks or several months. It's a lot like jogging. You don't become a marathon runner overnight, but your skill improves the longer you work at it.

ANSWER TO CBA EXERCISE ON PAGE 252

You could draw a line down the middle of a piece of paper. In the left-hand column you could list the advantages of thinking of yourself as a worthless nothing. How will this mind-set help you? In the right-hand column you could list the disadvantages of this attitude. How will this attitude hurt you? Weigh the advantages against the disadvantages on a 100-point scale.

ANSWER TO OLD TESTAMENT EXERCISE ON PAGE 255

This Old Testament passage suggests that our thoughts influence the way we think and behave. In Step 2 you learned that we FEEL the way we THINK. This means that our emotions result more from our Negative Thoughts and attitudes than from the bad things that happen to us. Unhealthy feelings, like depression, neurotic anxiety, and destructive anger, are caused by distorted, illogical thoughts. This may sometimes go against the grain, because we may feel like victims who have been treated unfairly by life. Nevertheless, it is an empowering and optimistic message, because we all have the potential to make positive and dramatic changes in the way we think, feel, and relate to others.

ANSWER TO COGNITIVE THERAPY EXERCISE ON PAGE 263

2. Negative feelings result from Negative Thoughts.

3. Some negative feelings are healthy and some are unhealthy. Unhealthy negative feelings nearly always result from thoughts that are distorted and illogical.

4. Self-defeating attitudes such as perfectionism or the need for approval can make you vulnerable to painful mood swings.

5. You can CHANGE the way you FEEL when you think about things in a more positive and realistic way.

ANSWER TO HEALTHY VS. UNHEALTHY EMOTION EXERCISE ON PAGE 263

1. Healthy negative feelings result from realistic thoughts, whereas unhealthy feelings result from distortions such as all-or-nothing thinking.

2. Unhealthy feelings are out of proportion to the upsetting event or may even come out of the blue.

3. Unhealthy emotions frequently involve feelings of hopelessness as well as a loss of self-esteem.

4. Unhealthy negative feelings make it difficult to function effectively and relate to other people.

5. Unhealthy negative feelings may go on and on indefinitely.

ANSWER TO HEALTHY NEGATIVE EMOTION EXERCISE ON PAGE 264

You can accept the feeling as a normal part of life. You can express what you feel and take constructive action based on your feeling.

ANSWER TO SELF-DEFENSE EXERCISE ON PAGE 265

You could point out your strong points and emphasize the many things you have accomplished.

ANSWER TO ACCEPTANCE PARADOX EXERCISE ON PAGE 265

You could remind yourself that although you have a number of strengths, you also have many weaknesses and shortcomings that you need to work on. You could accept your weakness with complete honesty and without any sense of shame or inferiority.

SUMMARY OF STEP 10

What did you learn in Step 10? Put a brief summary of several of the most important ideas we discussed here:

1. _____

_____

2. _____

_____

3. _____

_____

EVALUATION OF TEN DAYS TO SELF-ESTEEM

If you are in a Ten Days to Self-esteem group, please fill out the evaluation form on the following pages and turn it in before you leave. A review of the results will give your group leader valuable information about your experience. This feedback can help him or her make the next group even more effective.

PARTICIPANT EVALUATION FORM

Date: _____ Name: _____

Circle the number to the right that best describes how you feel	Agree Strongly	Agree	Neutral	Disagree	Disagree Strongly
1. The overall objectives of the program were met.	5	4	3	2	1
2. My personal goals for this experience were achieved.	5	4	3	2	1
3. The sessions were clear, understandable, and well organized.	5	4	3	2	1
4. The teaching methods were helpful to me.	5	4	3	2	1
5. The facility was comfortable and pleasant.	5	4	3	2	1
6. The program was a valuable learning experience.	5	4	3	2	1
7. This experience will be helpful in my personal life.	5	4	3	2	1
	Every Day	Frequently	Occasionally	Almost Never	Never
8. How often did you do the self-help exercises between sessions?	5	4	3	2	1
9. How often did you do the reading in *Ten Days to Self-esteem*?	5	4	3	2	1
	Very Helpful	Helpful	Neutral	Somewhat Unhelpful	Very Unhelpful
10. How helpful was the workbook (*Ten Days to Self-esteem*)?	5	4	3	2	1
11. How helpful were the self-help assignments between sessions?	5	4	3	2	1
12. How helpful were the discussions during the sessions?	5	4	3	2	1
13. How helpful were the group exercises?	5	4	3	2	1
14. How helpful and supportive was the group leader?	5	4	3	2	1

PARTICIPANT EVALUATION FORM (Page 2)

Circle the number to the right that best describes how you feel	Very Helpful	Helpful	Neutral	Somewhat Unhelpful	Very Unhelpful
15. How helpful and supportive were the other group members?	5	4	3	2	1
16. How helpful was the program in understanding your moods?	5	4	3	2	1
17. How helpful was the program in learning to change your moods?	5	4	3	2	1
18. How helpful was the program in developing better self-esteem?	5	4	3	2	1
19. How helpful was the program overall?	5	4	3	2	1

20. Please explain any low rating: _____
_____
_____

21. What did you like the *least* about the program? _____
_____
_____

22. What did you like the *most* about the program? _____
_____
_____

23. What did you learn that will be the most helpful to you? _____
_____
_____

24. General comments: _____
_____
_____
_____

EMPATHY SCALE*

Circle the number to the right of each statement that best describes how strongly you agree with it.

	Not at All	Somewhat	Moderately	A Lot
1. I felt that I could trust the group leader during the sessions.	0	1	2	3
2. The leader felt I was worthwhile.	0	1	2	3
3. The leader was friendly and warm toward me.	0	1	2	3
4. The leader understood what I said during the sessions.	0	1	2	3
5. The leader was sympathetic and concerned about me.	0	1	2	3
Total score on items 1–5 $\longrightarrow$				
6. Sometimes the leader did not seem completely genuine.	0	1	2	3
7. The leader pretended to like me more than he or she really does.	0	1	2	3
8. The leader did not always seem to care about me.	0	1	2	3
9. The leader did not always understand the way I felt inside.	0	1	2	3
10. The leader seemed condescending and talked down to me.	0	1	2	3
Total score on items 6–10 $\longrightarrow$				

APPENDIX OF SELF-HELP FORMS AND CHARTS

INSTRUCTIONS

This section contains three additional copies of many of the self-help forms you have learned to use in this book.

Make sure you keep at least one copy of each form blank! Do not make any marks on this set of master copies. Keep these master copies as originals so you can photocopy additional copies when you need more.

You have permission to reproduce these forms for your own personal use in working with your own mood problems. They have all been copyrighted. Permission to use them in a clinical practice or for any other purpose must be obtained in writing from David D. Burns, M.D.

MOOD TESTING

At the beginning of each step of this book, I asked you to fill out the Burns Depression Checklist, the Burns Anxiety Inventory, and the Relationship Satisfaction Scale. (The instructions and scoring key for each test can be found in Step 1.)

I realize that you may want to take the tests more frequently, or you may want to take them after you have completed the ten steps. Therefore, I have included an answer sheet for each of the three tests. When you use these versions of the tests that come with answer sheets, you can put your answers on the answer sheets instead of making check marks on the tests. Once you are done, put your total score at the bottom of the answer sheet, along with the date.

Please review the sample answer sheet on page 276. You can see that the woman who filled out the BDC on October 19 had a total score of 17, indicating a mild depression. One week later, her score was 15. This indicated that she still felt mildly depressed, but had improved a little bit. You will see that her improvement was in items 2 and 15 of the BDC, which assess hopelessness and suicidal impulses. Although she still felt quite unhappy, she felt more optimistic, and this lifted her mood.

Remember to use the answer sheets when you take the tests from this point on. **Do not make any marks on the tests themselves.** If you like, you can cover up your previous answers so that you won't be influenced by them when you take the tests again.

I have included three copies of each answer sheet. Make sure you leave one copy of each answer sheet blank so you can use it for photocopying.

THE BURNS DEPRESSION CHECKLIST*

On the answer sheet, indicate how much each of the following 15 symptoms has bothered you in the past several days. **Do not make any marks on this page.**

	0 Not at All	1 Somewhat	2 Moderately	3 A Lot
1. **Sadness:** Do you feel sad or down in the dumps?				
2. **Discouragement:** Does the future look hopeless?				
3. **Low self-esteem:** Do you feel worthless?				
4. **Inferiority:** Do you feel inadequate or inferior to others?				
5. **Guilt:** Do you get self-critical and blame yourself?				
6. **Indecisiveness:** Is it hard to make decisions?				
7. **Irritability:** Do you frequently feel angry or resentful?				
8. **Loss of interest in life:** Have you lost interest in your career, hobbies, family, or friends?				
9. **Loss of motivation:** Do you have to push yourself hard to do things?				
10. **Poor self-image:** Do you feel old or unattractive?				
11. **Appetite changes:** Have you lost your appetite? Do you overeat or binge compulsively?				
12. **Sleep changes:** Is it hard to get a good night's sleep? Are you excessively tired and sleeping too much?				
13. **Loss of sex drive:** Have you lost your interest in sex?				
14. **Concerns about health:** Do you worry excessively about your health?				
15. **Suicidal impulses:** Do you have thoughts that life is not worth living or think you'd be better off dead?†				

THE BURNS DEPRESSION CHECKLIST
ANSWER SHEET

Instructions: Put 0, 1, 2, or 3 in the space to the right of each of the 15 symptoms from the Burns Depression Checklist to indicate how much this type of feeling has bothered you in the past several days. Use this key: 0 = not at all; 1 = somewhat; 2 = moderately; 3 = a lot. Total your score at the bottom.

Today's Date	10/19	10/26				
	1. 1	1. 1	1.	1.	1.	1.
	2. 1	2. 0	2.	2.	2.	2.
	3. 2	3. 2	3.	3.	3.	3.
	4. 2	4. 2	4.	4.	4.	4.
	5. 1	5. 1	5.	5.	5.	5.
	6. 0	6. 0	6.	6.	6.	6.
	7. 2	7. 2	7.	7.	7.	7.
	8. 2	8. 2	8.	8.	8.	8.
	9. 2	9. 2	9.	9.	9.	9.
	10. 2	10. 2	10.	10.	10.	10.
	11. 0	11. 0	11.	11.	11.	11.
	12. 0	12. 0	12.	12.	12.	12.
	13. 1	13. 1	13.	13.	13.	13.
	14. 0	14. 0	14.	14.	14.	14.
	15. 1	15. 0	15.	15.	15.	15.
Total Score	17	15				

THE BURNS DEPRESSION CHECKLIST
ANSWER SHEET

Instructions: Put 0, 1, 2, or 3 in the space to the right of each of the 15 symptoms from the Burns Depression Checklist to indicate how much this type of feeling has bothered you in the past several days. Use this key: 0 = not at all; 1 = somewhat; 2 = moderately; 3 = a lot. Total your score at the bottom.

Today's Date						
	1.	1.	1.	1.	1.	1.
	2.	2.	2.	2.	2.	2.
	3.	3.	3.	3.	3.	3.
	4.	4.	4.	4.	4.	4.
	5.	5.	5.	5.	5.	5.
	6.	6.	6.	6.	6.	6.
	7.	7.	7.	7.	7.	7.
	8.	8.	8.	8.	8.	8.
	9.	9.	9.	9.	9.	9.
	10.	10.	10.	10.	10.	10.
	11.	11.	11.	11.	11.	11.
	12.	12.	12.	12.	12.	12.
	13.	13.	13.	13.	13.	13.
	14.	14.	14.	14.	14.	14.
	15.	15.	15.	15.	15.	15.
Total Score						

THE BURNS DEPRESSION CHECKLIST
ANSWER SHEET

Instructions: Put 0, 1, 2, or 3 in the space to the right of each of the 15 symptoms from the Burns Depression Checklist to indicate how much this type of feeling has bothered you in the past several days. Use this key: 0 = not at all; 1 = somewhat; 2 = moderately; 3 = a lot. Total your score at the bottom.

Today's Date						
	1.	1.	1.	1.	1.	1.
	2.	2.	2.	2.	2.	2.
	3.	3.	3.	3.	3.	3.
	4.	4.	4.	4.	4.	4.
	5.	5.	5.	5.	5.	5.
	6.	6.	6.	6.	6.	6.
	7.	7.	7.	7.	7.	7.
	8.	8.	8.	8.	8.	8.
	9.	9.	9.	9.	9.	9.
	10.	10.	10.	10.	10.	10.
	11.	11.	11.	11.	11.	11.
	12.	12.	12.	12.	12.	12.
	13.	13.	13.	13.	13.	13.
	14.	14.	14.	14.	14.	14.
	15.	15.	15.	15.	15.	15.
Total Score						

THE BURNS DEPRESSION CHECKLIST
ANSWER SHEET

Instructions: Put 0, 1, 2, or 3 in the space to the right of each of the 15 symptoms from the Burns Depression Checklist to indicate how much this type of feeling has bothered you in the past several days. Use this key: 0 = not at all; 1 = somewhat; 2 = moderately; 3 = a lot. Total your score at the bottom.

Today's Date						
	1.	1.	1.	1.	1.	1.
	2.	2.	2.	2.	2.	2.
	3.	3.	3.	3.	3.	3.
	4.	4.	4.	4.	4.	4.
	5.	5.	5.	5.	5.	5.
	6.	6.	6.	6.	6.	6.
	7.	7.	7.	7.	7.	7.
	8.	8.	8.	8.	8.	8.
	9.	9.	9.	9.	9.	9.
	10.	10.	10.	10.	10.	10.
	11.	11.	11.	11.	11.	11.
	12.	12.	12.	12.	12.	12.
	13.	13.	13.	13.	13.	13.
	14.	14.	14.	14.	14.	14.
	15.	15.	15.	15.	15.	15.
Total Score						

THE BURNS ANXIETY INVENTORY*

Use the answer sheet to indicate how much each of the following 33 symptoms has bothered you in the past several days. **Do not make any marks on this page.**

Category I: Anxious Feelings	0 Not at All	1 Somewhat	2 Moderately	3 A Lot
1. Anxiety, nervousness, worry, or fear				
2. Feeling that things around you are strange or unreal				
3. Feeling detached from all or part of your body				
4. Sudden unexpected panic spells				
5. Apprehension or a sense of impending doom				
6. Feeling tense, stressed, "uptight," or on edge				
Category II: Anxious Thoughts	**0** Not at All	**1** Somewhat	**2** Moderately	**3** A Lot
7. Difficulty concentrating				
8. Racing thoughts				
9. Frightening fantasies or daydreams				
10. Feeling that you're on the verge of losing control				
11. Fears of cracking up or going crazy				
12. Fears of fainting or passing out				
13. Fears of physical illnesses or heart attacks or dying				
14. Concerns about looking foolish or inadequate				
15. Fears of being alone, isolated, or abandoned				
16. Fears of criticism or disapproval				
17. Fears that something terrible is about to happen				

*Copyright © 1984 by David D. Burns, M.D., from *Ten Days to Self-esteem*, copyright © 1993.

THE BURNS ANXIETY INVENTORY (Continued)

Do not make any marks on this page. Use the separate answer sheet.

Category III: Physical Symptoms	0 Not at All	1 Somewhat	2 Moderately	3 A Lot
18. Skipping, racing, or pounding of the heart (palpitations)				
19. Pain, pressure, or tightness in the chest				
20. Tingling or numbness in the toes or fingers				
21. Butterflies or discomfort in the stomach				
22. Constipation or diarrhea				
23. Restlessness or jumpiness				
24. Tight, tense muscles				
25. Sweating not brought on by heat				
26. A lump in the throat				
27. Trembling or shaking				
28. Rubbery or "jelly" legs				
29. Feeling dizzy, lightheaded, or off balance				
30. Choking or smothering sensations or difficulty breathing				
31. Headaches or pains in the neck or back				
32. Hot flashes or cold chills				
33. Feeling tired, weak, or easily exhausted				

THE BURNS ANXIETY INVENTORY
ANSWER SHEET

Instructions: Put 0, 1, 2, or 3 in the space to the right of each of the 33 symptoms from the Burns Anxiety Inventory to indicate how much this type of feeling has bothered you in the past several days. 0 = Not at All; 1 = Somewhat; 2 = Moderately; 3 = A Lot. Total your score at the bottom.

Today's Date						
1.	1.	1.	1.	1.	1.	
2.	2.	2.	2.	2.	2.	
3.	3.	3.	3.	3.	3.	
4.	4.	4.	4.	4.	4.	
5.	5.	5.	5.	5.	5.	
6.	6.	6.	6.	6.	6.	
7.	7.	7.	7.	7.	7.	
8.	8.	8.	8.	8.	8.	
9.	9.	9.	9.	9.	9.	
10.	10.	10.	10.	10.	10.	
11.	11.	11.	11.	11.	11.	
12.	12.	12.	12.	12.	12.	
13.	13.	13.	13.	13.	13.	
14.	14.	14.	14.	14.	14.	
15.	15.	15.	15.	15.	15.	
16.	16.	16.	16.	16.	16.	
17.	17.	17.	17.	17.	17.	
18.	18.	18.	18.	18.	18.	
19.	19.	19.	19.	19.	19.	
20.	20.	20.	20.	20.	20.	
21.	21.	21.	21.	21.	21.	
22.	22.	22.	22.	22.	22.	
23.	23.	23.	23.	23.	23.	
24.	24.	24.	24.	24.	24.	
25.	25.	25.	25.	25.	25.	
26.	26.	26.	26.	26.	26.	
27.	27.	27.	27.	27.	27.	
28.	28.	28.	28.	28.	28.	
29.	29.	29.	29.	29.	29.	
30.	30.	30.	30.	30.	30.	
31.	31.	31.	31.	31.	31.	
32.	32.	32.	32.	32.	32.	
33.	33.	33.	33.	33.	33.	
Total Score						

THE BURNS ANXIETY INVENTORY
ANSWER SHEET

Instructions: Put 0, 1, 2, or 3 in the space to the right of each of the 33 symptoms from the Burns Anxiety Inventory to indicate how much this type of feeling has bothered you in the past several days. 0 = Not at All; 1 = Somewhat; 2 = Moderately; 3 = A Lot. Total your score at the bottom.

Today's Date						
1.	1.	1.	1.	1.	1.	
2.	2.	2.	2.	2.	2.	
3.	3.	3.	3.	3.	3.	
4.	4.	4.	4.	4.	4.	
5.	5.	5.	5.	5.	5.	
6.	6.	6.	6.	6.	6.	
7.	7.	7.	7.	7.	7.	
8.	8.	8.	8.	8.	8.	
9.	9.	9.	9.	9.	9.	
10.	10.	10.	10.	10.	10.	
11.	11.	11.	11.	11.	11.	
12.	12.	12.	12.	12.	12.	
13.	13.	13.	13.	13.	13.	
14.	14.	14.	14.	14.	14.	
15.	15.	15.	15.	15.	15.	
16.	16.	16.	16.	16.	16.	
17.	17.	17.	17.	17.	17.	
18.	18.	18.	18.	18.	18.	
19.	19.	19.	19.	19.	19.	
20.	20.	20.	20.	20.	20.	
21.	21.	21.	21.	21.	21.	
22.	22.	22.	22.	22.	22.	
23.	23.	23.	23.	23.	23.	
24.	24.	24.	24.	24.	24.	
25.	25.	25.	25.	25.	25.	
26.	26.	26.	26.	26.	26.	
27.	27.	27.	27.	27.	27.	
28.	28.	28.	28.	28.	28.	
29.	29.	29.	29.	29.	29.	
30.	30.	30.	30.	30.	30.	
31.	31.	31.	31.	31.	31.	
32.	32.	32.	32.	32.	32.	
33.	33.	33.	33.	33.	33.	
Total Score						

THE BURNS ANXIETY INVENTORY
ANSWER SHEET

Instructions: Put 0, 1, 2, or 3 in the space to the right of each of the 33 symptoms from the Burns Anxiety Inventory to indicate how much this type of feeling has bothered you in the past several days. 0 = Not at All; 1 = Somewhat; 2 = Moderately; 3 = A Lot. Total your score at the bottom.

Today's Date						
1.	1.	1.	1.	1.	1.	
2.	2.	2.	2.	2.	2.	
3.	3.	3.	3.	3.	3.	
4.	4.	4.	4.	4.	4.	
5.	5.	5.	5.	5.	5.	
6.	6.	6.	6.	6.	6.	
7.	7.	7.	7.	7.	7.	
8.	8.	8.	8.	8.	8.	
9.	9.	9.	9.	9.	9.	
10.	10.	10.	10.	10.	10.	
11.	11.	11.	11.	11.	11.	
12.	12.	12.	12.	12.	12.	
13.	13.	13.	13.	13.	13.	
14.	14.	14.	14.	14.	14.	
15.	15.	15.	15.	15.	15.	
16.	16.	16.	16.	16.	16.	
17.	17.	17.	17.	17.	17.	
18.	18.	18.	18.	18.	18.	
19.	19.	19.	19.	19.	19.	
20.	20.	20.	20.	20.	20.	
21.	21.	21.	21.	21.	21.	
22.	22.	22.	22.	22.	22.	
23.	23.	23.	23.	23.	23.	
24.	24.	24.	24.	24.	24.	
25.	25.	25.	25.	25.	25.	
26.	26.	26.	26.	26.	26.	
27.	27.	27.	27.	27.	27.	
28.	28.	28.	28.	28.	28.	
29.	29.	29.	29.	29.	29.	
30.	30.	30.	30.	30.	30.	
31.	31.	31.	31.	31.	31.	
32.	32.	32.	32.	32.	32.	
33.	33.	33.	33.	33.	33.	
Total Score						

RELATIONSHIP SATISFACTION SCALE*

Use the separate answer sheet to indicate how much satisfaction you have been feeling in your closest relationship. **Do not make any marks on this page.**

	0 Very Dissatisfied	1 Moderately Dissatisfied	2 Slightly Dissatisfied	3 Neutral	4 Slightly Satisfied	5 Moderately Satisfied	6 Very Satisfied
1. Communication and openness							
2. Resolving conflicts and arguments							
3. Degree of affection and caring							
4. Intimacy and closeness							
5. Satisfaction with your role in the relationship							
6. Satisfaction with the other person's role							
7. Overall satisfaction with your relationship							

Note: Although this test assesses your marriage or most intimate relationship, you can also use it to evaluate your relationship with a friend, family member, or colleague. If you do not have any intimate relationships at this time, you can simply think of people in general when you take the test.

RELATIONSHIP SATISFACTION SCALE
ANSWER SHEET

Instructions: Put a rating from 0 to 6 in the space to the right of each relationship area to indicate the amount of satisfaction you have recently felt in your closest relationship. Use this key:

0 = VERY DISSATISFIED
1 = MODERATELY DISSATISFIED
2 = SLIGHTLY DISSATISFIED
3 = NEUTRAL
4 = SLIGHTLY SATISFIED
5 = MODERATELY SATISFIED
6 = VERY SATISFIED

Today's Date						
	1.	1.	1.	1.	1.	1.
	2.	2.	2.	2.	2.	2.
	3.	3.	3.	3.	3.	3.
	4.	4.	4.	4.	4.	4.
	5.	5.	5.	5.	5.	5.
	6.	6.	6.	6.	6.	6.
	7.	7.	7.	7.	7.	7.
Total Score						

RELATIONSHIP SATISFACTION SCALE
ANSWER SHEET

Instructions: Put a rating from 0 to 6 in the space to the right of each relationship area to indicate the amount of satisfaction you have recently felt in your closest relationship. Use this key:

0 = VERY DISSATISFIED
1 = MODERATELY DISSATISFIED
2 = SLIGHTLY DISSATISFIED
3 = NEUTRAL
4 = SLIGHTLY SATISFIED
5 = MODERATELY SATISFIED
6 = VERY SATISFIED

Today's Date						
1.	1.	1.	1.	1.	1.	
2.	2.	2.	2.	2.	2.	
3.	3.	3.	3.	3.	3.	
4.	4.	4.	4.	4.	4.	
5.	5.	5.	5.	5.	5.	
6.	6.	6.	6.	6.	6.	
7.	7.	7.	7.	7.	7.	
Total Score						

RELATIONSHIP SATISFACTION SCALE
ANSWER SHEET

Instructions: Put a rating from 0 to 6 in the space to the right of each relationship area to indicate the amount of satisfaction you have recently felt in your closest relationship. Use this key:

0 = VERY DISSATISFIED
1 = MODERATELY DISSATISFIED
2 = SLIGHTLY DISSATISFIED
3 = NEUTRAL
4 = SLIGHTLY SATISFIED
5 = MODERATELY SATISFIED
6 = VERY SATISFIED

Today's Date						
	1.	1.	1.	1.	1.	1.
	2.	2.	2.	2.	2.	2.
	3.	3.	3.	3.	3.	3.
	4.	4.	4.	4.	4.	4.
	5.	5.	5.	5.	5.	5.
	6.	6.	6.	6.	6.	6.
	7.	7.	7.	7.	7.	7.
Total Score						

HOW TO USE THE DAILY MOOD LOG

The purpose of the Daily Mood Log is to help you overcome painful emotions such as loneliness, depression, anger, shyness, guilt, frustration, worry, and fear. There are three basic steps:

Step One: Describe the Upsetting Event. At the top of the sheet, write a brief description of the situation or problem that's bothering you. It might involve coming home to an empty house after work or having an argument with a friend.

Step Two: Record Your Negative Feelings. Identify your negative emotions and rate how intense they are, on a scale from 0% (for the least upset) to 100% (for the most upset).

Step Three: Use the Triple-Column Technique. Write down the Negative Thoughts associated with your feelings in the left-hand column. Number them consecutively. Indicate how much you believe each thought, from 0% (not at all) to 100% (completely). In the middle column identify the distortions in these thoughts, using the Distorted Thinking chart on the second page of the Daily Mood Log. In the Positive Thoughts column, substitute other thoughts that are more affirmative and realistic. Indicate how much you believe each of them, from 0% to 100%. Now reevaluate how much you believe each of your Negative Thoughts, from 0% to 100%. Finally, indicate how much better you feel by crossing out your original estimates (0% to 100%) for each negative emotion and writing new estimates.

DAILY MOOD LOG*

Step One: Describe the Upsetting Event _____

_____

Step Two: Record Your Negative Feelings—and rate them from 0% (the least) to 100% (the most). Use words like _sad, anxious, angry, guilty, lonely, hopeless, frustrated_, etc.

Emotion	Rating (0%–100%)	Emotion	Rating (0%–100%)	Emotion	Rating (0%–100%)

Step Three: The Triple-Column Technique

Negative Thoughts Write down the thoughts that make you upset and estimate your belief in each one (0%–100%).	**Distortions** Use the Distorted Thinking chart on the next page.	**Positive Thoughts** Substitute more realistic thoughts and estimate your belief in each one (0%–100%).

(Continued on next page)

DAILY MOOD LOG (Continued)

Negative Thoughts	Distortions	Positive Thoughts

DISTORTED THINKING*

1. **All-or-nothing thinking:** You look at things in absolute, black-and-white categories.
2. **Overgeneralization:** You view a negative event as a never-ending pattern of defeat.
3. **Mental filter:** You dwell on the negatives and ignore the positives.
4. **Discounting the positives:** You insist that your accomplishments or positive qualities don't count.
5. **Jumping to conclusions:** You conclude things are bad without any definite evidence.
   (a) **Mind reading:** You assume people are reacting negatively to you.
   (b) **Fortune-telling:** You predict that things will turn out badly.
6. **Magnification or minimization:** You blow things way out of proportion or you shrink their importance.
7. **Emotional reasoning:** You reason from how you feel: "I feel like an idiot, so I must be one."
8. **"Should" statements:** You criticize yourself or other people with "shoulds," "shouldn'ts," "musts," "oughts," and "have-tos."
9. **Labeling:** Instead of saying, "I made a mistake," you tell yourself, "I'm a jerk" or "a loser."
10. **Blame:** You blame yourself for something you weren't entirely responsible for, or you blame other people and overlook ways that you contributed to a problem.

DAILY MOOD LOG (Supplemental Sheet)

Negative Thoughts	Distortions	Positive Thoughts

DAILY MOOD LOG*

Step One: Describe the Upsetting Event _____

_____

Step Two: Record Your Negative Feelings—and rate them from 0% (the least) to 100% (the most). Use words like *sad, anxious, angry, guilty, lonely, hopeless, frustrated,* etc.

Emotion	Rating (0%–100%)	Emotion	Rating (0%–100%)	Emotion	Rating (0%–100%)

Step Three: The Triple-Column Technique

Negative Thoughts Write down the thoughts that make you upset and estimate your belief in each one (0%–100%).	Distortions Use the Distorted Thinking chart on the next page.	Positive Thoughts Substitute more realistic thoughts and estimate your belief in each one (0%–100%).

(Continued on next page)

DAILY MOOD LOG (Continued)

Negative Thoughts	Distortions	Positive Thoughts

DISTORTED THINKING*

1. **All-or-nothing thinking:** You look at things in absolute, black-and-white categories.
2. **Overgeneralization:** You view a negative event as a never-ending pattern of defeat.
3. **Mental filter:** You dwell on the negatives and ignore the positives.
4. **Discounting the positives:** You insist that your accomplishments or positive qualities don't count.
5. **Jumping to conclusions:** You conclude things are bad without any definite evidence.
   (a) **Mind reading:** You assume people are reacting negatively to you.
   (b) **Fortune-telling:** You predict that things will turn out badly.
6. **Magnification or minimization:** You blow things way out of proportion or you shrink their importance.
7. **Emotional reasoning:** You reason from how you feel: "I feel like an idiot, so I must be one."
8. **"Should" statements:** You criticize yourself or other people with "shoulds," "shouldn'ts," "musts," "oughts," and "have-tos."
9. **Labeling:** Instead of saying, "I made a mistake," you tell yourself, "I'm a jerk" or "a loser."
10. **Blame:** You blame yourself for something you weren't entirely responsible for, or you blame other people and overlook ways that you contributed to a problem.

DAILY MOOD LOG (Supplemental Sheet)

Negative Thoughts	Distortions	Positive Thoughts

DAILY MOOD LOG*

Step One: Describe the Upsetting Event _____

_____

Step Two: Record Your Negative Feelings—and rate them from 0% (the least) to 100% (the most). Use words like *sad, anxious, angry, guilty, lonely, hopeless, frustrated*, etc.

Emotion	Rating (0%–100%)	Emotion	Rating (0%–100%)	Emotion	Rating (0%–100%)

Step Three: The Triple-Column Technique

Negative Thoughts Write down the thoughts that make you upset and estimate your belief in each one (0%–100%).	Distortions Use the Distorted Thinking chart on the next page.	Positive Thoughts Substitute more realistic thoughts and estimate your belief in each one (0%–100%).

(Continued on next page)

DAILY MOOD LOG (Continued)

Negative Thoughts	Distortions	Positive Thoughts

DISTORTED THINKING*

1. **All-or-nothing thinking:** You look at things in absolute, black-and-white categories.
2. **Overgeneralization:** You view a negative event as a never-ending pattern of defeat.
3. **Mental filter:** You dwell on the negatives and ignore the positives.
4. **Discounting the positives:** You insist that your accomplishments or positive qualities don't count.
5. **Jumping to conclusions:** You conclude things are bad without any definite evidence.
    (a) **Mind reading:** You assume people are reacting negatively to you.
    (b) **Fortune-telling:** You predict that things will turn out badly.
6. **Magnification or minimization:** You blow things way out of proportion or you shrink their importance.
7. **Emotional reasoning:** You reason from how you feel: "I feel like an idiot, so I must be one."
8. **"Should" statements:** You criticize yourself or other people with "shoulds," "shouldn'ts," "musts," "oughts," and "have-tos."
9. **Labeling:** Instead of saying, "I made a mistake," you tell yourself, "I'm a jerk" or "a loser."
10. **Blame:** You blame yourself for something you weren't entirely responsible for, or you blame other people and overlook ways that you contributed to a problem.

DAILY MOOD LOG (Supplemental Sheet)

Negative Thoughts	Distortions	Positive Thoughts

FIFTEEN WAYS TO UNTWIST YOUR THINKING*

Method	Description of This Method	How to Use This Method/Question to Ask Yourself	Types of Distortions
1. Identify the Distortions	After you write down your Negative Thoughts, use the Distorted Thinking chart to identify the distortions in each.	"What are the distortions in this thought?"	any
2. The Straight-forward Approach	Substitute a more positive and realistic thought.	"Is this Negative Thought really true? Do I really believe this? Is there another way to look at the situation?"	any
3. The Cost-Benefit Analysis	List the advantages and disadvantages of a negative feeling (like getting angry when you're stuck in traffic), a Negative Thought (like "I'm such a loser"), or a Self-defeating Belief (like "I should try to be perfect").	"What are the advantages and dis-advantages of believing this (or feeling like this)? How will this attitude help me, and how will it hurt me?"	any
4. The Double-Standard Technique	Instead of putting yourself down, talk to yourself in the same compassionate way you might talk to a dear friend who was upset.	"Would I say such harsh things to a friend with a similar problem? What would I say to him or her?"	any
5. Examine the Evidence	Instead of assuming that your Negative Thought is true, examine the actual evidence for it.	"What are the facts? What do the data really show?"	jumping to conclusions; emotional reasoning; discounting the positives
6. The Survey Method	Do a survey to find out if your thoughts and attitudes are realistic. For example, if you believe that public speaking anxiety is abnormal, ask several friends if they ever felt that way.	"How do other people think and feel about this?"	jumping to conclusions

*Copyright © 1992 by David D. Burns, M.D., from *Ten Days to Self-esteem*, copyright © 1993.

FIFTEEN WAYS TO UNTWIST YOUR THINKING (Continued)

Method	Description of This Method	How to Use This Method/Question to Ask Yourself	Types of Distortions
7. The Experimental Method	Do an experiment to test the accuracy of your Negative Thought, in much the same way that a scientist would test a theory. For example, if you feel you are about to die of a heart attack during a panic attack, you could run up several flights of stairs. This would prove that your heart was healthy and strong.	"How could I test this Negative Thought to find out if it's really true?"	jumping to conclusions
8. The Pleasure-Predicting Method	Predict how satisfying various activities will be, on a scale from 0% (the least) to 100% (the most). After you complete each activity, record how satisfying it turned out to be.	This technique can help you get moving when you feel lethargic. It can also be used to test Self-defeating Beliefs, such as "If I'm alone, I'm bound to feel miserable."	fortune-telling; emotional reasoning
9. The Vertical Arrow Technique	Instead of disputing your Negative Thought, you draw a vertical arrow under it and ask why it would be upsetting to you if it was true. You will generate a series of Negative Thoughts that will lead to your underlying beliefs.	"If this thought was true, why would it be upsetting to me? What would it mean to me?"	any
10. Thinking in Shades of Gray	Instead of thinking about your problems in black-and-white categories, evaluate things in shades of gray.	When things don't work out as well as you hoped, think about the experience as a partial success. Try to pinpoint your errors instead of thinking of yourself as a total failure.	all-or-nothing thinking

FIFTEEN WAYS TO UNTWIST YOUR THINKING (Continued)

Method	Description of This Method	How to Use This Method/Question to Ask Yourself	Types of Distortions
11. Define Terms	When you label yourself as "inferior" or "a fool" or "a loser," ask yourself what you mean by these labels. You will feel better when you see that there is no such thing as a fool or a loser. Foolish behavior exists, but fools do not.	"What is the definition of a loser?" "What is the definition of an inferior human being?" "When I say I am hopeless, what claim am I making? What is my definition of someone who is hopeless?"	labeling; all-or-nothing thinking
12. Be Specific	Stick with reality and avoid judgments about reality.	Instead of thinking of yourself as totally defective, focus on your specific strengths and weaknesses.	overgeneralization; all-or-nothing thinking
13. The Semantic Method	You substitute language that is less colorful and emotionally loaded.	Instead of telling yourself, "I *shouldn't* have made that mistake," you can tell yourself, "It would be better if I hadn't made that mistake."	labeling; "should" statements
14. Reattribution	Instead of blaming yourself entirely for a problem, think about the many factors that may have contributed to it. Focus on solving the problem instead of using all your energy blaming yourself and feeling guilty.	"What caused this problem? What did I contribute and what did other people (or fate) contribute? What can I learn from the situation?"	all-or-nothing thinking; blame
15. The Acceptance Paradox	Instead of defending yourself against your own self-criticisms, find truth in them and accept your shortcomings with complete tranquillity. This is a powerful Buddhist idea—when you are nothing, you have nothing to lose. You can experience inner peace.	"Do I feel inadequate? I have *many* inadequacies. In fact, there is very little, if anything, about me that couldn't be improved considerably!"	any

ADDITIONAL TECHNIQUES THAT USUALLY REQUIRE THE HELP OF YOUR THERAPIST

The Socratic Method	The therapist asks a series of questions that lead you to understand the inconsistency of your negative belief. For example, he or she might ask, "When you say you are 'a failure at life,' do you mean you fail at some things some of the time or all things all of the time?"
The Externalization of Voices	You and the therapist take turns playing the roles of your Negative Thoughts and your Positive Thoughts. The person who is playing the Negative Thoughts attacks and the person who is playing the Positive Thoughts defends. Frequent role reversals can be used so the person who is defending does not get overwhelmed. This technique transforms intellectual understanding into emotional change at a gut level.
The Feared Fantasy Technique	You and the therapist act out your worst fears, such as being rejected because you're not smart enough or good enough. This can help you see that these fears really aren't as terrible as you thought. Your worst fears usually don't turn out to be real monsters, but simply hot-air balloons that can be punctured with a little logic, compassion, and common sense.
Therapeutic Empathy	Do you have some negative feelings about your therapist or about the therapy that you have not expressed? If so, this can sabotage your efforts, because you may subconsciously make the therapy fail. When you share your frustration openly, it can often get things back on track. Of course, the therapist must listen nondefensively to make this helpful to you!
Changing the Focus	Are you ruminating to avoid dealing with something upsetting? What is the real problem that is bothering you?
Agenda Setting	What are the specific problems in your life that you want help with? What steps are you taking for dealing with them? Do you want help in learning to deal with them more effectively? Are you willing to work hard between sessions to solve those problems? If not, why not?

HOW TO USE THE COST-BENEFIT ANALYSIS

The purpose of doing a Cost-Benefit Analysis is to help you change a self-defeating attitude, emotion, or behavior by balancing its advantages and disadvantages.

1. Attitude Cost-Benefit Analysis. List the thought or attitude you wish to change at the top of the sheet. It might be

- I need everyone's approval to be worthwhile.
- I should try to be perfect.

Then list the advantages and disadvantages of that attitude. Ask yourself, "How will it help me to believe this? And how will it hurt me?" For example, here are some advantages of believing that "I need love to be a happy and worthwhile human being." (1) I'll work hard to develop satisfying relationships. (2) When I feel loved, I'll feel terrific. The disadvantages might include: (1) My neediness might turn some people off. (2) When I'm alone or rejected, I'll feel miserable. (3) Other people will control my self-esteem.

After listing the advantages and disadvantages of the belief, weigh them against each other on a 100-point scale. Put your ratings in the circles at the bottom of the sheet. If the advantages of the attitude are considerably greater, you might put 70 and 30 in these circles. If the disadvantages are slightly greater, you might put 40 and 60 in them.

If the disadvantages of an attitude outweigh the advantages, try to revise your attitude so it will be more realistic and helpful to you. In the previous example, a revised attitude might be "It's okay to *want* a loving relationship, but I don't *need* a loving relationship to be worthwhile."

2. Emotion Cost-Benefit Analysis. Describe the emotion you wish to change at the top of the sheet. It might be loneliness, anger, resentment, sadness, depression, guilt, shame, bitterness, worry, fear, envy, or frustration. Then list the advantages and disadvantages of feeling this way. For example, if you're worrying about a test you have to take, ask yourself how it will help you to worry about it. One advantage of worrying is that you may study harder and do a better job. On the other hand, if you are worrying too much, you may not study as effectively.

After you've listed the advantages and disadvantages of the emotion, balance them against each other on a 100-point scale. If the disadvantages of the emotion are greater, use the Daily Mood Log to change your feelings. If the advantages of the emotion are greater, then your feelings may be healthy and appropriate. In this case, you can accept them and think about ways of expressing them effectively. For example, if you are angry with a friend, you might want to talk things over with him or her.

3. Behavior Cost-Benefit Analysis. Describe the behavior you want to change at the top of the sheet. It might be accepting a date with someone who perpetually calls at the last minute, procrastinating about cleaning up your room, or overeating or drinking excessively when you feel lonely.

List the advantages and disadvantages of the behavior and balance them as before. Try to be honest with yourself. Take subjective feelings and objective facts into account.

ATTITUDE COST-BENEFIT ANALYSIS*

The Attitude or Belief You Want to Change: _____

_____

Advantages of Believing This	Disadvantages of Believing This

ATTITUDE COST-BENEFIT ANALYSIS*

The Attitude or Belief You Want to Change: _____

_____

Advantages of Believing This	Disadvantages of Believing This

ATTITUDE COST-BENEFIT ANALYSIS*

The Attitude or Belief You Want to Change: _____

_____

Advantages of Believing This	Disadvantages of Believing This

EMOTION COST-BENEFIT ANALYSIS*

The Feeling You Want to Change: _____

_____

Advantages of Feeling This Way	Disadvantages of Feeling This Way

EMOTION COST-BENEFIT ANALYSIS*

The Feeling You Want to Change: _____

_____

Advantages of Feeling This Way	Disadvantages of Feeling This Way

EMOTION COST-BENEFIT ANALYSIS*

The Feeling You Want to Change: _____

_____

Advantages of Feeling This Way	Disadvantages of Feeling This Way

BEHAVIOR COST-BENEFIT ANALYSIS*

The Behavior You Want to Change: _____

_____

Advantages of This Behavior	Disadvantages of This Behavior

BEHAVIOR COST-BENEFIT ANALYSIS*

The Behavior You Want to Change: _____

_____

Advantages of This Behavior	Disadvantages of This Behavior

BEHAVIOR COST-BENEFIT ANALYSIS*

The Behavior You Want to Change: _____

_____

Advantages of This Behavior	Disadvantages of This Behavior

PLEASURE-PREDICTING SHEET*

Activity Schedule activities with the potential for pleasure, learning, or personal growth.	Companion If alone, specify *self*.	Predicted Satisfaction Record this *before* each activity on a scale from 0% to 100%.	Actual Satisfaction Record this *after* each activity on a scale from 0% to 100%.

PLEASURE-PREDICTING SHEET*

Activity Schedule activities with the potential for pleasure, learning, or personal growth.	Companion If alone, specify *self*.	Predicted Satisfaction Record this *before* each activity on a scale from 0% to 100%.	Actual Satisfaction Record this *after* each activity on a scale from 0% to 100%.

PLEASURE-PREDICTING SHEET*

Activity Schedule activities with the potential for pleasure, learning, or personal growth.	Companion If alone, specify *self*.	Predicted Satisfaction Record this *before* each activity on a scale from 0% to 100%.	Actual Satisfaction Record this *after* each activity on a scale from 0% to 100%.

ADDITIONAL RESOURCES

Other Books by Dr. Burns

Feeling Good: The New Mood Therapy (New York: Avon, 1992). Dr. Burns describes how to combat feelings of depression and develop greater self-esteem and joy in daily living. *This bestselling book* has sold over three million copies worldwide to date.

The Feeling Good Handbook (New York: Plume, 1990). Dr. Burns shows how you can use cognitive therapy to overcome a wide variety of mood problems such as depression, frustration, panic, chronic worry, and phobias, as well as personal relationship problems such as marital conflict or difficulties at work.

Intimate Connections (New York: Signet, 1985). Dr. Burns shows you how to flirt, how to handle people who give you the runaround, and how to get people of the opposite sex (or the same sex, if that is your preference) to pursue you.

Ten Days to Self-esteem: The Leader's Manual (New York: Quill, 1993). Dr. Burns provides you with clear, easy-to-understand instructions and specific tools so you can develop the Ten Days to Self-esteem program in hospitals, clinics, schools, and other institutional settings. Please note that you can obtain the patient workbook in quantities for your groups at generous discounts directly from the publisher (see page 331 for more information).

Workshops and Lectures by Dr. Burns

Dr. Burns offers workshops and lectures for mental health professionals and for general public audiences as well. For a list of dates and locations, visit Dr. Burns's web site at www.feelinggood.com.

Audiotapes for the General Public

Feeling Good. Dr. Burns describes ten common self-defeating thinking patterns that lead to depression, anxiety, frustration, and anger. He explains how to replace them with more positive and realistic attitudes so you can break out of bad moods and enjoy greater self-esteem now and in the future.

The Perfectionist's Script for Self-defeat. Dr. Burns helps you identify perfectionistic tendencies and explains how they work against you. He shows you how to stop setting unrealistically high standards and how to increase productivity, creativity, and self-satisfaction.

Audiotapes for Mental Health Professionals

Feeling Good: Fast & Effective Treatments for Depression, Anxiety and Therapeutic Resistance. 4 Cassettes—5.25 CE Credits Awarded. Dr. Burns describes the basic principles of CBT and illustrates state-of-the-art treatment methods for depression and anxiety disorders. He also illustrates how to deal with difficult, mistrustful, unmotivated, or angry patients who seem to sabotage treatment.

Feeling Good Together: Cognitive Interpersonal Therapy. 4 Cassettes—5.75 CE Credits Awarded. In this workshop, Dr. Burns shows how to modify the attitudes that sabotage intimacy and lead to anger and mistrust. He illustrates, step-by-step, how to work with individuals who can't get along with their spouses, family members, friends, or colleagues at work. He also explains how to deal with patients who blame others for their personal relationship problems.

Rapid, Cost-Effective Treatments for Anxiety Disorders. 4 Cassettes—5.5 CE Credits Awarded. In this workshop, Dr. Burns shows you how to integrate three powerful models in the treatment of the entire spectrum of anxiety disorders, including generalized anxiety, panic disorder (with or without agoraphobia), phobias, social anxiety, obsessive-compulsive disorder, and posttraumatic stress disorder (including victims of childhood sexual abuse).

Strategies for Therapeutic Success: My Twenty Most Effective Techniques. 8 Cassettes—12 CE Credits Awarded. In this two-day intensive workshop, Dr. Burns illustrates the most valuable therapy techniques he has developed during twenty-five years of clinical practice, training, and research.

You may order the audiotapes for professionals or for the general public by calling 001-800-810-9011 or by visiting the web site: www.lima-associates.com.

Treatment and Assessment Tools for Mental Health Professionals

Interactive Toolkit. An innovative software package that allows you to administer a variety of assessment instruments for on-line testing. The "Client Assessment Module" administers the assessment instruments and prints reports for patients and therapists. The "Therapist Module" allows you to add or create new tests and select particular tests for each client from a large selection of available instruments. All data are saved for easy input into statistical programs for analysis.

Therapist's Toolkit 2000. Includes hundreds of pages of state-of-the-art assessment and treatment tools for the mental health professional. Purchase includes licensure for unlimited reproduction in your clinical practice. Site licenses are available.

You may learn more or order these toolkits at Dr. Burns's web site: www.feelinggood.com.

TRAINING FOR GROUP LEADERS

Dr. Burns does workshops by invitation for mental health professionals on a variety of topics, as well as lectures for the general public. For a list of topics, cities, dates, and sponsoring agencies, please visit Dr. Burns's web site at www.feelinggood.com.

INDEX

Page numbers in **bold** refer to charts and tables. Page numbers in *italics* refer to exercise answers.

ABOUT DAVID D. BURNS, M.D.

David D. Burns, M.D., graduated magna cum laude from Amherst College, received his M.D. degree from Stanford University School of Medicine, and completed his psychiatry residency at the University of Pennsylvania. He has served as acting chief of psychiatry at the Presbyterian/University of Pennsylvania Medical Center and visiting scholar at Harvard Medical School. In 1995, Dr. Burns and his family returned to California. He is currently clinical associate professor of psychiatry and behavioral sciences at his alma mater, Stanford University School of Medicine, where he is actively involved in research and teaching. Dr. Burns is certified by the National Board of Psychiatry and Neurology.

Dr. Burns has received numerous awards, including the A. E. Bennett Award from the Society of Biological Psychiatry for his research on brain chemistry, and the Distinguished Contribution to Psychology Through the Media Award from the Association of Applied and Preventive Psychology. In 1998, he was named Teacher of the Year by the graduating psychiatric residents at Stanford.

You are invited to visit Dr. Burns's web site at www.feelinggood.com. This web site contains information about

- dates and locations for upcoming lectures and workshops by Dr. Burns
- audiotapes for the general public
- training tapes for mental health professionals (including CE credits)
- links for referrals to cognitive therapists around the country
- descriptions of Dr. Burns's new *Therapist Toolkit 2000* as well as his new *Interactive Toolkit*
- links to other interesting sites
- new information of potential interest to patients and therapists
- "Ask the Guru." You can submit questions to Dr. Burns about any mental health topic. Answers to selected questions are posted in a column format.

Vermilion books are available from all good bookshops
or call our mail order hotline number on:
01206 255 800

Postage and packing is free.

If you have enjoyed this book you might like these titles from Vermilion:

Love and Survival *Dr. Dean Ornish*	0 09 181618 1	£9.99	paper
How High Can You Bounce? *Roger Crawford*	0 09 181719 6	£8.99	paper
Families and How to Survive Them *Robin Skynner and John Cleese*	0 7493 1410 9	£7.99	paper
Life and How to Survive It *Robin Skynner and John Cleese*	0 7493 2320 5	£7.99	paper
Life Strategies *Dr. Phillip C. McGraw*	0 09 181999 7	£9.99	paper
Lessons at the Fence Post *Paul D. Cummings*	0 09 182592 X	£4.99	paper
Practical Intuition *Laura Day* *Introduction by Demi Moore*	0 09 181567 3	£7.99	paper
Be Assertive *Beverley Hare*	0 09 181396 4	£6.99	paper
The Power of Positive Thinking *Norman Vincent Peale*	0 7493 0715 3	£7.99	paper
The Power of Positive Living *Norman Vincent Peale*	0 7493 0821 4	£7.99	paper
You Can If You Think You Can *Norman Vincent Peale*	0 7493 1077 4	£7.99	paper
The Power of Positive Thinking for Young People *Norman Vincent Peale*	0 7493 0567 3	£7.99	paper
The Amazing Results of Positive Thinking *Norman Vincent Peale*	0 7493 0933 4	£7.99	paper
Courage and Confidence *Norman Vincent Peale*	0 7493 1341 2	£7.99	paper
Inspiring Messages For Daily Living *Norman Vincent Peale*	0 09 182666 7	£6.99	paper
The Power of Ethical Management *Norman Vincent Peale*	0 09 182665 9	£6.99	paper
The Positive Way to Change Your Life *Norman Vincent Peale*	0 7493 0858 3	£7.99	paper
Stay Alive All Your Life *Norman Vincent Peale*	0 7493 1430 3	£7.99	paper